# NEW OUTLINE-HISTORY

## OF THE

# UNITED STATES

### SINCE 1865

BY

## JOHN A. KROUT

*Professor of History, Columbia University*

*New York*

## BARNES & NOBLE, INC.

*Printed in the United States of America*

*By De Pamphilis Press, Inc., New York, N. Y.*

# PREFACE

In preparing this *Outline-History* of the United States since the Civil War, the author has been concerned primarily with the needs of college students. The arrangement of material follows no particular textbook on the subject, but is designed to provide a plan for the organization of the information which the student acquires from text and collateral reading. It should be especially useful in connection with general courses in which the instructor desires to make assignments in a wide range of historical literature. It is intended also to provide an up-to-date supplement to less recent textbooks, a manual for review and general reference, and a comprehensive digest for courses in American literature or other subjects needing a concise treatment of historical background.

The author hopes that college students will view the *Outline-History* as a guide to the most reliable secondary works, rather than as an easy short cut to historical knowledge. The general bibliography contains a selected list of titles with which every serious student of the history of the United States should become acquainted; the references at the close of each chapter give recommended readings on the immediate subject; and the Tabulated Bibliography supplies cross-references to latest editions of standard college textbooks. The paragraph method of presentation, which permits fuller explanations than the ordinary skeleton outline, the chronological devices, the review questions and the maps have been prepared as aids to an understanding of the development of the American nation since 1865. They will yield the largest returns when used in conjunction with the writings to which they are a guide.

J. A. K.

| Chapter in this Outline | Topic | Bassett | Beard | Dumond | Faulkner | Hacker and Kendrick | Harlow | Hicks American Nation |
|---|---|---|---|---|---|---|---|---|
| I | Reconstruction | **27–29** | 98–121 | 25 557–560 | 22 | **1–2** | **1–3** | **1–2** |
| II | Bases of a New Economic Order | **30** | 19 | 26–29 | 23–25 433–442 | **7–8** | 4 53–62 **6, 10** | 3, 6 |
| III | The Political Scene | **33** | **20, 23** | 613–622 | 443–463 | | 202–207 **14–15** | 7 191–19 |
| IV | Control of Transportation | 680–683 **35** | **20, 23** | 622–623 | 413–416 442–443 | **8, 14** | 7 | 164–17 |
| V | The Tariff and the Trusts | **35** | **23** | 624–631 | 463–467 29 | **15** 90–96 | 8 | 175–18 197–21 |
| VI | The Armies of Labor | 741–744 | **21** | 551 606–610 625–626 636, 642 | 406–410 | **12** | 9 | 180–19 260–26 |
| VII | The West in Revolt | 727–763 | **22, 23** | 31 | 443–449 29 | **16** | 16 | 11 268–27 |
| VIII | The Trend of Diplomacy | **37** | **24** | 32 | 30 | **6** | 62–68 17 | 299–30 333 |
| IX | Our Colonial Empire | 38 799–803 | 367–376 480–501 | 33 740 827–828 | 31 645–648 | **18, 19** | 67 **18–19** 531 | 306–31 15, 16 |
| X | At the Turn of the Century | **42** | **25, 31** | 666–667 34 | 28 516–518 34 | **13, 17** | **12** 280–284 | 276–2 |
| XI | The Era of Theodore Roosevelt | 819–834 | 504–517 **27** | 684–693 704 710–722 | **32–33** 586–594 | **20, 23** | **20, 23** 326–332 | 17 380–4 |
| XII | The Day of the Progressives | **40** | **27** | 706–709 722–730 | **33** 586–601 | 389–397 451–455 | 22 308–312 332–347 | 400–4 |
| XIII | Wilsonian Liberalism | **41** | **27** | 36 | 601–605 | **24–25** | 347–361 26 488–496 | 20 |
| XIV | The First World War | **43** | **28** | 37 | 36 | **26–27** | **27–31** | 21–23 |
| XV | War's Aftermath | **44–45** | 29–30 763–765 | 38–39 | 37–39 | **28–34** | 32–36 | 24–27 |
| XVI | The New Deal in Action | **46** | | 40 817–826 | 40 710–723 | **35–38** | 37–38 | 28–29 701–7 |
| XVII | Foreign Policy and World Power | | | 826–839 | 723–734 | | 39 579–588 | 711–7 |
| XVIII | The Second World War | | | | **42** | | 588–597 **41–42** | 734–7 |

Light-faced type indicates pages.

| Hicks Short History | Martin | Morison and Commager | Muzzey and Krout | Nichols Growth | Nichols Republic | Paxson | Schlesinger | Stephenson | Wirth-Forman |
|---|---|---|---|---|---|---|---|---|---|
| 20-21<br>428-439 | 1-4 | 1-2 | 12 | 15 | 1 | 1-2 | 1 | 1-2<br>34-36 | 25 |
| 439-442<br>23-25 | 6, 7 | 3-4 | 13 | 303-308<br>18-19 | 2, 4-5 | 2-3 | 2, 3, 5 | 3-8 | 526-533<br>26-27<br>30 |
| 26 | 8-10 | 10 | 13-14 | 308, 359<br>445 | 42-44<br>101<br>193-198 | 4-6 | 3-4 | 114-133 | 27 |
| 530-535 | | 5 | 521-524 | 19<br>448-449 | 6, 9 | 101-107<br>155-157 | 5 | 132-142 | 603-605 |
| 538-543 | 11 | 135-145<br>250-265 | 535-541 | 300-303<br>23 | 9 | 8, 15 | 4-5 | 140-166 | 588-599<br>609-613<br>30 |
| 543-553<br>568-574 | 159-163<br>216-223 | 7 | 524-529 | 293-296<br>385-389 | 25-33<br>130-134 | 7 | 5 | 103-113<br>177-181 | 599-603<br>606-609 |
| 28 | 13-15 | 9<br>236-249 | 15 | 21 | 7 | 9, 10,<br>11 | 8 | 162-169<br>13 | 636-640<br>31 |
| 404, 442<br>599-603 | 80-89<br>254-259 | 60-64<br>314-322 | 444-449 | 24 | 223-229 | 4 | 9-10 | 45-51<br>1-4 | 525, 552<br>653-658 |
| 30<br>850 | 16, 17 | 13-14 | 16 | 24<br>588-591<br>601-606 | 10<br>360<br>372-377 | 12, 14 | 9, 14 | 15-16<br>335-337 | 32 |
| 24<br>580 | 12 | 12 | | 462-465<br>26 | 216-220<br>11 | 11 | 6 | 17-18 | 575-587<br>674-677 |
| 31 | 20, 21 | 15-16 | 17 | 508-511<br>28, 30 | 257-261<br>14, 16 | 13-16 | 11 | 19-21<br>327-331 | 33 |
| 543-660 | 22 | 15, 17 | 18 | 27-32 | 15-16 | 18-19 | 12 | 22<br>322-334 | 729-755 |
| 660-672 | 23, 24 | 18-19 | 19 | 30-32 | 16 | 20-21 | 14 | 23 | 755-767 |
| 672-693<br>94 | 25-29 | 20 | 20 | 33-34 | 17-18 | 22-24 | 15-16 | 24-27 | 767-801 |
| 95<br>760-763<br>772-787 | 30-33<br>35 | 21-22 | 21 | 35-38 | 19-22 | 26-28 | 17-18 | 28-32 | 36-38<br>869-872 |
| 787-790<br>98 | 34 | 24-25 | 22 | 39<br>730-740 | 23-24 | 29-30 | 19-20 | 33-35 | 872-906 |
| 99<br>831-846 | | 26 | 22 | 740-750 | 25<br>572-588 | | 21 | | 40<br>921-932 |
| 846-859 | | 26 | 22 | | 588-605 | | | | 932-952 |

# Tabulated Bibliography
## of Standard Textbooks on
## the History of the United States

(See two preceding pages)

The following list gives the author, title, publisher, and date of the standard textbooks referred to in the table on the two preceding pages.

Bassett, *A Short History of the United States,* 3rd ed., Macmillan, 1939.

Beard and Beard, *The Rise of American Civilization,* new ed., Macmillan, 1934.

Dumond, *A History of the United States,* Holt, 1942.

Faulkner, *American Political and Social History,* 3rd ed., Crofts, 1944.

Hacker and Kendrick, *The United States since 1865,* Crofts, 1939.

Harlow, *The Growth of the United States, 1865-1943,* rev. ed., Holt, 1943.

Hicks, *The American Nation,* Houghton Mifflin, 1945.

Hicks, *A Short History of American Democracy,* Houghton Mifflin, 1943.

Martin, *History of the United States,* new ed., Vol. II, Ginn, 1938.

Morison and Commager, *The Growth of the American Republic,* 3rd ed., Vol. II, Oxford, 1942.

Muzzey and Krout, *American History for Colleges,* rev. ed., Ginn, 1943.

Nichols and Nichols, *The Growth of American Democracy,* Appleton-Century, 1939.

Nichols and Nichols, *The Republic of the United States,* Vol. II, Appleton-Century, 1942.

Paxson, *Recent History of the United States,* rev. ed., Houghton Mifflin, 1937.

Schlesinger, *Political and Social Growth of the American People,* 3rd ed., Macmillan, 1941.

Stephenson, *American History since 1865,* Harper, 1939.

Wirth, *Forman's Our Republic,* rev. ed., Appleton-Century, 1944.

# Table of Contents

## *Maps*

## CHAPTER I

# RECONSTRUCTION POLITICAL AND ECONOMIC

### CONSEQUENCES OF THE CIVIL WAR

The Civil War wrought a revolution in the life of the American people comparable to that which accompanied the War for Independence.

**The Problems of the Prostrate South.** As the veterans of the Confederate armies returned to their homes after Lee's surrender, they found destruction, destitution, and demoralization on every side.

ECONOMIC CONDITIONS. From Virginia to Texas were evidences of the grim realities of war. Farmhouses, barns, and mills had been burned; bridges and railroad tracks had been destroyed; towns had been looted and their inhabitants scattered. Business was at a standstill, save for speculative enterprises which preyed on the needs of the people. Plantation

I

owners, who had lost their property in slaves, found it almost impossible to borrow the capital with which to work their acres, now greatly diminished in value.

Social Readjustments. The war destroyed the whole structure of Southern society. The planter aristocracy, shorn of wealth and power in many sections, yielded reluctantly to the increasing influence of bankers, merchants, and small farmers. The Negroes, as they made the slow transition from the status of dependent slaves to that of free wage earners, raised serious problems of social relations.

Political Uncertainties. The collapse of the Confederacy threw all governmental processes into confusion. There was imperative need for the reorganization of local and state governments and for the resumption by new state governments of the normal relation between the state and the Union.

**The Process of Political Reconstruction.** While experts in constitutional law debated whether Congress or the President should direct the course of reconstruction, the conquest of Confederate territory by Union troops had compelled Lincoln to organize provisional governments.

Lincoln's Policy. Convinced that he should aid the Southern people to resume speedily their former allegiance, President Lincoln (1) set up provisional governments in Virginia, Tennessee, Louisiana, and Arkansas; (2) issued a Proclamation of Amnesty (1863), pardoning all (with a few exceptions) who would swear allegiance to the government of the United States; (3) authorized the establishment of a new state government for any state in which one-tenth of the qualified voters of 1860 should take the required oath of loyalty. He applied a "pocket veto" to the Davis-Wade Bill, which imposed more drastic conditions.

The "Johnson Governments." The burden of Lincoln's uncompleted task fell upon the shoulders of Andrew Johnson, a War Democrat who had been elected on the Union Republican ticket with Lincoln in 1864. The new President granted amnesty to former Confederates, except certain classes, who were willing to take an oath to "support, protect, and defend the Constitution." By successive proclamations he set up provisional governments in North Carolina, Mississippi, Georgia, Texas, Alabama, South Carolina, and Florida. He authorized the loyal white citizens to draft and ratify new constitutions, and to elect state legislatures, which were to repeal ordinances of secession, repudiate the Confederate debt, and ratify the Thirteenth Amendment freeing the slaves.

JOHNSON VERSUS CONGRESS. In December, 1865, the congressional leaders refused to seat the senators and representatives elected under the Johnson plan, and created a Joint Committee on Reconstruction.

a. *Hostility to Presidential Reconstruction.* Congressional opposition to Johnson's plans came from several sources: (1) fear of executive encroachment on the powers of Congress; (2) desire to safeguard the interests of the Negro by granting him the right to vote; (3) resentment over the speedy return of the ex-Confederates to political power in the South; (4) determination of the Republican politicians to create a Republican party in the South; (5) personal animosity of congressional leaders against President Johnson.

b. *Freedmen's Bureau Bill (1866).* In March, 1865, Congress had created the Freedmen's Bureau to protect the newly emancipated Negroes. Early in 1866 the national legislators passed a law extending the life of the Bureau indefinitely. Johnson vetoed the bill and the Radical Republicans in Congress could not override the veto.

c. *Civil Rights Bill (1866).* In April, 1866, the President's opponents passed over his veto a Civil Rights Act, conferring citizenship upon the Negroes and assuring them equality of treatment before the law.

THE CONGRESSIONAL PROGRAM. As the quarrel with Johnson progressed, the Radical Republican leaders grew more insistent in their demands for the political proscription of the ex-Confederates.

a. *The Fourteenth Amendment.* In April, 1866, the Joint Committee on Reconstruction proposed the Fourteenth Amendment, which Congress promptly referred to the states for ratification. Its provisions were: (1) citizenship was conferred on every person born or naturalized in the United States; (2) states which deprived the Negro of the ballot were to suffer a reduction of representation in Congress; (3) ex-Confederates were barred from holding national and state offices if they had filled similar posts before the war; (4) the Confederate debt was repudiated and the validity of the United States debt affirmed. Tennessee quickly ratified the amendment and was readmitted to the Union.

b. *The Congressional Elections (1866).* President Johnson and the Radical Republicans fought for control of Congress in the elections of 1866. The friends of the administration denounced the Fourteenth Amendment and urged a policy of conciliation toward the defeated South. The result was an overwhelming victory for the Radical Republicans.

c. *The Reconstruction Acts (1867).* Congress passed over the President's veto a Military Reconstruction Act (March 2, 1867), which was supplemented later in the year by acts outlining administrative routine. This legislation provided that (1) the ten states still unreconstructed were to be divided into five military districts with a major general in command of each; (2) constitutional conventions, elected by Negroes and loyal whites, were to frame constitutions providing for Negro suffrage; (3) these constitutions were to be acceptable to Congress; (4) qualified voters were to elect state legislatures pledged to ratify the Fourteenth Amendment; (5) with the ratification of the Fourteenth Amendment the states could apply for representation in Congress.

## THE FEDERAL GOVERNMENT

The "Reign of the Radicals," which was ushered in by the enactment of the Reconstruction Acts of 1867, was significant not only in the settlement of the Southern question but also in the determination of the political and economic policies of the federal government.

**The Impeachment of Andrew Johnson.** Not content with their victory at the polls in 1866, the congressional leaders strove to humiliate President Johnson by removing him from office.

THE TENURE OF OFFICE ACT. This act of March 2, 1867, was passed with the hope that the President would disobey it. He was forbidden to remove officeholders, including members of his cabinet, without the consent of the Senate. When Johnson in the spring of 1868 dismissed his Secretary of War, Edwin M. Stanton, the House of Representatives impeached the President for "high crimes and misdemeanors."

THE TRIAL OF THE PRESIDENT. Johnson's trial, which began in the Senate on March 4, 1868, was a notable victory for the defense counsel. Despite their use of political pressure, the Radicals failed by one vote to secure the two-thirds of the Senate necessary for conviction.

**The Election of 1868.** In the campaign of 1868 the Radicals within the Union Republican party became not only the champions of a vigorous Southern policy, but also the defenders of Northern financial and business interests against Western agrarians.

THE UNION REPUBLICAN CONVENTION. The delegates to the national convention adopted a platform which endorsed congressional reconstruction and demanded payment of the public debt in gold. The Radicals, having made sure that General Grant was one of their number, nominated him for President, and chose Schuyler Colfax of Indiana for Vice-President.

THE "OHIO IDEA." The Democratic party, seeking to recover its prewar strength, drafted a platform which denounced the congressional program of reconstruction as unconstitutional and pledged support to the "Ohio Idea," a proposal that government bonds, whenever possible, should be paid in greenbacks rather than in gold. But Democratic support of this Western financial policy was weakened by the nomination of Governor Horatio Seymour of New York, who repudiated the greenback plank.

GRANT'S VICTORY. In the electoral college Grant defeated Seymour by 214 to 80 votes, but his 300,000 popular majority was made possible only by the 650,000 Negro votes cast for him in the Southern states. The white voters of the country had not endorsed the Radical Republican program.

## THE SOUTHERN STATES

In the Southern states military reconstruction was responsible for a political regime, based upon Negro votes, which brought social confusion in its wake.

The "Carpetbag Governments." As the new state governments were set up in accordance with the legislation of 1867, the Negro vote was marshaled and controlled in many districts by ambitious and unscrupulous whites.

"CARPETBAGGERS" AND "SCALAWAGS." Politically inexperienced Negroes sat in the conventions which drafted the new constitutions. They were willing supporters of Northerners, who had come South with the expectation of achieving power and fortune ("carpetbaggers"), and of a few Southern whites, who sought political preferment and lucrative contracts by aiding the Radical program ("scalawags").

EXTRAVAGANCE AND CORRUPTION. Some legislatures elected in the Southern states (1868-1869) indulged in an orgy of extravagance and fraud which left its aftermath of exorbitant public debts and excessively burdensome taxes.

THE FIFTEENTH AMENDMENT. Arkansas, North Carolina, South Carolina, Florida, Alabama, and Louisiana were admitted to the Union by 1868, but Virginia, Georgia, Mississippi, and Texas were not able to satisfy Congress until 1870, when they were readmitted on condition that their legislatures ratify the Fifteenth Amendment, which forbade any state to deny the suffrage on the grounds of "race, color, or previous condition of servitude."

**The Undoing of Reconstruction.** Restored to their normal relations in the Union, the Southern states made slow but steady progress in their efforts to overthrow the "carpetbag governments" and restore white supremacy.

THE KU-KLUX KLAN. Secret societies — such as the Ku-Klux Klan, the Knights of the White Camelia, the Boys of '76 — were used as the instruments of a policy of terrorism which was designed to frighten the Negroes and compel them to renounce their new political power. The Klan, which became the most notorious of the organizations, was dominated in some districts by extremists who resorted to violence and brutality.

THE ENFORCEMENT ACTS. Southern resistance brought legislation for the enforcement of the congressional program. (1) An act of May, 1870, imposed heavy penalties for violation of the Fourteenth and Fifteenth amendments; (2) an act of February, 1871, placed congressional elections under the control of the federal authorities; (3) the Ku-Klux Act of the same year gave the President military powers to suppress violence in the Southern states.

THE RESTORATION OF WHITE RULE. The general Amnesty Act, passed by Congress in May, 1872, restored to thousands of ex-Confederates their political privileges and hastened the collapse of the carpetbag governments. The Negroes were kept from the polls, not by force, but by intimidating threats subtly conveyed. In 1875 only South Carolina, Florida, and Louisiana were still in the hands of the carpetbaggers, supported by federal troops. Two years later, with the withdrawal of the troops, these states also reverted to white control.

**The Solid South.** The most obvious political result of congressional reconstruction was the adherence of almost all Southern whites to the Democratic party. Seldom have the Republicans carried any of the former Confederate states in a national election.

**Economic Rehabilitation of the South.** The political confusion of the postwar decade retarded all the Southern states in their efforts to promote the economic well-being of their citizens.

THE DISRUPTION OF THE PLANTATION SYSTEM. The revolutionary changes effected by the war compelled the landholders of the Southern states to reduce the size of their plantations. Some sold off surplus acres, but the majority preferred to try a plan of cultivation on shares, with tenants who were unable to pay a cash rental. Owner and tenant entered into a partnership, one furnishing land, the other labor. But the cash necessary to finance the partnership was generally supplied by merchants or bankers who took mortgages on the crops as security for loans. It proved to be an expensive system of rural credits. Interest rates were too high; farmers were compelled to confine their production to staples like cotton and tobacco; and the agrarian group became virtually the tenants of the merchant-creditors.

INDUSTRIAL DEVELOPMENT. As the South of the great plantations disappeared, a new industrial order arose. The exploitation of coal, iron, phosphates, and lumber slowly gathered momentum. The less prosperous elements in the rural districts drifted into the towns to work in factories located where cheap water power was available. The increase in railroad mileage began to keep pace with the output of coal and pig iron and the multiplication of cotton spindles.

## REVIEW QUESTIONS

1. Compare Abraham Lincoln's attitude with that of Andrew Johnson toward the political questions involved in the reconstruction of the states of the secession.
2. Do you detect any inconsistency in the program of the congressional Radicals as set forth in the Fourteenth Amendment and the Reconstruction Acts of 1867?
3. Why were the politicians in the Union Republican party alarmed over the creation of the Johnson governments in the Southern states?
4. In what sense was the election of 1868 a victory of the business and financial interests in the North?
5. How do you account for the failure of the Radicals to secure a conviction in the impeachment proceedings against President Johnson?
6. Discuss the problems which confronted the Southern planter during the years immediately following the collapse of the Confederacy.
7. An eminent American historian has characterized the Civil War years as the period of a Second American Revolution. Do you see any justification for this view?

## SELECTED REFERENCES

Beale, H. K., *The Critical Year: A Study of Andrew Johnson and Reconstruction*

Bowers, C. G., *The Tragic Era*

Buck, Paul, *Road to Reunion*

Dunning, W. A., *Reconstruction, Political and Economic*

Fleming, W. L., *Sequel to Appomattox*

Henry, R. S., *Story of Reconstruction*

Lester, J. C., and Wilson, D. L., *Ku Klux Klan*

Milton, G. F., *The Age of Hate*

## Significant Dates

Completion of the Union Pacific
Railroad . . . . . . . 1869

Liberal Republican Campaign . 1872

Depression and Panic . . . . 1873

Resumption Act . . . . . . 1875

Centennial Exposition . . . . 1876

CHAPTER II

# THE BASES
# OF A NEW ECONOMIC ORDER

## EXPANSION OF BUSINESS ENTERPRISE

While the planters of the South were being humbled, the industrial and financial leaders of the nation, aided by a benevolent government, proceeded to lay the foundations of the new edifice of business enterprise.

**Opening the Trans-Mississippi West.** Possessed of abundant capital and able to secure an adequate labor supply, the business interests undertook the exploitation of the remarkable resources of the domain beyond the Mississippi.

OVERCOMING THE INDIAN MENACE. A necessary preliminary to the complete utilization of the natural resources of the West was the solution of the problem of those Indian tribes which relied for subsistence on the huge buffalo herds of the great plains.

10

a. *Military Conflicts.* While such tribes as the Crows and the Blackfeet were generally friendly to the white man, the Cheyennes, Apaches, and Sioux were particularly determined in their resistance to the encroachment of settlers on their lands. Hundreds of skirmishes occurred between United States troops and the "hostiles" in the decade after the Civil War. In 1876 the government's effort to clear the Black Hills country, which was marred by the massacre of General Custer's command on the Little Big Horn, finally resulted in the collapse of the Sioux confederacy. Sporadic outbreaks continued, however, until 1890.

b. *Governmental Policy.* An enlightened policy of dealing with the red man was formulated by government officials only after the record had been liberally sprinkled with needless wars and massacres, fraudulent seizures of Indian lands, and speculations of dishonest agents. For many years the War Department, which advocated "extermination" to overcome the treachery and cruelty of the savages, worked at cross-purposes with the Bureau of Indian Affairs, which made the mistake of confusing a program of pauperization with benevolent helpfulness. Late in the seventies Congress made the first tentative efforts to formulate a comprehensive plan for Indian education, and to control intelligently the activities of the reservation Indians.

c. *The Dawes Act (1887).* The initial measure in dealing with the problem of Indian lands was the Dawes Act, which conferred 160 acres of land and United States citizenship upon the heads of Indian families who should abandon their tribal allegiance. The motives back of this legislation were twofold: the desire to encourage Indians to take their proper place in the life of the nation, and the desire to satisfy the land hunger of Western settlers, by opening such parts of the reservation as were not needed in order to make the grants to the Indians.

THE MINING FRONTIER. During the fifties and sixties of the last century, the mineral deposits of the West, as they were revealed by venturesome prospectors, drew strange congregations into the wooden villages of the mining frontier.

a. *Output of Precious Metals.* During the fifties the California gold fields were rapidly exploited, gold was discovered in Colorado, and the Comstock Lode in Nevada proved to be rich in both silver and gold. From 1861 to 1865 the annual production of gold increased from $43,000,000 to $53,000,000. In 1874 gold was discovered in the Black Hills section of Dakota Territory. A few years later the great silver mines of Colorado were opened, and the mineowners became interested in the government's policy concerning the coinage of silver.

b. *New States.* Mining became the chief industry of the mountainous West. Upon it rested the economic structure of many communities which sought official recognition by applying for admission to the Union. Nevada (1864) and Colorado (1876) were accorded statehood on the basis of the population in their mining camps and hastily-built cities.

c. *Effect on the Currency.* The output of gold brought a welcome expansion in the currency, which otherwise would have been inadequate for the rapidly increasing needs of business enterprise. The tremendous quantities of silver, however, caused the price of that commodity to decline in the seventies and resulted in a persistent demand by the mineowners for a more abundant currency based on silver.

THE TRANSCONTINENTAL RAILROADS. Eastern business interests, Western miners, and settlers on the Pacific Coast enthusiastically sponsored plans to bind distant parts of the nation together with bands of steel.

a. *Governmental Aid.* In 1862 Congress granted a charter to the Union Pacific to construct a railroad from Nebraska to California. The promoters of the company were to receive a right of way, free use of timber and minerals on the public lands, and a grant of twenty sections of government land for every mile of track they constructed. In addition, Congress agreed to loan the company $16,000 for every mile built

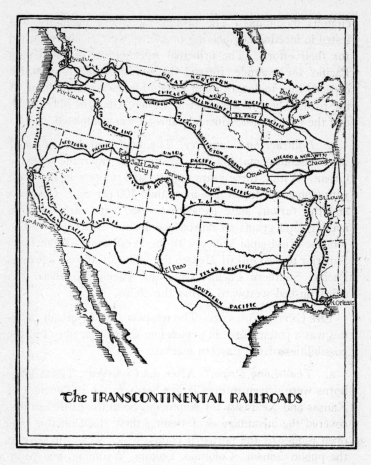

The TRANSCONTINENTAL RAILROADS

across the plains, $32,000 for every mile in the plateau regions, and $48,000 for every mile in the mountains. At the same time similar terms were accorded the Central Pacific, a California corporation, formed to build a line eastward to meet the Union Pacific.

**b.** *Construction Methods.* In 1867 the building of the transcontinental line began in earnest. The construction gangs worked feverishly to overcome the difficulties inherent in spanning a region of desert wastes, wooded plateaus, and precipitous mountains. The promoters, whose ingenuity was tested in meeting engineering problems, were richly rewarded for their efforts. The principal stockholders of the Union Pacific, for example, formed the Crédit Mobilier, in which capacity they took exorbitant profits for the actual building of the road. The two lines met at Ogden, Utah, in May, 1869, and the first transcontinental railroad was completed.

c. *Influence on Commerce.* The most immediate effect of the transcontinental line was to stimulate our trade with the Orient. Within three years exports and imports in the trade with China and Japan rose more than 100 per cent. Congress and the various state legislatures vied with each other in making land grants to railroad companies which planned to join the Mississippi Valley with the West Coast. From Lake Superior to the Gulf of Mexico the railheads of lines (Kansas Pacific, Southern Pacific, Gulf and Pacific, Northern Pacific) pushed westward across the plains.

THE CATTLE COUNTRY. The westward thrust of rail facilities was a potent force in persuading the cattlemen to test the possibilities of the Eastern markets.

a. *The "Long Drive."* After the Civil War, Texan longhorns were driven in ever larger herds to the rail centers of Kansas and Nebraska for shipment. Soon the cattlemen discovered the advantage of fattening their stock on the free, open ranges of the northern plains, which were still part of the public domain. Colorado, Dakota, Wyoming, and Montana contained excellent pasturage. During the two decades after 1865 more than 285,000 cattle annually were fattened on the free pasturage and shipped to Eastern stockyards.

b. *Collapse of the Cattle Industry.* The ten years prior to 1885 marked the heyday of the long drive, the cowboys, the open ranges, and the cattle barons. Boom times, however, did not survive (1) the advance of the farmers' frontier, which meant the fencing of the former grazing lands, (2) the state legislation providing for inspection, and prohibiting the driving of foreign cattle across state lines, (3) the competition of the livestock grown on the farms of the Middle West, and (4) the ability of the railroads and the commission men to dictate freight rates and prices. With the disappearance of the open range, Western ranching lost its most picturesque features.

THE ADVANCE OF THE HOMESTEADERS. The farmer, rather than the miner or the rancher, gradually became the dominant force in the "taming of the wild West."

a. *The Homestead Act (1862).* The policy of the United States in the disposal of its public lands had always been generous, but governmental generosity reached its zenith in the Homestead Act. This legislation provided that any citizen, or any alien who had declared his intention of becoming a citizen, might acquire 160 acres of surveyed land by residing on it for five years and paying a small entry fee. So rapid was the response to this invitation that by 1880 almost 20,-000,000 acres had been entered by those who claimed to be homesteaders. Despite many fraudulent entries, most of this land was soon under cultivation by bona fide settlers.

b. *Farmers' Frontier.* Prospective settlers, who could not qualify under the terms of the Homestead Act, had other opportunities to secure land, though too often they were victimized by speculative interests. The land-grant railroads offered much of their land at reasonable rates, and the state governments, which had received generous allotments under the Morrill Act for the encouragement of education, sold their acres on satisfactory terms. As a result, between 1870 and 1880, an area equal to that of Great Britain was brought under cultivation, and the agrarian frontier was pushed close to the limits of arable land.

c. *Agrarian Immigrants.* The bulk of the settlers in the "prairie states" came from the older states, attracted by cheap land, improved rail transportation, and larger crops which agricultural machinery made possible. Thousands, however, were foreign immigrants (Germans, Swedes, Norwegians, and Danes), who swelled the population of such states and territories as Nebraska, Kansas, Minnesota, and the Dakotas.

**Prosperity and Panic.** The process of exploiting the trans-Mississippi West had immediate repercussions in the marts of commerce and industry. For a dozen years after the firing on Fort Sumter, the business interests of the Northeast were caught up in the speculative and spectacular activities of boom times.

INDUSTRY. Two characteristics seemed to be common to most American industries: the trend toward large-scale production and the use of the corporate form of business organization.

a. *Large-Scale Production.* The evolution from the small shop to the extensive factory as the important unit in American industry was the result of numerous factors, such as (1) the tremendous extent of the domestic market within which American goods were protected from foreign competition by tariff barriers, (2) the far-flung transportation system which brought all parts of the market within reach of the industrial centers, (3) the abundant resources of coal, iron, copper, oil, and lumber, (4) the adequate supply of labor for factory and mill, (5) the accumulation of domestic and foreign capital available for industrial investments, and (6) the laissez-faire policy of the government which gave the industrialists a relatively free hand.

b. *Corporate Organization.* The form of business organization changed rapidly after 1850. The individual proprietorship and the partnership gave way before the corporation chartered under state law. During the fifties and sixties the obvious advantage of the corporate form — relative permanence of the organization, limited liability of the stockholders, and adequate capital for the promoters — induced the industrialists to seek charters for their enterprises. Upon these foundations were later erected the elaborate structures designed to insure monopolistic control of particular industries.

c. *Technical Improvements and Inventions.* The records of the Patent Office tell an impressive story of how old businesses were being revolutionized and new ones created by the invention and improvement of machinery and processes. In textile factories, steel mills, and oil refineries the increased production of labor enabled the manufacturers to sell their commodities widely and thus contribute to the material comfort of their countrymen.

d. *Territorial Location of Manufacturing.* Although the states of the Northeast, which had first felt the impulse of the Industrial Revolution, still retained their primacy in manufactured commodities, a second mill zone centering in the states of the old Northwest Territory was rapidly developing. For example, the seventies were marked by the beginning of territorial shifts which made Chicago the capital of the meat-packing domain, which carried flour-milling from up-state New York to Minneapolis, and which brought part of Pennsylvania's great iron and steel mills into Ohio and Illinois.

TRANSPORTATION AND COMMUNICATION. Of paramount importance in the new economic order were the railroads, as they performed their tasks of uniting all sections of the country, bringing raw materials and foodstuffs to the industrial centers, and carrying finished products to the domestic market and to ports of shipment for the foreign trade.

a. *Building the Railroads.* The construction of new lines, which had gone forward rapidly in the decade of the fifties, was checked temporarily by the Civil War, but even before the cessation of hostilities building had been resumed. Between 1865 and 1873 more than 30,000 miles of track was laid, and by 1880, despite the years of panic and depression, mileage in operation had reached 93,000. During the same period the railroad companies began to substitute steel for iron, to adopt the standard gauge for their tracks, and to improve their engines and rolling stock.

b. *The Railroad Systems.* During the sixties and seventies

the trend toward railroad consolidations established the nation's great rail systems: (1) the New York Central, which Cornelius Vanderbilt organized in 1869; (2) the Pennsylvania, which reached Cleveland, Chicago, and St. Louis in 1871; (3) the Erie, which suffered much from financial rogues like Daniel Drew and Jay Gould; (4) the Baltimore and Ohio, which pushed steadily beyond the Ohio River toward Chicago; (5) the New York, New Haven and Hartford, which came to dominate New England. West of the Mississippi the Union Pacific and the Southern Pacific spread their networks ever wider, while James J. Hill in 1878 secured the first unit in the Great Northern.

c. *Telegraphic Communication.* Operation of the railroads depended upon the telegraph. The lines in the country trebled within six years after the close of the war. As the railroads and the telegraph united the remote sections of the nation, so the Atlantic cable, successfully laid in 1866 by Cyrus W. Field, brought all the nations of the world into closer contact with each other.

d. *The Telephone.* One of the most interesting novelties exhibited at the Centennial Exposition in Philadelphia in 1876 was the "lover's telegraph," which proved to be Alexander Graham Bell's early model of the telephone. Within a few years it had revolutionized business routine in the great cities and had become a familiar convenience in thousands of American homes.

THE RISE OF THE CITY. A significant characteristic of the new economic order was the growth of cities both in size and in influence.

a. *A New Plutocracy.* The urban population grew rapidly as the offices and factories of prosperous business enterprises drew thousands of immigrants from Europe and other thousands of native-born Americans from the farms and villages. Many of these city dwellers speedily attained wealth through ingenious manipulation of investments in mines, railroads, factories, and banks. Their acquisitive methods were widely admired and widely imitated. Their power was recognized in all parts of the land, even if their standards of conduct and canons of taste left much to be desired.

b. *Municipal Problems.* While a majority of the plutocracy were busy adding to their fortunes, acquiring town houses and country estates, and winning social recognition and prestige, a select minority grappled with the difficult problems presented by the disorderly growth of the cities. They strove mightily, if not always effectively, to provide satisfactory housing, transportation, fire protection, and policing. A few rare spirits even attacked the squalor of the slum areas, or fought intemperance, disease, poverty, vice, and crime, which throve in the congested byways of the cities.

c. *Urban Influences.* If much of the city's population was drawn from the rural districts, the villages and farms fell more and more under the influence of urban manners and standards. Despite the antagonism toward the city often manifest by the agrarians, they succumbed gradually to urban standardization in habits of thought as well as in ready-made clothes.

THE PANIC OF 1873. The industrial boom of the postwar years was checked by the world-wide crisis and depression which marked the period from 1873 to 1878.

a. *Causes of the Panic.* The collapse of commercial prosperity in the United States was but a phase of the world depression resulting from (1) a series of costly international conflicts, culminating in the Franco-Prussian War, (2) an excessive expansion of railroads into central and eastern Europe, and (3) an inflation of national currencies which adversely affected international exchange. In this country the panic terminated a period of overproduction of raw materials and manufactured goods, of excessive construction of railroads and public works, of inflated currency and rising prices which stimulated highly speculative enterprises.

b. *Failure of Jay Cooke & Company.* The insolvency of the Philadelphia brokerage firm controlled by Jay Cooke, which had formed a syndicate to finance the Northern Pacific Railroad, precipitated the panic in September, 1873. Before the close of the year there were more than 5000 commercial failures, involving $228,000,000. In 1874 the bread lines lengthened, as three million men were thrown into the ranks of the unemployed. Prices fell and the farmer sold his grain below the cost of production.

c. *Proposals for Inflation.* Price levels remained low for several years after the first crisis. As a result numerous proposals were discussed in an effort to secure an inflation of the currency which would raise prices and stimulate trade. While many championed an issue of greenbacks (fiat money), some joined the mineowners in their demand for free and unlimited coinage of silver as well as gold.

**The Revolt of the Farmers.** The depressed prices of agricultural commodities following 1873 gave impetus to the mass protest of Western farmers against the political and economic conditions of the period.

THE "PATRONS OF HUSBANDRY." The Patrons of Husbandry, popularly known as the Grange, was a ritualistic society formed in 1867 by Oliver H. Kelley, a government clerk, who was anxious to promote rural social activity as an antidote to the loneliness and monotony of farm life. The meetings of the local granges soon became centers for the discussion of such agrarian problems as: (1) the declining prices of grain resulting from the rapid increase in the production of agricultural products; (2) the exorbitant prices which the manufacturer, protected from foreign competition by the tariff, charged for farm implements and other finished goods; (3) the excessive rates demanded by the commission merchants for the storage and handling of grain, and by the railroads for the transportation of crops to market; (4) the high interest on farm mortgages charged by most banks; (5) the heavy burden of taxation borne by farm lands and real estate generally, as compared with personal property; and (6) the lack of agrarian representation either in the state legislatures or in Congress.

THE CO-OPERATIVE MOVEMENT. The Grangers organized farmers' co-operatives in order to reduce the cost of the commodities which they purchased and to market more successfully the crops which they produced. In the decade of the seventies they were operating plow factories, harvester works, and retail stores as well as conducting grain elevators, packing plants, and loan and discount companies. Most of these co-operative ventures were wrecked on the rocks of inefficient management, internal dissension, and aggressive hostility of private competitors

THE GRANGER LAWS. By 1874 the Grangers reported more than 1,500,000 members, concentrated chiefly in the grain-growing states of the Middle West. Supporting third-party movements, under a variety of names, they fought for control of the state legislatures and won notable triumphs. In Illinois they wrote a law fixing the maximum railroad rates and maximum charges of elevator companies; in Wisconsin and Iowa they controlled the legislatures and enacted laws regulating freight rates; in Minnesota they formed a railroad commission to supervise public utilities, particularly railroads. Their political power in some of the prairie states enabled them to send delegations to Congress.

MUNN V. ILLINOIS (1876). When the Granger laws were tested in the state courts they were frequently held unconstitutional, but the Supreme Court of the United States in several cases in 1876 held that the courts were not competent to review rates of railroads and other public utilities, which had been fixed by state legislatures. In *Munn* v. *Illinois* the Supreme Court upheld the state's right to establish maximum fees to be charged by grain elevators. Within a decade, however, as we shall see, the federal judiciary modified its position concerning the competence of a state to regulate railroad traffic.

## THE POLITICAL DEBACLE

The economic and social issues presented by the Grangers during the heyday of their power (1873-1876) were not the chief concern of the nation's political leaders. The foundations of the new economic order were laid with slight directive counsel from government officials.

**Grantism.** President Grant's administrations were characterized by the low standard of public morality which had already become evident during the war years. Business leaders sought and received favors from the government for a price; government officials betrayed the interests of their constituents; politicians shamelessly used public office as a source of private profit.

GRANT'S ADVISERS. The cabinet contained only three men of outstanding ability: Hamilton Fish (State), J. D. Cox (Interior), and E. R. Hoar (Attorney-General). Cox and Hoar soon retired in disgust, and the President came under the influence of such astute politicians as Roscoe Conkling and Benjamin F. Butler. The civil service was filled with Grant's personal friends and relatives, and with the protégés of unimportant party workers.

THE GOLD CONSPIRACY. Neither by temperament nor by training was the President qualified to set a high standard of political ethics. Instead, his frank admiration for men of wealth involved him unwittingly in such scandals as that occasioned by the attempt of Jim Fisk and Jay Gould to corner the nation's gold supply. Grant's association with the conspirators made it impossible for him, however innocent, to denounce the plot which resulted in the financial ruin of a score of brokers on "Black Friday," September 24, 1869.

THE TWEED RING. Symptomatic of the conditions permeating political and business circles were the frauds committed against the city of New York by a gang of unscrupulous officials headed by William M. Tweed, boss of Tammany Hall. The persistent detective work sponsored by the *New York Times* and the striking cartoons of Thomas Nast in *Harper's Weekly* finally brought the destruction of the gang in 1871.

THE CRÉDIT MOBILIER SCANDAL. Ugly rumors of graft and political corruption in connection with the Crédit Mobilier, which built the Union Pacific, were partially verified in 1872. A congressional investigation (1873) produced evidence that Oakes Ames, a member of Congress from Massachusetts, had placed shares of Crédit Mobilier stock among government officials in order to influence legislation. Schuyler Colfax, Vice-President during Grant's first term, was one of those who retired from public life thoroughly discredited.

**The Liberal Republican Movement.** The groups within the Republican party which were hostile to Grant endeavored to prevent his re-election in 1872.

THE MISSOURI LIBERALS. The center of the anti-Grant movement was in Missouri, where such Republican leaders as Carl Schurz and B. Gratz Brown favored a more concilatory attitude toward the ex-Confederates in the state, and resented the dominance of the Radical Republicans in national affairs. The Missouri Liberals were especially critical of Grant's policy toward the South.

NOMINATION OF HORACE GREELEY. The convention of Liberals, which met in Cincinnati in May, 1872, contained champions of various political reforms. Besides the opponents of radical reconstruction, there were civil service reformers and advocates of lower tariff rates, as well as ardent crusaders against the corruption of the Grant regime. The delegates ignored Charles Francis Adams and Lyman Trumbull and unwisely selected Horace Greeley, editor of the *New York Tribune,* as the presidential nominee. The Democrats, without enthusiasm, accepted Greeley as their standard-bearer, because a fusion with the Liberal Republicans offered the only chance to defeat the nominee of the regular Republicans, President Grant.

Election of 1872. Greeley's defeat was overwhelming. He carried only three border states (Missouri, Kentucky, and Maryland) and three Southern states (Georgia, Tennessee, and Texas). The Liberal Republican movement, however, was not without results. It threw a sufficient scare into the administration to cause the President to advocate civil service reform, downward revision of the tariff, and modification of the Southern policy. Congress had already passed a general Amnesty Act in May, 1872.

**The Climax of Political Corruption.** Grant was either unwilling or unable to put the political house in order, and his second administration was marked by a distressing series of governmental scandals.

The "Salary Grab." The country was incensed by the action of Congress (March, 1873) in voting generous salary increases which included a 50 per cent increase for senators and representatives, to be effective as of December, 1871. The next Congress repealed this "back-pay steal."

The Sanborn Contracts. In May, 1874, it was discovered that Secretary of the Treasury Richardson had permitted J. D. Sanborn, a friend of Benjamin F. Butler, to retain exorbitant commissions for collecting unpaid internal revenue taxes. Richardson resigned in order to escape a vote of censure by the House.

The "District Ring." Despite the fact that Alexander Shepherd, governor of the District of Columbia, had enriched his friends through the "honest graft" of lucrative contracts, President Grant appointed him to the newly-created commission for the District in 1874. The Senate indignantly refused to ratify the appointment.

The "Whiskey Ring." By ingenious detective work Secretary Bristow, who had succeeded Richardson in the Treasury Department, revealed the existence of a conspiracy, with which Grant's private secretary, O. E. Babcock, was connected, to defraud the government of internal revenue taxes on whiskey.

THE BELKNAP SCANDAL. In March, 1876, Secretary of War Belknap suddenly resigned in order to escape impeachment for having accepted a bribe for several years from a federal officeholder.

**A Program of Deflation.** Eastern business interests, and the creditor class generally, were gratified by the financial policy of the Grant administration.

THE GREENBACK QUESTION. Ever since the early years of the war the trade of the country had been carried on largely through the medium of depreciated currency (greenbacks). Business and financial leaders advocated a policy of sound money which would gradually contract the volume of paper in circulation and redeem paper dollars at face value in gold. The process of retiring the greenbacks (deflation), begun in 1866, was abandoned two years later.

THE INFLATION BILL OF 1874. With the falling of prices, and the corresponding rise in the value of the dollar in terms of commodities, which marked the panic of 1873, the farmers of the West became leaders in a movement for cheaper currency through inflation. Congress passed a bill providing for the issuance of more greenbacks, but President Grant vetoed the measure.

RESUMPTION OF SPECIE PAYMENTS. In January, 1875, the Republicans passed the Resumption Act in an effort to reconcile the inflationist sentiment of the West with the sound money policies of the East. It provided that $346,681,000 of greenbacks should remain in circulation permanently, but that after January 1, 1879, they should be redeemable at face value in gold. A gold reserve of $100,000,000 was set up so that the notes could be redeemed whenever they were presented to the Treasury.

THE GREENBACK PARTY. The extreme inflationists answered the deflationary policy of the government by organizing the National Greenback party in 1875. Three years later in the congressional elections they cast one million votes, but their strength rapidly declined as the inflationists turned to free and unlimited coinage of silver.

**The Disputed Election (1876).** The Democrats, who had won significant victories in the mid-term elections of 1874, looked forward with confidence to the election of their presidential candidate in 1876.

TILDEN VERSUS HAYES. The Democratic national convention nominated Samuel J. Tilden, governor of New York, who had won a national reputation as a reformer by his successful prosecution of the corrupt "Canal Ring" in his state. The Republicans, after a bitter struggle between James G. Blaine, former Speaker of the House, B. H. Bristow, Secretary of the Treasury, and Roscoe Conkling, senator from New York, finally named Governor R. B. Hayes of Ohio.

THE INDECISIVE ELECTION. As a result of the balloting in November, Tilden carried states with 184 votes in the electoral college, one short of the necessary majority. Hayes received 165 undisputed votes. Twenty votes were in doubt: one in Oregon, because of the technical ineligibility of one of the Republican electors; and nineteen in three Southern states, South Carolina, Florida, and Louisiana, which were just passing from Negro-carpetbagger dominance to white rule. The balloting in these three states, and the counting and tabulating of the vote, was so clearly characterized by fraud on both sides that it is still impossible to determine whether Tilden or Hayes was entitled to the electoral vote.

THE ELECTORAL COMMISSION. To avert any possibility of violence, Congress created a special commission of fifteen to pass judgment upon the disputed votes. Five from the Senate (three Republicans and two Democrats), five from the House (three Democrats and two Republicans), and five justices of the Supreme Court were named to the Commission. The decision was eight to seven on every disputed point in favor of the Republican candidate, Hayes. The country acquiesced in the decision.

## REVIEW QUESTIONS

1. What factors do you consider important in determining the characteristics of large-scale industry in the United States after the Civil War? Why?

2. If you had been in a position to determine the policy of the government toward the Indians of the great plains, what changes would you have made in the policies which were actually applied?

3. To what extent are the grievances voiced by the Grangers still insistent problems of American agriculture? Was the Granger movement a failure?

4. How do you explain the fact that the Liberal Republican leaders and the revolting farmers did not make common cause against the Grant administration?

5. Why is the debtor class in any community generally in favor of a policy of inflation of the currency?

6. What evidence, if any, do you find to support the contention that the Grant administration was dominated by the banking and business interests of the Eastern states?

## SELECTED REFERENCES

Dick, Everett, *Sod House Frontier*
Giddens, P. H., *Birth of the Oil Industry*
Nevins, Allan, *Emergence of Modern America*
Osgood, E. S., *Day of the Cattleman*
Pelzer, Louis, *Cattlemen's Frontier, 1850-1890*
Schlesinger, A. M., *Rise of the City*
Thompson, Holland, *The New South*
Webb, W. P., *The Great Plains*

### CHAPTER III

# THE POLITICAL SCENE

### PARTISAN STRIFE

The professional politicians, who had been preoccupied with matters of patronage and partisan strife, were most reluctant to face the new issues raised by the economic revolution.

**New Issues.** As a result of the economic changes, which we have already noted, the most insistent national problems were those dealing with the control of railroad expansion, the regulation of industrial monopoly, the adjustment of disputes between wage earners and employers, and the maintenance of a monetary system which would protect the interests of the debtor as well as the creditor. Since these issues were apt to cut across party lines with devastating effect upon party discipline, the politicians either avoided them or dealt with them in evasive generalizations.

**Old Methods.** The political leaders were primarily concerned with controlling the party machinery, nominating candidates, winning elections, and distributing the patronage and other spoils. These were the vested interests of the politicians over which the party battles were really fought.

STALWARTS AND HALFBREEDS. Within the Republican ranks there developed during the seventies a bitter struggle for control. The two leading factions came to be known as Stalwarts and Halfbreeds. Stanch supporters of the Grant regime, the Stalwarts were led by Roscoe Conkling of New York, Don Cameron of Pennsylvania, and John A. Logan of Illinois, each of whom had an aggressive state organization. Among the Halfbreeds, John Sherman and James A. Garfield were outstanding, but James G. Blaine of Maine, an implacable foe of Conkling, finally assumed leadership. The reform element within the party was often strong enough to decide the factional quarrels. When it could not have its way such leaders as Carl Schurz, George William Curtis, B. H. Bristow, and Henry Ward Beecher were apt to bolt the ticket.

THE SOLID SOUTH. The distinctive feature of the Democratic organization was its strength in the states of the late Confederacy. After 1876 the Democrats could count upon the South to furnish the irreducible minimum of Democratic votes in the electoral college. The preponderance of Southerners, however, weakened the party in the Northeast and West, and it was difficult for the party leaders to maintain close cooperation between the Democracy of the Northern cities and of the Solid South.

## TRIUMPHANT REFORMERS

The narrow margin of Hayes's victory in 1876 gave strength to the reformers' demands that the Republican party correct the abuses which had resulted from the tactics of unscrupulous politicians.

**The Administration of Hayes.** In economic matters President Hayes represented the conservative business interests; in political affairs he was an earnest advocate of reform.

THE CABINET. The presidential advisers were unusually able men, and the reformers were pleased by the selection of William M. Evarts of New York (State), John Sherman of Ohio (Treasury), and Carl Schurz of Missouri (Interior). Hayes's conciliatory attitude toward the South was shown by his appointment of David Key, a Tennessee Democrat, as Postmaster-General, and his withdrawal of federal troops from South Carolina, Florida, and Louisiana.

CIVIL SERVICE REFORM. President Hayes cast his lot with the enemies of the spoils system. He issued an executive order forbidding financial assessments on federal officeholders for party purposes; he gave Carl Schurz a free hand to try the merit system in making appointments in the Interior Department; he named T. L. James, a champion of civil service reform, to the postmastership of New York City; and he removed Chester A. Arthur and A. B. Cornell from their posts in the New York customhouse for the good of the service.

FINANCIAL POLICY. Despite the pressure from the Western wing of his own party, Hayes refused to yield to the demands of the inflationists.

a. *The Bland-Allison Act.* In 1878 Congress passed the Bland-Allison Act, which authorized the Treasury Department to purchase between $2,000,000 and $4,000,000 worth of silver bullion each month and coin it into silver dollars. Hayes vetoed the bill, on the ground that it substituted cheaper dollars in the payment of obligations contracted before 1878, but the measure was passed over his veto.

b. *Resumption of Specie Payments.* In conformity with the Resumption Act of 1875, Secretary of the Treasury Sherman announced on January 1, 1879, that the greenbacks would be redeemed at face value in gold.

THE QUARREL WITH CONGRESS. Hayes's relations with Congress were far from happy, for the Democrats controlled the House during his entire administration and the Senate from 1879 to 1881.

a. *The Potter Committee Investigation.* The Potter Committee of the Democratic House of Representatives was instructed to investigate Hayes's title to the presidency. It was a political move to keep the disputed election fresh in the minds of the electorate. The investigation was abruptly terminated when the Republicans published certain telegrams sent during the campaign of 1876 by prominent Democratic politicians.

b. *Federal Election Laws.* Partisanship, likewise, was important in the dispute between the President and Congress over the federal election laws. The Democrats demanded that the federal government abandon the use of federal troops in supervising elections in the Southern states. To accomplish this purpose, Congress attached "riders" to essential appropriation measures, hoping that Hayes would not dare to veto them. After a protracted controversy during which the President vetoed five bills, Congress yielded. Hayes insisted that he was merely protecting the government against unjustifiable congressional tactics, but his spirited defense of the federal election laws contained a strong suggestion of partisanship.

**The Passing of the Stalwarts.** The Stalwart faction made a vigorous bid for power in the campaign of 1880, but failed to reassert its control over the Republican organization. Thereafter its influence steadily waned in party councils.

THE ELECTION OF GARFIELD. Hayes's disinclination to serve another term in the presidency seemed to remove the chief obstacle in the way of the Stalwarts, who were determined to force Grant upon the party and the country.

a. *Republican Convention of 1880.* In the Republican national convention, however, a deadlock developed between Grant's Stalwart supporters and the friends of James G. Blaine. Not until the thirty-sixth ballot did Grant's opponents concentrate their strength and lead a stampede of delegates to the standard of James A. Garfield.

b. *The Campaign.* The animosities of the convention were not easily forgotten during the campaign; but Grant and Conkling reluctantly agreed to speak for Garfield in order to present a united front against the Democrats, who had nominated a Civil War general, Winfield S. Hancock of Pennsylvania.

c. *The Influence of Blaine.* As soon as he had been elected, by 214 to 155 votes in the electoral college, Garfield indicated that James G. Blaine, whom he appointed Secretary of State, would exercise a commanding influence in the new administration. The result was an unseemly quarrel between Senator Conkling and the President. When Garfield used the patronage in New York in such a way as to build a Garfield-Blaine machine, Conkling defied the administration. This controversy was still acute when the President was assassinated by Guiteau, a misguided supporter of Conkling's Stalwart faction.

**Arthur's Administration.** The assassination of Garfield elevated to the presidency Vice-President Chester A. Arthur, who had been one of Conkling's lieutenants in New York.

REORGANIZING THE CABINET. President Arthur surprised those skeptical observers who doubted whether he was equal to the tasks of the presidency. He refused to use his high office to reward his former political associates, and he frowned upon the continuation of factional strife within the party. Gradually the cabinet was reorganized and the influence of Blaine's friends declined. F. T. Frelinghuysen of New Jersey replaced Blaine in the State Department; C. J. Folger of New York became Secretary of the Treasury in place of William Windom of Minnesota; but Robert T. Lincoln, son of the former President, was retained as Secretary of War.

DEFEATING THE SPOILSMEN. Arthur's first message indicated that he was prepared to co-operate with Congress in effecting a drastic modification of the spoils system.

a. *Background of Civil Service Reform.* Despite a few feeble protests, the country in the sixties generally accepted the doctrine that appointments to positions in the civil service were legitimate political spoils to be distributed by the victorious party. But there were signs of the slow permeation of the idea that merit alone should be the test for public office: (1) T. A. Jenckes of Rhode Island, a student of the civil service of Great Britain, introduced a bill into Congress (1865) calling for competitive examinations; (2) a commission appointed by Grant (1871) experimented futilely with examinations for certain positions; (3) Secretary Schurz effected important reforms in the Interior Department; (4) the National Civil Service Reform League, founded in 1881 by George William Curtis, served to unite the efforts of many publicists and political reformers.

b. *The Pendleton Act (1883).* The assassination of President Garfield, which seemed to be the result of factional quarrels over political appointments, shocked the country into a realization of the evils of the spoils system. Popular indignation became widespread as revelations of political jobbery and corruption marked the trial of Garfield's assassin, Guiteau. The result was the Pendleton Act, passed by a Congress in which the Republican majority supported the measure in the hope that it would safeguard Republican officeholders in the event of Democratic success the next year.

c. *The Civil Service Commission.* The purpose of the Pendleton Act was (1) to substitute merit for political influence in federal appointments, and (2) to protect officeholders from financial assessments against their salaries for party campaign funds. The President was authorized to appoint a commission of three to advise him in classifying the grades of service, and in supervising competitive examinations to establish fitness of candidates for office. Arthur named the Civil Service Commission and placed 15,573 employees under the merit system.

CHINESE EXCLUSION. Chinese immigration, which had increased rapidly after 1850, began to arouse hostility in the decade of the seventies.

a. *The Burlingame Treaty (1868).* Chinese coolies were welcomed on the Pacific coast, so long as their labor was needed in such work as the construction of the Central Pacific railroad. The Burlingame Treaty granted Chinese subjects unrestricted rights of immigration as well as equality of treatment with immigrants from other countries.

b. *Demand for Exclusion.* Shortly after 1870, as it became apparent that the Chinese were competing with American laborers, a movement developed in California for revision of our policy of free immigration. The Chinese were socially unassimilable and were endangering American standards of living by virtue of their own low economic standards. Congress abrogated the Burlingame Treaty, but Hayes vetoed the measure and sent a commission to China to secure modification of the treaty.

c. *Act of 1882.* After President Arthur had vetoed an exclusion bill, Congress passed an act excluding Chinese laborers for a period of ten years. Temporary exclusion was extended in 1892 and became the permanent policy of the government.

"PORK BARREL" APPROPRIATIONS. As the government receipts from high customs duties and internal revenue taxes piled up a surplus in the treasury, the members of Congress were encouraged to support appropriations for improvements and public works in their respective districts. Between 1870 and 1880 such "pork barrel" appropriations more than doubled. When the bill of 1882 called for the expenditure of $18,000,000 in hundreds of river and harbor projects of dubious value, President Arthur courageously vetoed it. The senators and representatives passed the measure over his veto.

## A DEMOCRATIC VICTORY

The election of 1884 brought a political upheaval which marked the return of the Democratic party to power for the first time since the administration of James Buchanan.

**The "Mugwump" Campaign.** Ever since the scandals of the Grant administration the Republicans had been on the defensive in the interparty battle. In 1884 defections from their own ranks contributed largely to their defeat.

THE NOMINATION OF BLAINE. The Republican convention refused to grant the nomination to President Arthur, though he desired it and deserved it. Instead the delegates, disregarding the small but vigorous reform element, yielded to the magnetism of Blaine and on the fourth ballot named him for the presidency in a frenzy of rejoicing.

THE MUGWUMPS. The Republican reformers, nicknamed "mugwumps," in considerable numbers announced that they would bolt the ticket if the Democrats nominated a candidate to whom they could give their support. The answer of the Democratic convention was the nomination of Grover Cleveland, who had won distinction as an independent governor of New York State.

THE ELECTION OF GROVER CLEVELAND. There were numerous reasons for the success of the Democrats in the campaign of 1884: (1) the belief, inspired by the revelations of the "Mulligan Letters," in 1876, that Blaine had used his political position to further his private financial interests; (2) the refusal of many independent Republicans to support the ticket; (3) hostility to Blaine on the part of some of the former Stalwarts; (4) the vote polled by the Prohibitionist candidate in the normally Republican counties of upstate New York; (5) the resentment of the Catholic voters, especially in the crucial state of New York, over the speech of Rev. S. D. Burchard, a Blaine supporter, who characterized the Democrats as the party of "Rum, Romanism, and Rebellion." Cleveland was stronger than his party, for he embodied the hopes of the political reform element, irrespective of party affiliation, throughout the country.

**Cleveland's Policies.** President Cleveland's task was made extremely difficult by the hostility of petty politicians within his own party and by the partisan tactics of the Republicans in Congress.

THE OFFICEHOLDERS. The President found it embarrassing to defend the merit system against the pressure of his party associates, who were enjoying their first national victory in twenty-eight years and who desired a division of the federal offices among the party workers.

a. *The Cabinet.* Cleveland's official family was composed of men who were inexperienced but capable. Thomas F. Bayard of Delaware (State), William C. Whitney of New York (Navy), and L. Q. C. Lamar of Mississippi (Interior) were outstanding. The administration tried to give Southerners, who had been proscribed since the Civil War, equality with Northerners in the federal offices.

b. *The Civil Service.* With the Democratic chieftains demanding that the 100,000 federal jobs be apportioned among the party workers, Cleveland reluctantly permitted partisan removals to satisfy the demand. He showed his interest in reform, however, by adding almost 12,000 positions to the classified service which was on a merit basis.

THE REPEAL OF THE TENURE OF OFFICE ACT. When Cleveland removed a federal district attorney in Alabama, the Senate, invoking the Tenure of Office Act (see page 5) demanded that the President submit the papers relative to the removal. This Cleveland refused to do, insisting that the right of removal of federal officers was a purely executive function. The Senate censured the President, but in 1887 repealed the Tenure of Office Act.

THE PENSION CONTROVERSY. The mounting treasury surplus enabled Congress to be generous in granting pensions to the veterans of the Civil War who had served the federal government.

a. *Arrears of Pension Act (1879)*. The modest appropriations for pensions, which had been granted to veterans disabled in war service, increased rapidly after the passage of the Arrears of Pensions Act. This law permitted the successful applicant to receive back-pensions from the date of his discharge from the army to the time of filing his claim. Soon pension agents and brokers were touring the country persuading veterans to file claims, and the pension roll by 1885 numbered 345,125.

b. *Private Pension Bills*. Claimants whose cases were not approved by the Bureau of Pensions were accustomed to turn to Congress, where willing legislators sponsored private bills, many of which were outrageous frauds. These private bills President Cleveland tried to investigate, and his researches led him to veto more than two hundred measures. Despite the charge that he was hostile to the veterans, Cleveland did his utmost to keep the pension list a roll of honor.

c. *Dependent Pension Bill (1887)*. Congress abandoned the test of service-disability in the general Dependent Pension Bill, which provided that any ex-soldier who had served three months and was incapable of earning a livelihood was entitled to a pension, regardless of whether he had suffered disability in the war. Cleveland vetoed the measure on the ground that it would tend to "pauperize" the veterans and that it was too soon after the war for so comprehensive a pension policy.

d. *Minor Legislation*. Many of Cleveland's recommendations to Congress were either ignored by the legislators or blocked by the Republican leaders. He urged without success (1) the repeal of the Bland-Allison Act, (2) the revision of the tariff schedules, and (3) the husbanding of the diminishing acreage of public lands. Among the nonpartisan measures enacted were: (1) the Presidential Succession Act, fixing the succession to the presidency in the event of the death of both the president and the vice-president; (2) the Electoral Count Act, authorizing the states to decide contests over presidential electors; (3) the Dawes Act (see page 11); and (4) an act establishing the Department of Agriculture. The most significant piece of legislation, the Interstate Commerce Act, was not, as we shall see, the result of Cleveland's leadership.

## REVIEW QUESTIONS

1. Do you find any distinctions, based on economic theory or political principle, between the Stalwarts and the Halfbreeds?
2. How do you account for the fact that the politicians avoided the new issues engendered by the economic revolution?
3. Discuss the political and economic forces responsible for the passage of the Bland-Allison Act of 1878. Why did President Hayes veto the measure?
4. Explain the contribution of each of the following to the cause of civil service reform: Thomas A. Jenckes, Carl Schurz, Chester A. Arthur, and George William Curtis.
5. Why has the Pendleton Act been called the "Magna Carta" of civil service reform?
6. Who were the "mugwumps"? Explain their attitude in the campaign of 1884.
7. Did the "return of the Democrats to power" cause any change in the economic policies of the government? What were its most obvious results in the realm of politics?

## SELECTED REFERENCES

Burgess, J. W., *The Administration of President Hayes*
Fish, C. R., *Civil Service and the Patronage*
Haworth, P. L., *Hayes-Tilden Election*
Josephson, Matthew, *The Politicos, 1865-1896*
Ross, E. D., *Liberal Republican Movement*
Seitz, E. D., *The Dreadful Decade*
Sparks, E. E., *National Development*
Thomas, H. C., *The Return of the Democratic Party to Power*

## CHAPTER IV

# THE CONTROL
# OF TRANSPORTATION

### THE ATTACK ON THE RAILROADS

In spite of the obvious benefits resulting from the rapid extension of the railroad network into all parts of the country, the public protests against the methods of the builders and operators of the transportation system constantly increased.

**Popular Indictment of the Railroads.** The charges against the common carriers included various aspects of the promotion, construction, and management of the roads.

SPECULATIVE PROMOTION. The achievements of the railroad builders during the sixties and seventies were sometimes marred by men who were speculators rather than railroad operators. They were guilty of (1) promoting lines in regions where absence of competition enabled them to charge exorbitant rates; (2) unloading the securities of unsuccessful roads

39

on the residents of the localities which the roads pretended to serve; (3) imposing an excessive capital burden on new projects by paying huge profits to themselves as directors of construction companies which laid the tracks.

FINANCIAL ABUSES. The practises of some owners and managers embraced a wide range of chicanery and dishonesty.

a. *Fraudulent Sale of Securities.* In some instances powerful railroad directors sold bonds and pocketed the proceeds, thus increasing the corporation's liabilities without adding to its assets.

b. *Manipulation of Securities in the Market.* Jay Gould, Jim Fisk, and Daniel Drew were typical of some owners who used valuable railroad properties as devices for building up private fortunes through the unscrupulous manipulation of securities on the stock exchange. They knew little, and cared less, about honestly managing a transportation system.

c. *"Stock-Watering."* Shippers complained that in prosperous years the railroad directors concealed excessive profits by the process of declaring stock dividends, which increased the outstanding capital stock of the enterprise without adding a dollar of new capital to the existing investment. When traffic tended to fall off, the directors increased the freight rates with the plea that they had to earn enough to pay dividends on the total capital stock. The public realized that it paid high rates for service in order to return dividends on stock certificates which represented no real investment in the road. In 1883, for example, it was estimated that the roads of the country were carrying an indebtedness of $7,500,000,-000 of which $2,000,000,000 was "water."

POLITICAL CORRUPTION. There was a growing concern during the seventies and eighties over the interference of powerful railroad lobbies with the course of state legislation. Pressure was exerted in various ways to secure favors from legislators or to block restrictive legislation. By the resort to (1) extensive distribution of free passes among politicians and officeholders, (2) generous contributions to party campaign funds, and (3) outright bribery of legislators, the railroads gained "protection" but also incurred popular ill will.

GRIEVANCES CONCERNING RATES. In the eyes of the shippers the greatest sins of the common carriers were their rate-making policies.

a. *Pooling Agreements.* In order to prevent rate wars and cutthroat competition many of the roads entered into pooling agreements, which provided either for a distribution of territory among the members of the pool or for a pro rata division of the profits at the end of the fiscal year. Thus genuine competition among the roads was eliminated, and rates remained as high as traffic could bear.

b. *Discrimination between Localities.* The "long-and-short-haul evil" grew out of the tendency of the roads to favor shippers who resided at important terminal points where there was competition between lines. As a result, rates from one terminal point to another were low, while the shipper using way stations, where there was no competition between carriers, paid a proportionately higher rate for the same service. The same shipment could be sent from New York to Chicago at a lower rate than was charged for the shorter distance between Rochester, New York, and Toledo, Ohio.

c. *Secret Rebates.* The small shipper bitterly complained that his larger competitor was the recipient of favors from the railroads in the form of secret rebates, which brought freight costs far below the rates advertised by the roads in their published schedules. We shall see in our consideration of the growth of "big business" that this discriminatory practise was forced upon the carriers by the powerful industrial enterprises in their war on the independent producers.

**State Control of Rates.** Popular protests against the railroads resulted first in the attempt of state legislatures to regulate the practises of the common carriers.

RAILROAD COMMISSIONS. In 1869 Massachusetts created the first commission with supervisory powers. Its record of correcting abuses through investigation and conference caused other Eastern states, notably New York and New Hampshire, to set up similar bodies to hear complaints and report discriminatory practises.

LEGISLATIVE RATE-MAKING. The Western states, under the impulse of the Grangers and various agrarian parties (see page 62), passed laws fixing maximum rates for the transportation of freight and passengers. Illinois set up a commission which was given power to prepare rate schedules; Wisconsin, Minnesota, and Iowa established carrying charges by direct legislative action; several other states adopted constitutional amendments empowering the legislature to deal with railroad abuses.

**Judicial Review of State Legislation.** The railroads appealed to the courts to protect them against state regulation, but the trend of the early decisions was against the carriers.

THE GRANGER CASES. During the seventies the Supreme Court of the United States held that when property becomes "clothed with a public interest," its owner must "submit to be controlled by the public for the common good."

a. *Munn* v. *Illinois*. In the autumn of 1876 the Court decided that an Illinois law fixing the maximum rates for the storage of grain in elevators did not deprive the warehouse owners of property rights without due process of law.

b. *Peik* v. *The Chicago and Northwestern Railroad*. In 1877 the Court, distinguishing between intrastate commerce and interstate commerce, maintained the right of Wisconsin to regulate railroad rates within the state even though such regulation might incidentally affect persons outside the state. A majority of the judges believed that the states should be permitted to handle their railroad problems without judicial interference "until such time as Congress should legislate on this matter."

THE WABASH RATE CASE. The principles established in the Granger cases were apparently reversed by the Supreme Court in 1886 when it handed down the decision in *Illinois* v. *Wabash, St. Louis and Pacific Railroad*. A statute of Illinois which attempted to prevent rate discrimination on shipments to various points within the state was held unconstitutional on the ground that the state was interfering with interstate commerce, over which the power of Congress was exclusive. The effect of the decision was to limit the state's jurisdiction to intrastate commerce and to render ineffective most of the rate-making legislation of the previous fifteen years.

## CONGRESS AND THE RAILROADS

For years before the Wabash decision crippled the power of the states over interstate commerce, Congress had been considering proposals for federal regulation of the railroads.

**Early Movement for Federal Control.** Every presidential campaign since 1868 had been marked by the demand of the minor parties that Congress regulate rates. The Labor Reform party (1872), the Prohibitionists (1876), the Greenbackers (1880), and the Greenback-Labor party (1884) cited the outstanding railroad abuses and called upon the national government to take action. Within the two major parties there was considerable sentiment favoring congressional legislation. The Windom Report (1874) to the Senate, the McCrary Bill (1874) passed by the House, and the Reagan Bill (1878), which the Senate refused to consider, all kept the issue alive.

**The Cullom Committee Investigation.** In 1885 the Senate appointed a special committee of five, headed by Senator Shelby M. Cullom of Illinois, to investigate the subject of federal control of interstate commerce. This committee after protracted hearings in every section of the country filed a two-thousand page report which reached the conclusion that "upon no public question is public opinion so nearly unanimous as upon the proposition that Congress should undertake in some way the regulation of interstate commerce."

**The Interstate Commerce Act (1887).** The congressional debates over the Cullom Report finally brought the first important attempt of the national government to control private business enterprise in the public interest.

Provisions of the Act. The Interstate Commerce Act forbade the railroads (1) to grant special rates, secret rebates, or drawbacks; (2) to discriminate between persons, places, and commodities in rate-making; (3) to charge more for a short haul than a long haul under the same conditions of traffic; (4) to form pooling agreements; (5) to deny the public the right to inspect schedules and rates. A Commission of five was created to supervise the accounting systems, rate schedules, and business methods of the roads, to hear complaints from shippers, and to assist the Attorney-General in prosecuting offenses against the law in the federal courts.

Enforcement. Despite the conscientious work of an able Commission, the law proved to be disappointing as a corrective of the abuses against which the shippers had protested for years. Effective regulation was impossible because of (1) the inability of the Commission to compel witnesses to testify, (2) the prolonged litigation in the federal courts over rulings of the Commission, (3) the success of the railroad attorneys in winning their appeals from the Commission's orders, and (4) the tendency of the Supreme Court to interpret the Interstate Commerce Act in such a way as to restrict the Commission's control over discriminatory rates and the long-and-short-haul evil. For twenty years the country waited for Congress to remedy the situation by further railroad legislation.

## REVIEW QUESTIONS

1. How do you account for the arrogant attitude adopted by many of the promoters of the early railroads toward the shippers and the general public?
2. What types of discriminatory rate-making aroused the most vigorous protests throughout the country?

3. Discuss the relation of the Granger movement to the control of interstate commerce.
4. What constitutional safeguards did the legal counsel for the railroads invoke in order to nullify state regulatory enactments?
5. In what sense was the Supreme Court's decision in the Wabash rate case a reversal of the principles set forth in the opinion in *Peik* v. *The Chicago and Northwestern Railroad?*
6. Why was Congress reluctant to attempt a program of federal control of the common carriers?
7. How was the Interstate Commerce Commission frustrated in its efforts to carry out the purpose of the act of 1887?

## SELECTED REFERENCES

Adams, C. F., Jr., *Chapters of Erie*
Buck, S. J., *The Granger Movement*
Corey, Lewis, *House of Morgan*
Haney, L. H., *Congressional History of Railways*
Hedges, J. B., *Henry Villard and the Railways of the Northwest*
Moody, John, *Railroad Builders*
Riegel, R. E., *Story of the Western Railways*
Trottman, Nelson, *History of the Union Pacific*

CHAPTER V

# THE TARIFF AND THE TRUSTS

## THE BATTLE OVER TARIFF REVISION

In 1887, the year in which he reluctantly signed the Interstate Commerce Act, President Cleveland sent a forceful message to Congress demanding immediate downward revision of the tariff schedules.

**The Trend of Tariff Legislation.** During the Civil War the Republican party had redeemed its campaign pledges by raising custom duties to protective levels, and those levels were maintained after the war emergency had passed.

TINKERING WITH THE SCHEDULES. Protection, justified at first as a compensation to industry for the increased internal revenue taxes, was generally accepted as an important factor in the growth of American industry. Such modification of rates as occurred in 1870, 1872, and 1875 was designed to meet sectional demands and protests without changing the protective principle.

ACT OF 1883. During the campaign of 1880 there was much talk of taking the tariff out of politics and revising schedules to meet the needs of domestic producers on a scientific basis. Two years later a tariff commission of nine members, after

46

conducting a thorough investigation, surprised the country by recommending "a substantial reduction of tariff duties." Congress, however, ignored the sound advice of the experts and finally enacted (1883) a bill which was a caricature of genuine reform. The reductions in rates scarcely averaged 2 per cent in various schedules.

**The Problem of the Surplus.** Cleveland regarded the tariff question as one phase of the government's fiscal policy, which was accumulating treasury surpluses through an indefensible program of taxation.

Surplus Revenue. From 1880 to 1890 the excess of government receipts over expenditures averaged $100,000,000 annually. This surplus was embarrassing because (1) it indicated that the taxpayers were bearing an unnecessary burden; (2) it reduced the amount of currency available for normal business needs; and (3) it was a constant temptation to Congress to make "pork-barrel" appropriations of doubtful public value.

Cleveland's Tariff Message (1887). President Cleveland was opposed to any wholesale increase in government expenditures in order to reduce the surplus; he feared the effect of paying off the public debt by purchasing government bonds before they fell due; he believed that the internal revenue taxes had been sufficiently reduced. Consequently, the tariff remained as the obstacle in the way of tax reform. In his message to Congress in 1887 the President not only denounced the existing customs duties as "a vicious, inequitable, and illogical source of unnecessary taxation," but he also maintained that the protective principle was responsible for the growth of industrial combinations which increased prices by stifling competition.

Controversy in Congress. Presidential pressure persuaded the Democratic House to pass the Mills Bill, providing for drastic reduction of tariff rates, but the Republican Senate replied with the Aldrich Bill (1888), containing the elements of high protection.

**The Republican Revival.** Cleveland's attitude tended to make the tariff a party issue, and the Republicans were eager to appear before the country as the protectors of American business against the cheap labor and cheap goods of Europe.

THE CAMPAIGN OF 1888. The Democrats renominated President Cleveland, while the Republicans named Benjamin Harrison of Indiana, after Blaine declined to become a candidate. To a remarkable degree party lines were kept intact on the tariff issue. The Democrats were placed on the defensive by the aggressive and well-financed Republican campaign. Cleveland was accused, without justification, of being a free-trader whose tariff policy would benefit British manufacturers at the expense of American industrialists. Though the President had a popular plurality of more than 100,000 votes, he lost the electoral college to Harrison by 233 to 168.

THE HARRISON ADMINISTRATION. The new Republican president leaned heavily upon Blaine, whom he named Secretary of State, Thomas B. Reed of Maine, who became Speaker of the House, and William McKinley of Ohio, chairman of the House Committee on Ways and Means.

a. *The Reed Rules.* The Democrats sought by parliamentary tactics to prevent the Republicans in the House from going forward with their legislative program. By arbitrary rulings, which conflicted with long-established parliamentary precedents, Speaker Reed defeated the opposition. In 1890 the House accepted Reed's rules by agreeing (1) that actual attendance should be the basis for determination of a quorum, and (2) that the Speaker should entertain no dilatory motions.

b. *The Civil Service.* Harrison's support of the merit system was purely nominal during the first years of his administration. Wholesale removals of officeholders in the postal service brought protests even from Republican leaders. Late in 1892 the President, already defeated for re-election, added a few offices to the classified service.

c. *The "Billion Dollar Congress."* Despite Harrison's plea that the problem of the surplus be solved by a reduction in taxation, the Republican leaders in Congress dissipated the surplus through increased expenditures. The appropriations of the Fifty-first Congress, which exceeded $1,000,000,000, included (1) the return to the Northern states of the direct tax collected during the Civil War; (2) an extensive program of river and harbor improvement; (3) additional sums for the construction of a steel navy, which had been started in 1883; and (4) a dependent pension bill (1890), which almost doubled the annual cost of pensions.

d. *The Legislation of 1890.* The attempt of the protectionists to revise tariff schedules was delayed in Congress because it became entangled with other legislation. Western Republicans, more interested in inflation than in protection, demanded that their party endorse free and unlimited coinage of silver. To preserve party harmony and to insure the passage of the tariff act, the Republican managers accepted the Sherman Silver Purchase Act, which authorized the government to purchase 4,500,000 ounces of silver each month and to issue treasury notes, redeemable in gold or silver, against the silver bullion. Complications also developed when the Republicans sought to compel the South to permit the Negro to vote. A Federal Election Bill passed the House, but was sidetracked in the Senate in order to clear the way for the tariff act.

THE McKINLEY TARIFF. The legislation designed to fulfill the Republican pledge of tariff revision was guided by William McKinley of Ohio, chairman of the House Committee on Ways and Means.

a. *Protective Schedules.* On the theory that prosperity flowed directly from protection, McKinley and his colleagues raised the general level of duties. Rates in the woolen goods, cotton goods, and steel products schedules were increased, while the protective principle was extended to the products of American farms.

b. *Sugar Subsidy*. To satisfy the producers of raw sugar, as well as the American Sugar Refining Company, the legislators put raw sugar on the free list and granted a bounty of two cents a pound to domestic producers of raw sugar. This strategy also reduced revenues and thus decreased the treasury surplus.

c. *Reciprocity*. At the suggestion of Secretary Blaine, the Senate included reciprocity provisions in the tariff act. The President was empowered to impose duties on such commodities as coffee, tea, molasses, sugar, and hides, whenever the nations exporting these articles discriminated against the products of the United States. Blaine used this provision to negotiate several reciprocity agreements with Latin American countries.

d. *Opposition to Protection*. As soon as the McKinley Bill became law, prices of protected commodities were raised by manufacturers, wholesalers, and retailers in anticipation of the effect of the protective schedules. The Democrats used this "increase in the cost of living" as an effective weapon against the Republicans in the congressional elections of 1890. The Democratic landslide was partly a repudiation by the electorate of the apparent effects of the protective tariff.

## FEDERAL REGULATION OF BUSINESS

The Republican leaders, who regarded protection as a necessary guarantee of the continued prosperity of American industry, reluctantly yielded to the popular demand that the government impose restraints upon the methods of the more powerful industrialists.

**The "Trust Problem."** The remarkable industrial growth recorded during the generation following the Civil War (see pages 16-17) resulted not only in large-scale production with its attendant advantages to producer and consumer, but also in huge business combinations which often became monopolies.

PROCESS OF ATTAINING MONOPOLY CONTROL. Various devices were used by the great corporations as they strove to secure a dominant position in their particular fields of production.

a. *Pools*. The pool, which was early used by the railroads, generally took the form of an agreement by which several supposedly competing firms established prices, regulated output, and divided markets. Such agreements were easily broken and often proved unsatisfactory.

b. *Trusts*. This form of combination first was tested in the organization of the Standard Oil Trust (1879). John D. Rockefeller's ingenious attorneys worked out a plan whereby a group of corporations, engaged in the refining and transporting of petroleum, entrusted their stocks to a small board of trustees, which was authorized to vote the stocks and control the combination. The original stockholders received "trust certificates" on which they were entitled to dividends from the earnings of the trust. As revised in 1882, the Standard Oil Trust included forty companies, the stock of which was held in trust by a board of nine men. The forty companies represented 90 per cent of the oil refineries and pipe lines of the country. The Standard device was followed in modified form by groups which organized the "Sugar Trust," the "Beef Trust," the "Whiskey Trust," and a score of others.

c. *Holding Companies*. When some of the states prosecuted these trustees on the ground that they were restraining trade, industry began to abandon the trust device and experimented with the holding company. The latter agency was able to dominate a particular industry by (1) purchasing the physical properties of competing plants, (2) securing control of companies through purchase of a majority of the capital stock, and (3) leasing facilities or patent rights which were essential to success. The holding company became important after 1889, as New Jersey, Delaware, West Virginia, and other states modified their corporation laws to permit the chartering of such combines.

Economic Liberalism and State Regulation. The trend toward monopoly in industry had gone far before governmental authorities, either state or federal, could be persuaded to intervene. One reason was the dominant theory of economic liberalism, which in the United States had been summarized in the slogan, "The government of business is no part of the business of government." Freedom of competition in industry would insure fair prices for the consumer and would compel efficient methods on the part of the producer. Not until it became fully apparent that unrestrained competition was leading straight toward monopoly did the states apply the rules of the common law forbidding agreements or contracts in restraint of trade. Louisiana (1887) moved against the Cottonseed Oil Trust; New York (1889) challenged the agreement of the Sugar Trust; Ohio (1890) began a dissolution suit against Standard Oil.

**The Doctrine of Public Interest.** During the eighties and nineties the prevailing theory that the government should abstain from meddling in business affairs was challenged by those who believed that governmental regulation of the economic life of the nation was essential for the welfare of the people. The campaign to protect the "public interest" against the "private interests" was stimulated by (1) the resentment of small business enterprises against the tactics of the great corporations, (2) the complaints of consumers who discovered evidences of monopolistic price-fixing, (3) the revelations of the methods employed by such organizations as Standard Oil, (4) the attacks upon monopoly of such publicists as Henry George, Henry D. Lloyd, and Edward Bellamy, (5) the propaganda of the minor parties in the Western and Southern states.

**Antitrust Legislation.** The first action against the trusts came in state antitrust laws.

State Antitrust Laws. In 1889 Kansas enacted an antimonopoly statute, and within the next year fifteen states had defined in somewhat specific terms the corporate practices which would be punished as actions in restraint of trade. These laws were of little effect because (1) corporations chartered in states which had no restrictive legislation might trade across state lines, and (2) the federal courts had shown a tendency, ever since Roscoe Conkling's plea in *San Mateo County* v. *Southern Pacific Railroad* (1882), to interpret the Fourteenth Amendment in such a way as to protect corporations against any state legislation which might deprive them of "life, liberty, or property without due process of law."

SHERMAN ACT (1890). So powerful was the popular sentiment against the "trusts" in 1889 that President Harrison recommended action by Congress, and the Republican leaders followed his recommendation. The Sherman Antitrust Act, reiterating one of the principles of the common law of England, declared illegal "every contract, combination in the form of trust or otherwise, or conspiracy, in restraint of trade or commerce among the several states, or with foreign nations." It authorized prosecutions by federal district attorneys and suits for damages by any person or corporation injured by a company in restraint of trade.

ENFORCEMENT AND THE COURTS. During the first eleven years of the law's enforcement the federal government was far from aggressive in filing bills in equity and securing criminal indictments. The inactivity of the federal prosecutors can be blamed neither on the indefiniteness of the statute, which was not well phrased, nor on the attitude of the courts. In 1895 the Supreme Court did hold (*U.S.* v. *E. C. Knight Co.*) that the control by the Sugar Trust of 95 per cent of the refining of sugar was not an illegal restraint on interstate trade, but in subsequent decisions a majority of the Court prepared the way for successful prosecutions. The administrations from Harrison to Theodore Roosevelt, however, were not really interested in a vigorous campaign against the trusts.

## REVIEW QUESTIONS

1. Why did an accumulating surplus in the treasury of the United States constitute a financial problem of great importance for the government?

2. In what ways was the problem of the surplus related to the question of customs duties?

3. Explain Cleveland's reasons for demanding that Congress undertake a revision of the tariff schedules.

4. What difficulties did the Republican leaders have to overcome before they could redeem their campaign pledges concerning the tariff?

5. What features of the McKinley Bill were unusual in the history of American tariff-making?

6. What is meant by the "trust problem"?

7. Discuss the obstacles which made it difficult to formulate a comprehensive program of governmental control of business enterprise.

8. To what extent did the Sherman Antitrust Act accomplish the purpose for which it was enacted?

## SELECTED REFERENCES

Dewey, D. R., *National Problems*
Ford, H. J., *The Cleveland Era*
Hendrick, B. J., *The Age of Big Business*
Lloyd, H. D., *Wealth versus Commonwealth*
Moody, John, *The Truth About the Trusts*
Stanwood, Edward, *American Tariff Controversies,* II
Tarbell, Ida, *The Nationalizing of Business*
Walker, A. V., *History of the Sherman Law*

CHAPTER VI

# THE ARMIES OF LABOR

## ORGANIZING THE WORKERS

From the Civil War to the close of the nineteenth century American workingmen, in confused and fumbling fashion, endeavored to organize and guide a labor movement based upon the workers' role in the new industrial order.

**Trade-Unionism.** By the decade of the sixties American workers began to appreciate the effects of machine industry upon the handicrafts. The consequent demand for more aggressive labor organizations was further stimulated by the fact that wages had lagged behind prices during the war years. As a result, trade-unions on a national scale were formed rapidly between 1861 and 1866. In the latter year the National Labor Union, largely under the guidance of W. H. Sylvis, attempted to bring national unions and other labor associations into a great federation pledged to promote the solidarity of labor and to encourage social reforms. Its career, marked by bitter quarrels over questions of policy and objectives, was terminated in 1872 after the leaders had entered politics as sponsors of the National Labor Reform party.

**The Knights of Labor.** For fifteen years after the collapse of the National Labor Union the forces of labor were represented by the Noble Order of the Knights of Labor, a secret society formed by Uriah S. Stephens in 1869 among the garment cutters of Philadelphia.

CHARACTERISTICS. The Knights stressed (1) industrial unionism rather than trade-unionism, (2) the inclusion of all workers in one great organization, (3) the formation of local assemblies on the basis of residence rather than the craft affiliation of the worker, and (4) the highly centralized control of the local assemblies by the General Assembly.

OBJECTIVES. In furthering industrial brotherhood the Knights pledged themselves "to secure for the workers the full enjoyment of the wealth they create, and sufficient leisure in which to develop their intellectual, moral, and social faculties." Their program included such specific objectives as: (1) the eight-hour day, (2) arbitration in industrial disputes, (3) equal pay for equal work for both sexes, (4) the prohibition of child labor, (5) the establishment of bureaus of labor statistics, (6) the enactment of safety and health codes for industry, (7) laws compelling employers to pay laborers weekly, (8) the recognition of the incorporation of labor unions, (9) the prohibition of contract foreign labor, (10) the abolition of national banks, (11) the imposition of an income tax, (12) government ownership of railroads and telegraph lines.

METHODS. In politics the Knights fought aggressively for their program, but not until their influence was waning did they view favorably the idea of a labor party. The creation of producers' and consumers' co-operatives accomplished less than their idealistic leaders anticipated. Although arbitration was one of their main tenets, the Knights relied increasingly upon the strike and the boycott to win victories.

GROWTH AND DECLINE. The organization of the Knights, which expanded rapidly under the leadership of Terence V. Powderley, reached its greatest strength in 1886 when 5,892 locals reported 702,924 members. A series of unsuccessful strikes in 1886 marked the beginning of the Order's decline. Its complete collapse was hastened by (1) the growing belief that many of the Knights favored violence in industrial disputes, (2) the hostility of the skilled workers toward an organization which minimized the interests of the trade-union, (3) the failure of most of the producers' co-operatives in which the Knights had invested funds, (4) the confusion of counsel among the leaders, many of whom were unsympathetic with the idealism of the social reformers within the organization, (5) the revolt against centralized control by many of the local assemblies, and (6) the inability of the Order to handle the large numbers of unskilled and transient workers.

**The American Federation of Labor.** The increasing dissatisfaction of skilled craftsmen with the aims and methods of the Knights of Labor resulted in the formation in 1881 of the Federation of Organized Trades and Labor Unions, changed in 1886 to the American Federation of Labor.

AIMS AND METHODS. Samuel Gompers and Adolph Strasser, who had revived the International Cigarmakers' Union, were influential in formulating the philosophy of the new Federation. Its structure was based upon the national craft union; the authority of the central body did not encroach unnecessarily upon the autonomy of the national craft union; the membership was confined to those who belonged to "trades and labor unions." The specific objectives of the Federation were quite similar to those of the Knights, and for a time the two organizations co-operated. Gradually, however, the Federation leaders concentrated their efforts upon the campaign for shorter hours, higher wages, and improved conditions of employment within the various crafts. Their weapons came to be collective bargaining, the strike, and the boycott. Refusing to sponsor an American labor party, they used their political power to secure immediate objectives rather than to champion a comprehensive program of economic reorganization.

GROWTH AND ACCOMPLISHMENTS. Despite the presence of a small minority of Socialists, the American Federation remained conservative, and defended the capitalistic system while denouncing its imperfections. The achievements of the Federation included (1) the development of strong national unions with full treasuries and effective schemes of sickness and unemployment benefits, (2) the establishment of the eight-hour day in several trades, (3) the recognition of labor's right of collective bargaining by an increasing number of employers, and (4) the slow but steady growth of labor's strength in the state legislatures and in Congress. The membership of the Federation increased from 190,000 in 1890 to 550,000 in 1900 and slightly more than 2,000,000 in 1914. The majority of American workers, however, were not affiliated with the A.F. of L.

**Difficulties of Labor Organization.** If the leaders of labor were less successful than the captains of industry in mobilizing and leading their forces, it was because their task was more difficult. In their attempts to weld the nation's workers into a united and class-conscious group, they had to cope with (1) the ever-increasing armies of aliens, divided by language, religion, and national tradition, (2) the doctrinaire radicals enamored of theories for the reorganization of the social order, (3) the large number of underpaid women workers in certain crafts, and (4) the entrance of the Negroes, both skilled and unskilled, into the ranks of labor.

## LABOR UNREST

In the running warfare between capital and labor during the last quarter of the nineteenth century the governments of the states and the nation seldom interfered, and then only as defenders of property rights.

**Industrial Violence.** If American laborers were little inclined to challenge the bases of the capitalistic system, they were nevertheless quick to use the strike and the boycott in order to compel capitalists to grant shorter hours and higher wages. Between 1880 and 1900 the industrial warfare each year averaged: 1,190 strikes, affecting 330,500 workers in 6,372 establishments with a loss of $22,500,000. Many of these disputes were marked by widespread violence.

**The Railroad Strike of 1877.** Symptomatic of the extensive labor unrest in the seventies was the great railroad strike of 1877, which started when employees of the Baltimore and Ohio Railroad struck because of a reduction in wages. Soon most of the roads lying east of the Mississippi were involved. Rioting in Baltimore, Pittsburgh, and other cities was more than the local authorities could handle and militia companies were called into action. Finally President Hayes authorized the use of federal troops to restore law and order.

**The "Great Upheaval."** Despite the failure of the workers to win the railroad strikes, industrial warfare grew more intense. Between 1884 and 1886, "the great upheaval," the forces of labor launched a great drive for the eight-hour day. In May of the latter year a mass meeting of strikers in Chicago was broken up by the police, several of whom were killed by the explosion of a bomb. Eight anarchists were found guilty of the crime. This Haymarket Square affair injured the cause of labor throughout the country, for many openly accused the Knights of Labor of condoning violence and affiliating with anarchistic organizations.

**Employers' Counteroffensive.** As organized labor learned to use the strike effectively, employers fought vigorously against the power which the unions wielded through collective bargaining.

THE HOMESTEAD STRIKE (1892). The attempt of the Carnegie Steel Company to break the grip of the union in its Homestead (Pennsylvania) plant resulted in open warfare between strikers and Pinkerton guards, who had been employed by the company to protect its strikebreakers. After the state militia restored order the strike was called off and the strong union of iron and steel workers collapsed.

THE PULLMAN STRIKE (1894). A strike of the employees of the Pullman Palace Car Company was followed by the refusal of the workers in the American Railway Union to handle trains carrying Pullman cars. As the boycott spread from Chicago over the Middle West and Far West, the Railroad Managers' Association fought back vigorously. Two developments were of particular importance: (1) President Cleveland, without consulting Governor Altgeld of Illinois, sent United States troops to Chicago, and (2) Attorney-General Olney instructed the federal attorneys in Chicago to obtain an injunction against the American Railway Union on the ground that it was conspiring to obstruct interstate commerce. As a result of federal intervention the workers lost the strike and Eugene V. Debs, president of the American Railway Union, was sentenced to prison for six months because he violated the judicial injunction. Thenceforth the American Federation of Labor campaigned aggressively against the injunction in labor disputes.

### REVIEW QUESTIONS

1. Contrast the organization, methods, and objectives of the Knights of Labor with those of the American Federation of Labor.
2. How do you account for the failure of the leaders of American labor to sponsor the formation of an American labor party?
3. Why has the policy of the American Federation of Labor been essentially hostile to European radicalism?
4. What influence, if any, did the labor disturbances of 1885-1886 have upon the American labor movement?
5. Why was the policy of the federal government in the Pullman Strike so bitterly resented by many labor leaders?
6. Do you consider the use of injunctions in labor disputes justifiable?

## SELECTED REFERENCES

Adamic, Louis, *Dynamite, The Story of Class Violence*
Beard, Mary R., *Short History of the American Labor Movement*
David, Henry, *History of the Haymarket Affair*
Gompers, Samuel, *Seventy Years of Life and Labor*
McMurray, D. L., *Coxey's Army*
Orth, S. P., *Armies of Labor*
Powderly, T. V., *Thirty Years of Labor*
Wolman, Leo, *Growth of American Trade Unions*

## Significant Dates

CHAPTER VII

# THE WEST IN REVOLT

### THE AGRARIAN CRUSADE

The political power of the industrialists was seriously threatened during the decade of the nineties as the farmers of the West and South, joined by many wage earners of the East, launched a frontal attack against the bulwarks of big business.

**Farmer-Labor Politics.** The grievances of the farmers and laborers, as we have already noted, resulted in the formation of numerous third parties which won occasional local victories but failed to unite the forces of discontent under one national banner. From the formation of the Greenback-Labor party in 1878 until 1884 a fusion of the agrarian and labor forces of the country was the great objective. From 1884 to 1888 the labor organizations seemed to assume leadership in guiding the minority parties. After 1889 the agrarian element became aggressive in politics.

**The Currency Question.** A continuing note sounded by the minority parties was hostility to the deflationary policy implicit in the National Banking Act (1863) and the Resumption Act (1875). The demand was for inflation, as a means of increasing the price of the farmer's commodities and the laborer's services, and as a guarantee that the debtor would not pay back more valuable dollars than he had borrowed.

THE GREENBACK MOVEMENT. Many of the inflationists championed an increase in the amount of legal-tender notes, or greenbacks, in circulation. Their program included repeal of the Resumption Act, abolition of the national-bank notes, and issuance of legal tenders convertible into government bonds. In 1876, the Greenbackers nominated Peter Cooper; in 1880, the Greenback-Labor party nominated James B. Weaver of Iowa; in 1884, Benjamin F. Butler was the nominee; in 1888, the Greenbackers joined the Union Labor party and supported A. J. Streeter of Illinois. In none of these campaigns did they poll more than 310,000 votes. Some of the leaders, however, achieved greater success under the Populist banner.

THE FREE-SILVER MOVEMENT. More popular than the proposals of the Greenbackers was the inflationary program of those who demanded free and unlimited coinage of silver. The Coinage Act of 1873 omitted silver dollars from the list of standard coins for the simple reason that silver, which was worth more in the commercial market than it was worth for coinage purposes at the mint, had not been in circulation for some forty years. Shortly after the act was passed, however, new mines were discovered in the Far West and the rising output of silver caused the price of the bullion to decline on the commercial market (pages 11-12). Then the mineowners joined the debt-burdened farmers and wage earners, suffering from the panic of 1873, in denouncing the new coinage act as a "crime" perpetrated by the financial interests to prevent inflation of the currency and thus benefit the creditors at the expense of the debtors. The silverites, working through both of the major parties, demanded free and unlimited coinage of silver at a ratio of sixteen to one with gold at all government mints. They succeeded in committing the government to purchases of silver in the Bland-Allison Act (see page 30) and the Sherman Silver Purchase Act (see page 49). Many of them finally joined the Populists in a desperate attempt to secure free and unlimited coinage.

**The Populists.** The political climax of the agrarian discontent of the seventies and eighties was the organization of the People's Party of America, in which were enrolled many who had seen service as Grangers, Greenbackers, Laborites, and champions of free silver.

AGRARIAN GRIEVANCES. As in the heyday of the Granger movement, the farmer still complained of excessive freight rates, high interest charges, and exorbitant taxes. His basic grievance, however, was the declining price of his grain, livestock, or cotton. This he explained in terms of the inadequate money supply, which kept commodity prices low. He failed to appreciate the effects of increased farm production, which resulted from cheap land, abundant immigration, and labor-saving machinery, or of the growing competition of Canadian, Russian, and Argentine farmers.

PROBLEMS OF POLITICAL ORGANIZATION. During the decade of the eighties there was a phenomenal growth, in the Western and Southern states, of powerful agrarian organizations such as the Farmers' Union, Agricultural Wheel, Northwestern Alliance, and the National Farmers' Alliance and Industrial Union. Among these groups there was agreement concerning objectives, but dissension over tactics and procedure. The chief difficulties were to reconcile conflicting views of (1) the desirability of forming a third party; (2) the advisability of co-operating with the representatives of the industrial wage earners; (3) the role of Negro farmers in the movement.

THE OMAHA PLATFORM. A series of conventions, beginning in 1889, worked out the broad outlines of a political program to be supported by the Alliance men, and paved the way for the formal organization of the People's party at St. Louis on February 22, 1892. At Omaha on the following July 4, the new party announced its platform. The program of economic reform called for: (1) free and unlimited coinage of silver and gold at the ratio of sixteen to one; (2) increase of the currency in circulation to $50 per capita; (3) enactment of a graduated income tax; (4) reduction of state and national taxes; (5) the establishment of postal savings banks by the government; (6) government ownership and operation of railroads, telegraph, and telephone lines; (7) prohibition of alien ownership of land; (8) the appropriation by the government of all land held by railroads and other corporations in excess of their actual needs; (9) use of government funds to facilitate marketing of farm products and to extend short-term rural credits. As an invitation to the wage earners the Populists resolved that they favored: (1) restriction of undesirable immigration; (2) the eight-hour day for governmental employees; (3) the abolition of private detective agencies, such as that which figured in the Homestead strike. The political reforms included: (1) single term for the President; (2) popular election of senators; (3) adoption of the initiative and referendum by the states; (4) the Australian secret ballot.

**The Campaign of 1892.** The Populists put their first ticket in the field in 1892, nominating James B. Weaver of Iowa, a former Greenbacker, for President and James G. Field of Virginia for Vice-President. Weaver's popular vote was 1,041,600. He received the entire electoral vote of Kansas, Colorado, Idaho, and Nevada, and one vote in the states of North Dakota and Oregon, making a total of twenty-two. In South Carolina the Populists captured the Democratic organization, while in several other states of the Solid South they co-operated with the Republicans in an effort to defeat the dominant Democrats. In the Middle West, third-party strategy dictated an alliance with the Democrats against the dominant Republicans, but the Populists were no more sympathetic toward Grover Cleveland, who was elected, than toward Benjamin Harrison, who was defeated in 1892.

## THE PLIGHT OF INDUSTRY

During Cleveland's second administration the hostility of the West and South toward the industrial East grew more intense as a result of the panic of 1893 and the policies of the government in economic matters.

**The Panic of 1893.** Cleveland had scarcely been inaugurated (March 4, 1893) before the country was in the grip of a panic comparable to that of 1873.

CAUSES. As in the case of previous depressions the fundamental causes of the crisis of 1893 were obscure, but certain factors gave warning of the coming storm. (1) There had been an excessive conversion of liquid capital into fixed forms, often for purely speculative purposes; (2) governmental expenditures had mounted, while income remained stationary, until the treasury surplus was changed to a deficit; (3) confidence in the government's ability to meet its obligations in gold waned as a result of the additional burden placed upon the gold reserve fund by the Sherman Silver Purchase Act of 1890; (4) the tendency to hoard gold increased as European investors began to sell their American securities in order to secure the yellow metal, and as foreign business houses demanded the settlement of trade balances in gold; (5) the fears of the business community became acute in April, 1893, when the gold reserve in the treasury fell for the first time below the $100,000,000 mark.

FINANCIAL DEPRESSION. The panic, precipitated by the failure of the National Cordage Company early in May, was one of the most severe the country had ever experienced. Within two months nineteen national banks and a large number of state banks in the Southern and Western states had suspended operations. Between May and October, 1893, more than 8000 business houses failed, and 156 railroads fell into the hands of receivers. By the spring of 1894 unemployment had grown acute, as bands of men and boys roamed the countryside. Some, organized as "armies," sought relief from state and national governments. One such army under the leadership of "General" Jacob Coxey, of Ohio, marched to Washington to present its petition for inflation of the currency and a government program of public works.

**Cleveland's Financial Policies.** Despite the demand from the South and West for a more abundant currency, President Cleveland was a determined foe of inflation. He insisted that the government meet its obligations in gold, that the federal budget be balanced by reduction of expenditures, and that tariff barriers be lowered to promote trade revival.

REPEALING THE SILVER PURCHASE ACT. The President informed a special session of Congress (August, 1893) that the panic was directly traceable to the fear that the country was going to substitute silver for gold as its monetary base. This fear had been engendered by the generous purchases of silver under the Sherman Act and by the drain on the gold reserve as treasury notes, issued to buy silver, were presented at the Treasury for redemption in gold. He called for prompt repeal of the Sherman Act. With the aid of the Eastern Republicans the President won, but he incurred the bitter animosity of the Western and Southern contingents in his own party.

THE WILSON-GORMAN TARIFF. As a result of the battle over the repeal of the Sherman Act, Congress was in a bitter mood when it turned (December, 1893) to consider the Cleveland recommendations for tariff reform. The Wilson Bill, which passed the House, provided for (1) the inclusion of raw materials like iron ore, coal, lumber, wool, and sugar in the free list; (2) the reduction of the duties in such schedules as cotton and woolen goods, iron and steel products, and silks and linens; (3) the repeal of the bounty granted under the McKinley Tariff to the domestic producers of raw sugar; and (4) imposition of a tax of 2 per cent on incomes of $4000 or over in order to make up the loss in revenue from the reduced duties. The Senate accepted 634 amendments to the Wilson Bill and the resulting Wilson-Gorman Tariff bore marked resemblance in many of its schedules to the McKinley Tariff. President Cleveland denounced the action of the protectionists in the Senate and refused to sign the act, but it became law without his signature. Within a year the Supreme Court held that its income tax provision was unconstitutional (*Pollock* v. *Farmers' Loan and Trust Company*).

MAINTAINING THE GOVERNMENT'S CREDIT. Cleveland's determination to meet governmental obligations in gold compelled him to watch closely the treasury's gold resources.

a. *The Dwindling Gold Reserve.* The greenbacks and the treasury notes of 1890, which were redeemable in gold, constituted an endless drain upon the gold reserve. Once presented for redemption this paper currency could not be cancelled but was put back into circulation. Therefore, bankers and business men used it whenever they needed gold to draw sums from the treasury, and the government was never relieved of its obligation. When the Treasury tried to maintain its reserves by selling bonds to the public for gold, the subscribers paid gold, received their bonds, and then presented notes for redemption which immediately drew out the gold which had just been paid for in bonds.

b. *The Morgan Contract.* In February, 1895, with the reserve standing at only $41,340,181, President Cleveland reached an agreement with J. P. Morgan and a financial syndicate whereby the bankers agreed to furnish the government with 3,500,000 ounces of gold coin for which they were to receive 4 per cent thirty-year bonds. During the operation of the contract the syndicate protected the treasury against withdrawals of gold. Cleveland was bitterly denounced for appealing to the "Wall Street interests" and permitting a group of private bankers to realize $7,500,000 profit from the resale of the bonds. While the President's action seemed necessary to save the gold reserve, it alienated a majority within his own party who were rapidly veering toward free silver as the solution of the nation's financial ills.

## THE DEFEAT OF THE AGRARIANS

The political battle for the control of the government in 1896 was a momentous test in the struggle between "the farmer and the financier, the plow holder and the bond holder, the debtor, and the creditor, the West and the East."

**Populist Hopes.** The country was in sullen mood in the spring of 1896. The plight of the farmer was still acute; unemployment or declining wages was the lot of the wage earners; business enterprise had not yet recovered from the depression of 1893. The Populists viewed with high hopes these evidences of economic unrest and the consequent crumbling of old party lines throughout the West and South. Having increased their total vote by 40 per cent in the congressional elections of 1894, they looked forward to 1896 as a year of national victory, for they expected the Democratic and Republican parties to remain under the control of conservative leaders committed to a policy of sound currency based on the gold standard.

**The Republicans.** Though many Western Republicans favored free silver, the party was under the control of the industrial and financial interests of the nation.

MARCUS ALONZO HANNA. No Republican leader was more influential in 1896 than Mark Hanna, the Cleveland capitalist, whose career in Ohio politics had demonstrated the intensity of his conviction that there should be a close union between "big business" and the Republican party. He was determined that his close friend, Governor William McKinley of Ohio, should be presidential nominee, and that the platform should pledge maintenance of the gold standard.

THE PLATFORM. Hanna adroitly handled a threatened revolt on the part of the free-silver men of the West. In the end a gold plank was adopted and only thirty-four delegates, led by Senator Teller of Colorado, bolted the convention. The platform also contained planks favoring (1) a protective tariff; (2) generous pensions for Civil War veterans; (3) enlargement of the navy; (4) American control of the Hawaiian Islands; and (5) compulsory arbitration of labor disputes in interstate commerce.

THE NOMINEE. So effectively had Hanna lined up the Republican delegates that the convention required only one ballot to nominate William McKinley for President. The nominee was a veteran of the Civil War, who had served fourteen years in Congress, where he had become the leading champion of the protective tariff. As late as 1890 he had been a "silverite," but he finally "repented" of his heresy and agreed with the Eastern financial interests that the gold standard would correct the nation's monetary ills.

**Democratic Strategy.** The smooth functioning of the Republican machine under Hanna's expert manipulation contrasted sharply with the confusion within the Democratic organization. The Western and Southern Democrats were frankly in revolt against the Cleveland administration.

THE VICTORY FOR SILVER. The Democratic convention held in Chicago in July, 1896, was dominated by the friends of free silver. The Cleveland administration was repudiated. The platform, adopted after spirited debate, demanded the "free and unlimited coinage of both gold and silver at the present legal ratio of sixteen to one." Other planks included (1) opposition to the emission of national-bank notes; (2) criticism of the Supreme Court for its decision against the income tax; (3) support of tariffs for revenue only; (4) denunciation of "government by injunction"; and (5) the demand for enlargement of the powers of the Interstate Commerce Commission.

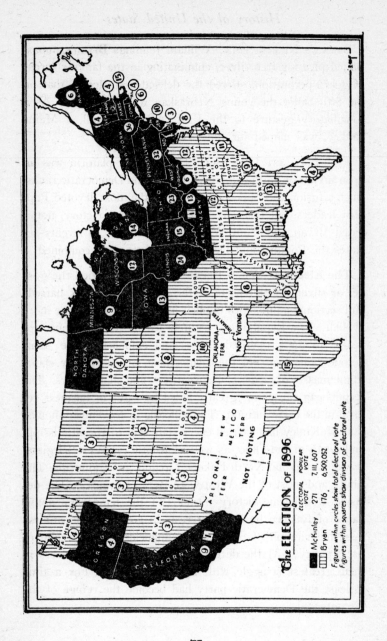

The ELECTION OF 1896

|  | ELECTORAL VOTE | POPULAR VOTE |
|---|---|---|
| McKinley | 271 | 7,111,607 |
| Bryan | 176 | 6,500,052 |

Figures within circles show total electoral vote.
Figures within squares show division of electoral vote.

BRYAN'S NOMINATION. William Jennings Bryan's impassioned plea for free silver, culminating in the famous "cross of gold" peroration, stirred the delegates so deeply that on the fifth ballot the young Nebraskan was nominated. As a conciliatory gesture to the East, Arthur Sewall, a Maine banker, was named for the vice-presidency.

THE POPULIST DILEMMA. The Chicago plaform was an open invitation to the Populists to join the Democratic ranks. Such a fusion was opposed by some of the most devoted Populist leaders, but the rank and file, eager for victory, nominated Bryan and Tom Watson of Georgia. In twenty-six states the Populist and Democratic tickets were combined.

**The Election.** When Bryan vigorously carried the gospel of silver into all parts of the country, the class hatreds and sectional animosities implicit in the struggle became more evident. The Republicans, astutely led by Mark Hanna, appealed to the propertied classes and emphasized the "dangerous radicalism" of the Democrats. Bryan frankly spoke to the masses of farmers, wage earners, and shopkeepers. The Republican cause was greatly aided by signs of business revival in the early autumn. The balloting in November showed that McKinley had carried every state east of the Mississippi and north of the Ohio, as well as Kentucky, West Virginia, Iowa, Minnesota, North Dakota, Oregon, and California. The South and most of the West were Byran's country. The decisive Republican victory meant (1) the temporary dominance of Eastern business interests in governmental affairs; (2) the triumph of conservative financiers in the realm of fiscal policy; (3) the defeat of the farmers and laborers in their greatest struggle with the industrialists. For a time at least the Democratic party had become the refuge of the discontented.

## REVIEW QUESTIONS

1. Why was it difficult to organize the agrarian and labor elements of the country as an effective political party?
2. Discuss the basic grievances of the farmers at the opening of the decade of the nineties.
3. What was Populism's remedy for the farmer's plight?
4. Why did Cleveland's policies during his second term disrupt the Democratic party?
5. If you had been a Populist leader in 1896 would you have advocated union with the Democrats? Why?
6. What philosophy of government was exemplified by Marcus A. Hanna?
7. How do you explain William J. Bryan's nomination by the Democrats in 1896?
8. The campaign of 1896 was far more significant then a mere party battle over free silver. Discuss.

## SELECTED REFERENCES

Beer, Thomas, *The Mauve Decade*

Bizzell, W. B., *The Green Uprising: An Historical Survey of Agrarianism*

Bryan, W. J., *The First Battle*

Buck, S. J., *Agrarian Crusade*

Fine, Nathan, *Labor and Farmer Parties in the United States*

Hicks, J. D., *Populist Revolt*

Peck, H. T., *Twenty Years of the Republic*

Simkins, F. B., *Tillman Movement in South Carolina*

CHAPTER VIII

# THE TREND OF DIPLOMACY

## POLITICAL DIPLOMATS

During the three decades which followed the Civil War the United States had no purposeful foreign policy. Our relations with the outside world were either wholly fortuitous or else determined by the exigencies of domestic politics.

**The State Department.** Our remoteness from the currents of European diplomacy was fully revealed by the attitude of various Secretaries of State, thirteen of whom served between 1865 and 1898. With the possible exception of Hamilton Fish they were all politicians much more concerned with the political scene at home than with diplomatic developments abroad. In particular controversies they were apt to be aggressively nationalistic, but their methods were generally straightforward and honorable.

**The Foreign Service.** Our representatives in foreign lands, too often chosen because of conspicuous services to

74

the party in power, were occasionally men of outstanding ability. The stakes of diplomacy were so inconsequential, however, that they seldom had opportunity to distinguish themselves. The changing administrations were more concerned with the work of our consular agents, who were charged with promotion of our export and import business. Their services made possible after 1880 the *Monthly Consular Report* for the benefit of our steadily expanding foreign trade.

## LEGACIES FROM THE CIVIL WAR

The attitude of France and Great Britain toward the government of the United States during the Civil War left a legacy of bitterness which affected our foreign relations during the era of reconstruction.

**The Collapse of the French Empire in Mexico.** The assistance given indirectly by Napoleon III to the Confederacy increased the resentment of the Lincoln, and later the Johnson, administration against French intervention in Mexico. Near the close of the Civil War, Napoleon, in flagrant violation of the Monroe Doctrine, had placed Maximilian of Austria upon a tottering Mexican throne. Secretary Seward, whose protests had been ignored during the war, now vigorously demanded immediate withdrawal of French troops. War was imminent, but Seward avoided resort to force and won a diplomatic victory when Napoleon finally agreed to withdraw and reluctantly carried out his pledge in the spring of 1867. Without French support Maximilian lost his throne and was executed by his former subjects.

**Settlement of the *Alabama* Claims.** Great Britain's failure during the Civil War to enforce strictly its neutrality laws had made possible the construction in British shipyards of cruisers which were destined for the service of the Confederacy. The damages inflicted by these cruisers, the most famous of which was the *Alabama,* upon American shipping came to be known as the *Alabama* Claims. Secretary Seward pressed Great Britain for settlement.

THE FENIAN MOVEMENT. Late in 1865 the Fenians, Irish-American champions of the independence of Ireland, sought to compel Great Britain to recognize Ireland's demands by launching sporadic attacks upon Canada from bases of operations on American soil. Impressed by the effective manner in which the United States government suppressed these lawless ventures, British statesmen indicated their desire to settle outstanding differences with us.

JOHNSON-CLARENDON CONVENTION. In 1868 Reverdy Johnson, our ambassador at London, negotiated an agreement with Lord Clarendon, providing for the submission of claims of citizens of either country against the other to a joint high commission. This convention the Senate refused to ratify, fearing that the commission would consider only direct damages and not the indirect damages ($2,000,000,-000), which Senator Sumner insisted could be satisfied only by the cession of Canada to the United States.

TREATY OF WASHINGTON. Neither President Grant nor Secretary Fish believed that the extravagant claims for indirect damages were justified. Consequently, in May, 1871, the Senate ratified the Treaty of Washington which contained (1) a new arrangement concerning the Newfoundland fisheries; (2) settlement by arbitration of the boundary in Vancouver Sound; and (3) submission of the *Alabama* Claims to a joint tribunal.

THE GENEVA AWARD (1872). The tribunal, which met at Geneva, Switzerland, excluded the indirect claims of the United States but awarded direct damages of $15,500,000, which the British government promptly paid.

**The Purchase of Alaska.** Unlike France and Great Britain, Russia had been openly a friend of the United States government during the Civil War. When the Czar in 1867

decided to sell Alaska he found Secretary Seward kindly disposed toward the proposition. The Senate promptly ratified
a treaty setting the price of the territory at $7,200,000.

## RELATIONS WITH LATIN AMERICA

One of the serious defects in American diplomacy was its
failure to establish cordial relations with the republics of
Latin America.

**Mediation in Boundary Disputes.** For more than a half-
century after the promulgation of the Monroe Doctrine
(1823) our interest in Latin America was merely to prevent interference by European governments with the republics of the New World. Boundary disputes, constituting a
menace to peace, caused the United States to offer its services frequently as an impartial mediator. (1) In 1876 the
United States arbitrated a dispute between Argentina and
Paraguay; (2) in 1880 our good offices were accepted by
Colombia and Chile in all controversies which they could not
settle by direct negotiation; (3) the following year we helped
Mexico and Guatemala as well as Chile and Argentina settle
boundary disputes; (4) at the same time we intervened in
the quarrel between Chile and Peru over the provinces of
Tacna-Arica and earned the ill will of the latter nation by
our efforts for compromise.

**Blaine's Pan-American Policy.** James G. Blaine, imi-
tating the policies of Henry Clay, was eager (1) to unite
the American republics into some sort of Pan-America association under the "benevolent leadership" of the United
States and (2) to establish closer commercial contact between
the United States and Latin America.

First Pan-American Congress (1889). During his brief
secretaryship under President Garfield, Blaine had arranged
for a conference of the American nations at Washington, but
his successor, F. T. Frelinghuysen, abandoned the project.
Later under President Harrison, Secretary Blaine presided
over the deliberations of the first Pan-American Congress.

The sole tangible result was the establishment of the Bureau of American Republics (Pan American Union) to facilitate the interchange of commercial information.

THE CHILEAN CONTROVERSY (1891). Much of Blaine's work for more cordial relations with Latin American countries was nullified by his handling of certain misunderstandings between the United States and Chile. When our minister in Chile, Patrick Egan, assumed a truculent attitude toward the new government which had seized power by force, Blaine supported him. Later in the year Blaine used a brawl between Chilean and American sailors in Valparaiso as a pretext for a tone of belligerency which brought us to the verge of war with a determined Chilean government. While Blaine secured proper apologies from Chile, his attitude created an unfortunate impression of aggressiveness in Latin America.

## CONTROVERSIES WITH GREAT BRITAIN

Despite the Treaty of Washington (1871) and the Geneva Award, relations between the United States and Great Britain were far from friendly during the next quarter-century.

**Reasons for Anti-British Sentiment.** American ill will toward Great Britain may be attributed to (1) the tradition, growing out of two wars and perpetuated by American publicists and historians, that the English had been and still were our most powerful enemy; (2) the fact that the governing classes in England had apparently desired the disruption of the Union during the Civil War; (3) the belief of many politicians that the best way to cultivate the Irish-American vote was to "twist the British lion's tail"; (4) the resentment against the patronizing, or critical, attitude of many English commentators on things American.

**Anglo-American Controversies.** These fundamental antagonisms were aggravated by diplomatic disputes often extremely difficult to settle amicably.

NORTHEASTERN FISHERIES DISPUTE. When the convention of 1871 (see page 76) expired in 1885, American fishing rights in British North American waters were protected only by the unsatisfactory provisions of a treaty of 1818. The Canadian government was unwilling to sign a new treaty unless the United States granted more favorable customs treatment to Canadian goods. The seizure by Canada of several American fishing smacks so angered Congress that President Cleveland was given discretion to close American ports to Canadian ships and goods. The State Department, however, finally worked out a *modus vivendi* which remained in operation until a written convention was accepted in 1910.

BERING SEA CONTROVERSY. The attempt of the United States government to protect the herds of Alaskan seals in the Bering Sea led to an acrimonious exchange of diplomatic notes between Secretary Blaine and Lord Salisbury beginning in 1889. Not until each of the diplomats had threatened the other with the use of force was the controversy submitted to arbitration. In 1893 a commission ruled against the contentions of the United States on every point.

VENEZUELA BOUNDARY QUESTION. Venezuela and British Guiana had been involved in a boundary dispute ever since 1876. Three times the United States (1886, 1890, 1894) had offered its services as mediator and had been refused. Finally, in 1895, when it appeared that Great Britain was using the boundary controversy to acquire additional territory, Secretary Olney sent several sharp notes to London in which he asserted (1) that the United States was bound under the Monroe Doctrine to protect the territorial integrity of Venezuela; (2) that the United States was practically sovereign on this continent and that its fiat was law upon the subjects to which it confined its interposition; and (3) that peaceful arbitration was the only way to settle the boundary line. When Lord Salisbury denied the applicability of the Monroe Doctrine and refused to submit the disputed boundary to arbitration, President Cleveland asked Congress to approve the appointment of a commission to draw the boundary line which it would be the duty of the United States to defend against any possible British aggression. The war spirit engendered by the President's message to Congress was quieted when it became evident that responsible leaders on both sides of the Atlantic desired peace. A treaty was finally signed in February, 1897, under which an arbitral tribunal found most of the British contentions valid.

## AMERICAN INTERESTS IN THE PACIFIC

During the generation following the Civil War, American interests in the Pacific grew constantly more important. Like our advance across the continent these ventures into the islands of the Pacific were quite fortuitous and wholly unrelated to any orderly program of expansion.

**The Samoan Islands.** First stimulated by the China trade, American contacts with the Samoan Islands were marked by (1) harbor privileges for American ships in the islands (1872); (2) exclusive right to use the harbor of Pago Pago (1878); (3) condominium with Great Britain and Germany (1889); and (4) occupation of the island of Tutuila (1899).

**Hawaii.** The acquisition of the Hawaiian Islands revealed the processes of American expansion in the Pacific.

EARLY CONTACTS. As early as 1820 New England missionaries had established themselves in Hawaii, where their descendants were joined by Yankee ship captains, traders with the Orient, and sailors on the whaling ships, who steadily augmented the American population in the islands.

THE SUGAR PLANTERS. Sugar became the chief interest of Americans in Hawaii. The sugar planters, a majority of whom were Americans, worked indefatigably for closer relations with the United States. In 1875 they secured a treaty of reciprocity between this country and the islands which greatly stimulated their sugar trade.

OVERTHROW OF THE HAWAIIAN MONARCHY (1893). The American faction in the Hawaiian Islands, led by the great planters and financed by foreign capital, staged a successful revolt against Queen Liliuokalani in 1893. The provisional government persuaded the Harrison administration to sign a treaty of annexation. This treaty was still before the Senate when Cleveland assumed office, and after investigation the President refused to urge its ratification. He did, however, recognize the Hawaiian Republic proclaimed in 1894.

ANNEXATION. During the Spanish-American War, Congress passed a joint resolution annexing the Hawaiian Islands, which President McKinley signed on July 7, 1898.

**Minor Possessions in the Pacific.** Almost a score of small Pacific islands came under our jurisdiction during the last two decades of the nineteenth century. Some offered possibilities as naval bases, for example, Wake and Midway, but most of them were valuable merely for their deposits of guano.

## REVIEW QUESTIONS

1. Why did the United States encounter difficulty in settling the *Alabama* Claims with Great Britain?
2. Was the action of Napoleon III in Mexico a violation of the Monroe Doctrine? Explain.
3. What were the objectives of Blaine's policy toward Latin America? Did he accomplish his purpose?
4. How do you explain the developing interest of the United States in the Pacific after the Civil War?
5. Do you consider James G. Blaine an able diplomat? Why?
6. What relation did Secretary Olney seek to establish between the Monroe Doctrine and Great Britain's quarrel with Venezuela?
7. Was President Cleveland justified in manifesting a belligerent attitude toward Great Britain during the Venezuelan crisis? Why?

## SELECTED REFERENCES

Carpenter, E. J., *America in Hawaii*
Dennett, Tyler, *Americans in Eastern Asia*
Dunning, W. A., *British Empire and the United States*
Foster, J. W., *American Diplomacy in the Orient*
Mahan, A. T., *From Sail to Steam*
Nichols, J. P., *Alaska*
Perkins, Dexter, *Monroe Doctrine, 1867-1907*
Ryden, G. F., *Foreign Policy of the United States in Relation to Samoa*

CHAPTER IX

# OUR COLONIAL EMPIRE

## CONFLICT WITH SPAIN

The Spanish-American War set in motion a train of events which started the United States along the path of empire.

**The Cuban Situation.** During the nineteenth century the United States government frequently manifested concern over the fate of Spain's chief possession in the Caribbean, Cuba.

OUR CUBAN POLICIES. The attitude of the State Department shifted with changing circumstances. Early in the century there was great fear lest the sovereignty of Spain in the island should be replaced by that of a more formidable European power. For a decade after 1850 there was much discussion of the possibility of acquiring Cuba either by purchase or seizure. Finally, in the last quarter of the century, as American commercial contacts and financial investments increased, our State Department was inclined to support any policy which gave promise of promoting stable political conditions in the island.

THE TEN YEARS' WAR (1868-1878). This prolonged revolt of the Cubans against Spanish authority not only devastated the island but also brought the United States to the verge of a war with Spain. When the Spanish authorities captured the American-built steamer *Virginius* carrying aid to the Cuban insurgents, and executed members of its crew, Secretary Fish had difficulty in settling the affair without resort to force. The termination of the war in 1878 left the insurgents sullenly resentful over unfulfilled promises of the Spanish government and sent many Cuban leaders to the United States, whence they carried on a propaganda for Cuban independence.

CUBAN WAR OF INDEPENDENCE (1895). Discontent in Cuba flared into revolt when the declining prices of sugar and tobacco, partly induced by American customs duties under the Wilson-Gorman Tariff, brought widespread economic depression to the island. The demand of the insurgents for independence was not supported by the conservative classes in Cuba, nor by most Americans who had economic interests at stake.

SPANISH "RECONCENTRATION" POLICY. Unable to cope with the guerilla tactics of the revolutionary forces, which were terrorizing the countryside, Governor-General Weyler tried to confine the operations of the insurgents to a limited area and to concentrate the population of many districts in camps under the control of Spanish troops. This "reconcentration" policy, resulting in great suffering for the noncombatant Cubans, was vigorously denounced in the United States.

**The Demand for Intervention.** While the government of the United States was scrupulously neutral, the American people were openly sympathetic with the Cuban revolutionists.

CLEVELAND'S ATTITUDE. During the closing months of his administration, President Cleveland strove to maintain genuine neutrality, and to persuade the Spanish government that the grant of Cuban autonomy was the surest means of establishing peace and political stability. He feared, however, that the demand for intervention would compel his successor, McKinley, to act.

THE WAR FACTION. American intervention in the Cuban situation was not desired by those who had the largest financial interests in the island. The groups most enthusiastic for a war to secure Cuban independence included: (1) those who believed that Spanish policy, as exemplified by Weyler, had been "brutal and inhuman"; (2) certain jingoes who felt that war was the highroad to commercial and industrial prosperity; (3) partisan politicians who hoped that a successful struggle with Spain would quicken patriotic support of the administration; (4) a few public officials, like Roosevelt and Lodge, who were eager to have the United States assume its place as a world power; and (5) a powerful portion of the press, which was fattening its circulation by publishing exaggerated stories of Spanish "atrocities" and erroneous accounts of the Cuban situation.

THE DE LOME LETTER. The war faction was strengthened on February 9, 1898, when Hearst's *New York Journal* published a letter which the Spanish minister, Dupuy de Lome, had written to a friend in Cuba. The letter contained offensive slurs against President McKinley which aroused widespread indignation. De Lome promptly resigned.

THE SINKING OF THE "MAINE." On February 15 the battleship *Maine,* which had been sent to Havana in case Americans there needed protection, was sunk at her moorings with the loss of 260 officers and men. Though it was impossible to determine whether the sinking had been the work of Spanish loyalists or Cuban insurgents, or was entirely accidental, the war faction immediately made "Remember the *Maine*" a slogan.

McKINLEY'S DECISION. President McKinley was genu-
inely desirous of averting war, but he realized that a "peace
at any price" policy might split his party and wreck his administration. Therefore, on April 11 he sent a war message to
Congress, charging that the Spanish government was unable
to suppress the Cuban rebellion and unwilling to grant an
armistice. Actually, Spain had yielded to McKinley's demands after he wrote his message, but before he sent it to
Congress. Spanish action came too late. The war resolution,
as signed by the President on April 20, 1898, contained the
so-called Teller Resolution, which pledged the United States
to withdraw from Cuba as soon as its independence had been
established and political stability assured.

**The War with Spain.** The hostilities were short and
highly successful, despite the serious blunders made by our
government in the conduct of the war.

THE ARMY AND NAVY. The brunt of the war fell naturally
upon the navy, which was well prepared for the emergency.
It was the first test of the new steel navy, construction of
which had been going forward since 1883. In addition to the
Atlantic Fleet under Admiral Sampson, the Flying Squadron
under Commodore Schley, and the Asiatic Squadron under
Commodore Dewey, the Navy Department had put into service more than one hundred auxiliary ships acquired during
the spring of 1898. Thirty million dollars had been expended,
the personnel of officers and men had been doubled, and con
tracts had been placed for munitions and supplies. The War
Department, on the other hand, was ill-prepared for the conflict. Its administrative routine broke down when it tried
to double the size of the regular army and prepare 200,000
volunteers for the conflict. Inferior food, inappropriate clothing, and inadequate medical service took a far heavier toll
than did the actual fighting on the field of battle.

THE PHILIPPINE CAMPAIGN. The first blow for Cuban
independence was struck in the far-distant Philippines. Com-

modore Dewey's squadron, which was in Asiatic waters as a
result of Assistant Secretary Theodore Roosevelt's efforts,
steamed from Hong Kong to Manila and destroyed the Spanish fleet in Manila Bay. Dewey was compelled to wait from
May 1 until August 13 for reinforcements which enabled the
American troops to capture the city of Manila.

THE BLOCKADE OF CUBA. Meanwhile, Admiral Sampson
and Commodore Schley had established an effective blockade
of all Cuban ports. They were not able, however, to prevent
Admiral Cervera, with the most important Spanish fleet, from
taking a position under the batteries of Santiago harbor.
Lieutenant Hobson's attempt to sink the collier *Merrimac*
across the mouth of the harbor failed, and the fleet waited
for the arrival of American troops before beginning the Cuban campaign in earnest.

SANTIAGO. The campaign against Santiago was brief and
decisive. Its two phases were (1) the operations of the
American expeditionary forces to the north and east of the
city and (2) the destruction of Cervera's fleet. On June 14,
1898, seventeen thousand troops under command of General
W. R. Shafter embarked at Tampa, Florida. Within three
weeks General J. F. Kent's division had taken San Juan Hill,
General H. W. Lawton's division had reached El Caney, and
General Wheeler's dismounted cavalry, with the Rough Riders, had stormed Kettle Hill. Admiral Cervera, learning that
the Americans controlled the heights above Santiago, made a
desperate effort to escape. His entire fleet was destroyed,
while the American casualties were one killed and sixteen
wounded. On July 17 Santiago surrendered.

THE "CONQUEST" OF PUERTO RICO. After the termination
of the Santiago campaign General N. A. Miles undertook to
pacify Puerto Rico. So feeble was the military resistance in
the island that Mr. Dooley described the "campaign" as
"Gin'ral Miles' Gran' Picnic an' Moonlight Excursion." It
was cut short by the peace protocol.

**The Peace of Paris.** The terms of the treaty with Spain contained provisions of tremendous significance for the future of the American people.

NEGOTIATIONS. Through the good offices of the French government a peace protocol was signed by the United States and Spain calling for a conference at Paris on October 1, 1898. McKinley named a delegation of five (Secretary of State W. R. Day, Whitelaw Reid, publisher of the *New York Tribune,* and Senators C. K. Davis, W. P. Frye, and George Gray). The payment of the Cuban debt and the status of the Philippines caused the most serious disagreement among the negotiators.

TREATY PROVISIONS. The chief clauses of the treaty which was finally signed on December 10 were: (1) the grant of Cuban independence and assumption of the Cuban debt by Spain; (2) the cession to the United States of Puerto Rico, Guam, and the Philippines; (3) the payment by the United States of $20,000,000 for the Philippines. McKinley decided that the country favored the retention of the Philippines. This overseas expansion was the result of many motives: the desire to increase our national prestige, to promote new business enterprises, to tap the expanding trade with the Orient, to frustrate the designs of Germany in the Pacific, and to "uplift and civilize" the population of the islands.

RATIFICATION. President McKinley encountered great difficulty in persuading the Senate to ratify the treaty. A few Republicans, led by Senator Hoar of Massachusetts, denounced any attempt to subjugate and rule distant Oriental possessions. The Democrats sought to make political capital out of the situation. Not until Bryan personally appealed to his party associates did the Administration get the treaty ratified with the aid of Democratic votes.

## THE BEGINNING OF IMPERIALISM

As a consequence of its war with Spain the United States began to play a more vigorous part upon the world stage than at any previous period in its history.

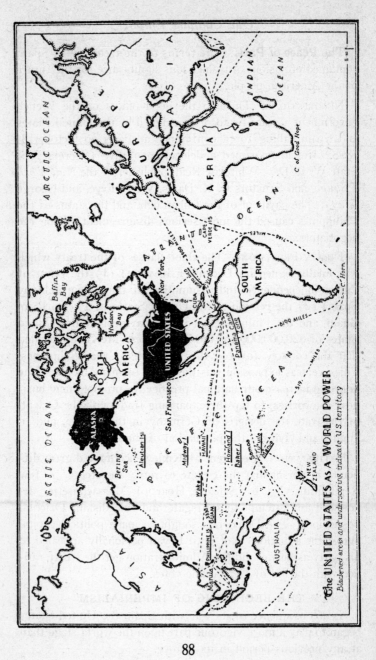

The UNITED STATES AS A WORLD POWER

Blackened areas and underscoring indicate US territory

**Hay's Foreign Policy.** John Hay, who succeeded William R. Day as Secretary of State in 1898, was eager to make American influence more potent in world affairs.

First Hague Conference. The international conference, which met at the Hague in 1899 at the invitation of Nicholas II of Russia, created a tribunal for the adjudication of international disputes which was in large part the work of the American delegation under Andrew D. White. In all the deliberations dealing with disarmament and the modification of the laws of war the United States was an active participant.

The "Open Door" (1899-1900). Alarmed by the activity of the European powers in establishing "spheres of influence" in China, Secretary Hay requested Great Britain, Germany, Russia, France, Italy, and Japan to agree to the principle of the "open door." His proposals included (1) noninterference with the twenty-two treaty ports in China; (2) universal application of the Chinese tariff laws within the foreign concessions; (3) equal railroad rates and harbor dues within any given "sphere" for merchants of all nations. Reluctantly, the European powers agreed to Hay's principle of equality of opportunity in China in commercial matters, thus insuring to American traders equality of treatment with the nationals of the countries which had received concessions from the Chinese government. The protection of the territorial integrity of China was incidental.

The Boxer Rebellion (1900). Resentment of the Chinese against the commercial and financial exploitation of their country by foreigners resulted in an attack upon the foreign settlement in Peking by an antiforeign society known as the Boxers. At Secretary Hay's insistence an international relief force was organized which fought its way to Peking in time to save the majority of those besieged in the legations. The United States assumed the lead in determining the punishment to be imposed upon China for the Boxer outrages, and succeeded in restraining those nations which desired to wreak summary vengeance upon the Celestial Empire. Again Hay demonstrated the extent of American interest and influence in world affairs.

**Imperialists and Anti-Imperialists.** Many Americans attributed the emergence of the United States as a world power to the desire of our government to imitate the imperialistic policies of the European nations.

THE ANTI-IMPERIALISTS. Even before the treaty of Paris was signed an Anti-Imperialist League had been organized in Boston (November, 1898). Its members, led by Charles Francis Adams, W. G. Sumner, and Carl Schurz, denounced the acquisition of colonial possessions as a policy which would conflict with democratic principles, impose heavy burdens upon the national treasury, and compel us to conquer millions of people hostile to our rule. The literature of protest sent out by the Anti-Imperialists was generally inspired by the Eastern "intellectuals."

THE CAMPAIGN OF 1900. Imperialism became the paramount issue in the political battle for the presidency in 1900.

a. *McKinley and Roosevelt.* The Republicans renominated McKinley with great enthusiasm, drafted Theodore Roosevelt against his wishes for the vice-presidency, and praised the administration for its successful conduct of a "righteous war" and for its courageous assumption of our "moral duty" in the Philippines.

b. *The Democrats.* William Jennings Bryan, nominated by acclamation, endeavored to spread the gospel of anti-imperialism. Denunciation of the trusts, condemnation of high protection, and support of free silver received less attention from the Democratic candidate than the challenge to the country to repudiate the course of empire upon which the Republicans had entered.

c. *Endorsement of McKinley.* Bryan's cause was hopeless. The country was enjoying heightened prestige abroad and widespread prosperity at home. The electorate was ready to assume the burdens imposed by our new possessions and to reward the party which had brought a revival of commercial and industrial activity. Bryan carried only four states outside the Solid South, and received 155 electoral votes to 292 for McKinley.

## GOVERNING AN EMPIRE

The organization and administration of our colonial empire raised serious political, economic, and constitutional problems which had to be settled in the decade after the Spanish War.

**The Insular Cases.** A vital question concerning the status of our island dependencies was this: Does the Constitution follow the flag? The Supreme Court gave a somewhat involved answer in a series of cases dealing with the effect of American tariff laws upon our distant possessions (*De Lima* v. *Bidwell,* 1901; *Downes* v. *Bidwell,* 1902; *Hawaii* v. *Mankichi,* 1903). These so-called Insular cases laid down the proposition that the Constitution is theoretically in force wherever the sovereign power of the United States is exerted, but certain "fundamental" provisions of the Constitution "are not always and everywhere applicable." In effect this doctrine has given Congress exclusive and almost unlimited power to govern our insular possessions.

**Puerto Rico.** While the population of Puerto Rico had been reasonably contented under Spanish rule, it accepted the authority of the United States without protest.

FORAKER ACT (1900). By the terms of the Foraker Act, Congress (1) made the population of the island "citizens of Puerto Rico"; (2) established a civil government consisting of a governor and council appointed by the president, and a house of delegates elected by qualified native voters; (3) regulated the commercial relations of the island with the United States.

JONES ACT (1916). Puerto Rico occupied the position midway between that of a territory and a colony until 1917, when the Jones Act of the previous year went into effect. By its provisions (1) Puerto Ricans were made citizens of the United States; (2) the Council was replaced by an elected Senate of nineteen members. There has been constant protest against the tendency of American presidents to treat the governorship as a political "plum." Some Puerto Ricans favor statehood, while others desire complete autonomy.

ECONOMIC CONDITIONS. The material progress of the island under American rule has been superficially impressive, but the masses of the native peasantry are still landless and a large proportion live perilously near the starvation line. During the depression of the 1930's almost 60 per cent of the inhabitants were unemployed.

**The Philippines.** The most severe test of American colonial policy and administration has been made in the Philippine Islands.

AGUINALDO'S INSURRECTION. Emilio Aguinaldo, who had revolted against Spanish control of the islands in 1896, co-operated with the American forces two years later in the hope that he would be installed as president of the new Philippine Republic. When he realized the direction of American policy, he organized an insurrection which was ruthlessly suppressed by the army in 1902.

THE PHILIPPINE COMMISSIONS. McKinley's first commission, headed by President Schurman of Cornell, reported in 1899 that the Filipinos were not ready for self-government. The second commission, under the leadership of Judge William H. Taft, laid the foundations of the political structure of the islands, and in 1901 was intrusted with powers of civil government.

THE ORGANIC ACT OF 1902. This enactment outlined the conditions under which the Filipinos were to be admitted to larger participation in the government. In 1907, after

Governor Taft's administration had prepared the way, elections were held for a popular assembly which was to share with the appointed council the legislative function.

THE JONES ACT (1916). In this act the Democrats moved toward that "ultimate independence" which their platforms had stressed since 1900. The appointive council was replaced by an elective senate, thus enabling the Filipinos to control both houses of the legislative body. Five of the administrative departments were to be filled by competent natives. Only the governor-general and the vice-governor were to be Americans.

THE INDEPENDENCE MOVEMENT. The Jones Act and the liberal administration of Francis B. Harrison (1913-1921) gave impetus to the demand for immediate independence. Despite the reports of the Wood-Forbes Commission (1921) and the Thompson Committee (1926) that the islands were not yet ready for self-government, the agitation for independence continued both in the islands and in the United States. Those who opposed our control on the ground that we were denying liberty to the Filipinos were joined by others who argued that our financial investments in the islands had been disappointing, that duty-free sugar from the Philippines was competing with American-grown sugar on an unfair basis, that the islands had not enabled us to increase our trade with the Orient, and that they constituted a liability rather than an asset from the angle of national defense.

THE HAWES-CUTTING BILL (1933). Although the Hoover administration was opposed to "cutting the Philippines adrift," sentiment for independence in Congress grew rapidly. In January, 1933, the legislators passed over the President's veto a bill providing for Philippine independence after a twelve-year probationary period. The Philippine legislature refused to ratify this measure but finally accepted (May, 1934) the Tydings-McDuffie Bill, which fixed 1946 as the date for the severance of economic ties between the islands and the United

States. In 1935 Manuel Quezon became president of the Philippine Commonwealth inaugurating the transition to complete independence. Japan's attack on Pearl Harbor and her subsequent conquest of the Philippines compels a reconsideration of the subject by both Filipinos and Americans.

**Relations with Cuba.** Although the United States withdrew its military forces from Cuba as soon as peace and order had been established, it imposed upon the island certain conditions which in effect would have kept it under our control.

THE PLATT AMENDMENT. After a military government under General Leonard Wood had started Cuba along new paths, a convention of Cuban delegates met in 1901 to draft a constitution. At the insistence of Congress the convention was compelled to incorporate in the constitution the so-called Platt Amendment: (1) that Cuba should make no international agreements impairing its sovereignty without the consent of the United States; (2) that it should contract no debts unless the interest could be met out of current revenues; (3) that it should welcome the intervention of the United States whenever necessary to preserve the independence or political stability of the island; (4) that it should grant two naval stations to the United States.

INTERVENTIONS. Factional difficulties in Cuba in 1906 caused the establishment of a provisional government which was supported for three years by American military forces. In 1912 our marines were sent to the island to quell disorders which had grown out of race riots in one province. Five years later the Cuban elections were supervised by American marines, some of whom were not withdrawn for several years. The turbulent nature of President Machado's regime between 1930 and 1933 caused our State Department to exert diplomatic pressure which finally resulted in Machado's resignation. On May 31, 1934, however, the Platt Amendment was abrogated by the action of the United States, so far as its direct intervention in Cuban internal affairs is concerned.

ECONOMIC PENETRATION. Since the Spanish War our financial investments in Cuba and our commercial contacts with the island have increased rapidly. In 1930 almost 80 per cent of the sugar industry was controlled by Americans, while the total investment of our capital was in excess of $1,500,000,000.

## REVIEW QUESTIONS

1. What is meant by "imperialism"? Does American "imperialism" differ in any respect from that of the European powers?
2. Why did the United States intervene in Cuba? To what extent did economic motives affect our national attitude?
3. Who were the Anti-Imperialists? Explain the nature of their protest against imperialism.
4. Has the Platt Amendment made Cuba a protectorate of the United States? Justify your answer.
5. Do you regard the decisions in the Insular cases as important contributions to our constitutional law? Discuss.
6. What principles seem to have been "fundamental" in the policies which we have applied in our colonial possessions?
7. Do you favor independence for the Philippine Islands? Why?

## SELECTED REFERENCES

Clements, P. H., *The Boxer Rebellion*
Diffie, B. W. and J. W., *Porto Rico: A Broken Pledge*
Forbes, W. C., *The Philippine Islands*
Jenks, L. H., *Our Cuban Colony*
Mahan, A. T., *Lessons of the War with Spain*
Millis, Walter, *The Martial Spirit*
Pratt, J. W., *The Expansionists of 1898*
Snow, A. H., *The Administration of Dependencies*

CHAPTER X

# AT THE TURN
# OF THE CENTURY

## ECONOMIC PROSPERITY

At the threshold of the twentieth century the United States experienced a return of prosperity which mightily increased the prestige of the Republican party and the McKinley administration, although it brought problems which were later to confound business and political leaders.

**The Revival of Agriculture and Industry.** Mark Hanna's proud boast that McKinley was "the advance agent of prosperity" seemed to be substantiated during the period of McKinley's first administration. Several factors were responsible for the upward trend in business: (1) the increased output of gold, resulting from the discoveries in the Klondike, in western Alaska, and in South Africa, which caused commodity prices to rise steadily; (2) the heavy demands for farm

96

products and finished goods both in the American market and in the trading centers of Europe, which was partially induced by the extraordinary needs of the United States during the Spanish War and of Great Britain during the Boer War; (3) the abundant harvests throughout the American grain belt in the closing years of the century, which increased the purchasing power of the large farm population. Although individual farmers were more prosperous, agriculture as a whole failed to keep pace with industry. The lion's share of the benefits from the economic revival went to the captains of industry.

**Concentration of Capital.** That consolidation of industrial enterprise, which we have already noticed (see page 51), reached its climax at the opening of the twentieth century.

TRANSPORTATION. In 1900 the railroad network included approximately 200,000 miles, of which fully 70 per cent was in the hands of the groups represented by Vanderbilt, Gould, Hill, Morgan, Rockefeller, and Harriman. The par value of the securities based upon these great systems was estimated to be in excess of $15,000,000,000.

INDUSTRY. Despite the fact that the Sherman Antitrust Law had been on the statute books for a decade, industrial combines were more numerous in 1900 than they had ever been before. Eighteen trusts with an aggregate capital of $288,000,000 were reported in the decade 1880-1890, while in the next ten years 157 trusts with a capital of $3,150,000,-000 were listed. The general characteristics of this trend toward industrial concentration were well illustrated in the case of the United States Steel Corporation. Under the direction of J. P. Morgan, eleven great companies were absorbed, giving the new concern control of 70 per cent of the iron and steel production of the nation. Although Morgan's creation had physical assets of only $682,000,000, common and preferred stock to the amount of $1,000,000,000 was issued and $300,000,000 worth of bonds were sold. Almost half the capitalization represented present discounting of possible future profits.

BANKING. The unprecedented combinations in transportation and industry were made possible by the increasing concentration of credit facilities in the hands of a few groups of powerful financiers. Both the public banking systems in state and nation and the private banking institutions were divided among these groups. Although the extent of the affiliations was not fully known, there were already mutterings against the "money trust" which like a great octopus had its tentacles fastened on every phase of the economic life of the nation.

**Republican Legislation.** The McKinley administration, eager to promote the prosperity of the nation through the instrumentality of big business, refrained from invoking the antitrust laws to curb concentration, and sponsored legislation which the industrialists and financiers desired.

THE DINGLEY TARIFF (1897). Just what contribution, if any, the Dingley Tariff made toward the prosperous conditions at the turn of the century it is impossible to determine, but the measure was clearly the handiwork of the representatives of big business. Its schedules, which remained in force until 1909, restored the protective levels of the McKinley Act of 1890.

THE GOLD STANDARD ACT (1900). More tardily, but none the less completely, the Republicans met the wishes of the business interests on the currency question. After a feeble and futile effort to do something for silver by international agreement, the McKinley administration pushed through Congress the Gold Standard Act, which provided that the gold dollar was the basic unit of value (thus ratifying what had really been done in the Coinage Act of 1873); that greenbacks and treasury notes of 1890 would be redeemed in gold; and that a gold reserve of $150,000,000 would be set aside for redemption purposes. For the time being, at least, sound money had triumphed.

## A SCIENTIFIC REVOLUTION

The American people at the turn of the century were beginning to realize the social and economic implications of those changes in the various fields of applied science which constituted a veritable scientific revolution.

**Preventive Medicine and Public Health.** This generation reaped the fruits of long years of experimentation in medicine and surgery. The public health movement, which grew constantly more comprehensive and efficient, endeavored (1) to destroy the sources of disease by supervising water supplies, compelling pasteurization of milk, or eliminating the breeding places of the mosquito carriers of malaria and yellow fever; (2) to immunize whole communities against particular diseases such as smallpox, anthrax, and diphtheria by the use of serums; (3) to prevent foreign epidemics by a rigid enforcement of quarantine regulations in dealing with immigration; (4) to spread through the schools and public health services a knowledge of proper personal hygiene.

**Applied Science and Modern Conveniences.** By 1900 two forms of energy were beginning to revolutionize man's relation to his physical environment — electricity and the internal combustion engine.

ELECTRICITY. Although the speed of communication by telegraph and telephone had become a commonplace, it was not until 1901 that the pioneer work of Guglielmo Marconi gave promise of wireless telegraphy and telephony. Through the genius of Thomas A. Edison it had become possible to use the incandescent lamp for illuminating homes as well as city streets. So rapidly were the dynamo and the electric motor developed that within a decade after 1890 it was feasible to electrify street railways in any part of the United States. The hydroelectric industry, not even listed in the census of 1880, was beginning its challenge to steam power.

THE INTERNAL COMBUSTION ENGINE. This important power possibility was devised in practical form by the French as early as 1860, but it was not applied successfully until late in the century. It made possible two significant inventions, the motor car and the airplane. In 1900 the automobile, which Charles E. Duryea of Springfield, Massachusetts, and Elwood Haynes of Kokomo, Indiana, had begun to manufacture in 1892, was already passing out of the category of a novelty. The airplane, on which Samuel P. Langley began to work in 1895, was first tested in 1903 when Orville and Wilbur Wright made a short successful flight at Kitty Hawk, North Carolina.

MECHANICAL INVENTIONS. The list of mechanical inventions of the period would be voluminous, for the Patent Office issued more than 400,000 patents every year during the decade following 1890.

## EDUCATION AND RELIGION

The generation which reached maturity in 1900 inherited a tradition of philanthrophic benevolence, humanitarian striving, and social progress which it expected to carry on.

**Public Education.** By the opening of the new century it was evident that the democratic theories of education were bringing the masses within the influence of the school system, which was being constantly adapted to the needs of the times.

ELEMENTARY AND SECONDARY SCHOOLS. Between 1870 and 1900 the number of students in the public schools increased from 6,900,000 to 15,500,000. Every section except the South, which was tardily rebuilding its educational facilities, felt the influence of the improved grammar schools and the new high schools with their growing emphasis on vocational training.

COLLEGES AND UNIVERSITIES. Higher education was stirred by revolutionary forces in the last quarter of the nineteenth century. (1) Many states used their shares of the land grants under the Morrill Act (1862) to establish state universities, which broadened and deepened the meaning of collegiate instruction. (2) A group of progressive college presidents (Andrew D. White of Cornell, F. A. P. Barnard of Columbia, Charles W. Eliot of Harvard, Daniel C. Gilman of Johns Hopkins) interpreted anew the role of the college in society. (3) Generous philanthropists, too numerous to mention, made possible the foundation of additional colleges, the improvement of equipment and accommodations in existing institutions, and the beginning of adequate training in the professions.

LYCEUMS AND CHAUTAUQUAS. Adult education of a popular sort, which had early been organized as the lyceum, became nationwide with the development of the idea sponsored by the Chautauqua Literary and Scientific Circle (1873). By 1910 Chautauqua reading circles were to be found in all parts of the country, while the summer season witnessed the Chautauqua assembly under the brown top, listening to lectures, concerts, and dramatic sketches.

THE PUBLIC LIBRARY. One of the most important educational influences was the spread of the public library, which was stimulated by public action and private philanthropy. By 1900 thirty-seven states had enabled the towns within their borders to levy taxes for the establishment and support of libraries. Andrew Carnegie, who set the standard for many benefactions, had given $62,500,000 to aid communities in making books and magazines freely available to their citizens.

THE NEWSPAPER PRESS. As the school system slowly won its battle against illiteracy, the low-priced press became an ever more potent force in molding public opinion. If the day of the great editors (Greeley, Bryant, Bowles, Bennett, Dana) was past, there was some compensation in the improved methods of news-reporting, particularly as developed by the Associated Press (1900), which made the daily paper at once more interesting and more instructive. The tendency toward cheap sensationalism, which Pulitzer and Hearst were inclined to carry to extremes, was regrettable, but both these aggressive editors were willing to take up the cudgels for the common man and to champion important, though unpopular, social reforms. Astounding circulation figures, which showed some New York dailies near the million mark, indicated the possibilities of the press as an instrument controlling public opinion on political and economic questions.

**Religious Trends.** American churches were slow to meet the challenge of changed social conditions, and there was considerable dissent among conservative members when a social gospel was finally emphasized.

DENOMINATIONAL GROWTH. The phenomenal expansion of Roman Catholicism, which resulted from the large immigration of Germans, Irish, and Italians, was recorded in the census of 1900 which listed 9,000,000 Catholic communicants, most of them in the larger cities. Rural America was still dominated religiously by a bewildering variety of the denominations of evangelical Protestantism — the Methodists, Baptists, and Presbyterians constituting the largest groups.

EVANGELISM. The leaders of Protestantism in the generation after the Civil War were concerned chiefly with (1) the warfare between science and religion which developed as a result of the publication of Darwin's hypothesis and the finding of geologists, botanists, anthropologists, and other scientists concerning the nature of the physical world; (2) doctrinal controversies which had their origin in that careful examination and evaluation of the Scriptures, popularly called the "higher criticism"; (3) the work of personal evangelism which was carried forward through the agency of periodic revivals, such as those of Dwight L. Moody and his countless imitators, and through the efforts of the Sunday schools, the young people's societies, and the Christian Associations.

SOCIAL SERVICE. Late in the nineteenth century the religious organizations began to stress social service not only as a prelude to evangelical work, but also in its own right. Urban congregations, particularly, became conscious of the under-privileged in their midst and strove to make the church a community center rather than merely a place of worship. The Y.M.C.A. and the Y.W.C.A. tried to develop comprehensive programs to meet the social problems of youth. From the pulpits came a gospel which found much to criticize in the fruits of industrialization and urbanization. The Salvation Army supplemented its evangelism with the practical approach of food depots, lodging houses, and employment agencies.

**Organized Philanthropy.** As the benefactions of private philanthropists increased, efforts were made to guide intelligently the assistance given to the poor and distressed.

Social Settlements. Such pioneer ventures as Andover House in Boston, Jane Addams' Hull House in Chicago, and the Henry Street Settlement in New York, which were widely imitated in other cities, strove to study the needs of particular neighborhoods and then to formulate programs which would open new vistas of achievement and opportunity to the families of the poor. Most of the settlement houses became agencies for the translation of benevolence into constructive action.

Charity Societies. By the decade of the nineties the haphazard relief of the poor, which had been carried on by public agencies and benevolent persons, was being rapidly institutionalized. Charity organization societies in most of the larger cities were making systematic studies for the purpose of separating the "worthy poor" from professional paupers, of eliminating duplication of effort, and of finding the proper method of dealing with each case.

## THE BROADENING OF CULTURE

While there was much that was barren and dull in the cultural tradition of the American people at the turn of the century, there were brilliant workers in letters and art of whose masterpieces the nation could be proud.

**Intellectual Leaders.** Preoccupation with money, as the symbol of the gain spirit, was the distinctive trait of the average American of this period, but there were many who rose above the average and there was a goodly company which made original contributions to the life of the spirit. Difficult as it is to select those whose work bore some evidence of the touch of genius, one may mention such scientists as Lewis H. Morgan in anthropology, Asa Gray in botany, Josiah Willard Gibbs in physics, Wolcott Gibbs in chemistry, and Simon Newcomb in astronomy; such philosophers as Josiah Royce, William James, and Charles S. Peirce; such economists and critics of the contemporary scene as Henry George, Thorstein Veblen, and Henry Adams.

**Literature.** Most Americans of the post-Civil War generation read an unbelievable amount of trash, but it was not because of the sterility of American letters. Even if the highest praise be denied William Dean Howells, Hamlin Garland, and Frank Norris for their novels, and Bret Harte, Stephen Crane, and Ambrose Bierce for their short stories, there still remain such brilliant creative artists as Walt Whitman, Henry James, and Mark Twain (Samuel L. Clemens). That they received recognition in their own lifetime is a credit to the generation which often showed an amazing lack of discrimination in its literary preferences.

**Painting, Sculpture, and Architecture.** No other period in the history of American painting was so productive of great creative work. There were the landscapes of Winslow Homer, George Inness, Homer Martin, and A. H. Wyant; the murals of La Farge, Abbey, and Vedder; and the portraits of John S. Sargent and William M. Chase. Among American sculptors Augustus St. Gaudens stood supreme. His work, together with that of Daniel Chester French and George Grey Barnard, constituted an impressive contribution during this period to the plastic arts. The architects partially atoned for their sins at the close of the nineteenth century. After the grotesque imitations of French chateaux and Persian villas, which characterized domestic architecture, and the massive ugliness of many public buildings, the original conceptions of H. H. Richardson, Louis H. Sullivan, and John Roebling were an earnest expression of the best that later American architects were to achieve. Quite as important as the work of these great artists was the fact that popular canons of taste were gradually improving, as increasing thousands enjoyed the collections of art in such galleries as the Museum of Fine Arts in Boston, the Corcoran in Washington, and the Metropolitan Museum in New York (1880).

**Music.** Appreciation of good music was notable, even if American composers fell far short of the standard set by the great masters of Europe. Music lovers were grateful for (1) the concerts of great European musicians, made possible by the support of wealthy philanthropists; (2) the symphony orchestras — Boston (1881), Chicago (1891), Cincinnati (1895), Philadelphia (1900) — which followed the example of the New York Philharmonic (1845); (3) the successful operatic performances made possible by the establishment of the Metropolitan Opera House in New York (1883); (4) the pleasing, if not profound, work of Edward MacDowell, Horatio Parker, Arthur Foote, and George Chadwick.

**The Theatre.** At the opening of the twentieth century the American theatre had not yet entered upon its golden age. Show houses were numerous, but there were few works of merit by American dramatists which were produced behind their footlights. Traveling companies still relied upon Shakespeare, *Uncle Tom's Cabin,* or sure-fire melodramas long tested on the British stage. In New York Augustin Daly eagerly sought new talent, while Charles Frohman brought the greatest European plays to the American stage both in the metropolis and on the road.

## REVIEW QUESTIONS

1. How do you explain the economic revival which marked the closing years of the nineteenth century?
2. What significance do you attach to the legislation of McKinley's administration?
3. Discuss the tendencies in industry and finance which were exemplified by the formation of the United States Steel Company.
4. What effect, if any, did the "scientific revolution" have upon industrial enterprises?
5. What did the generation at the turn of the century mean by "social reform"?
6. What do you consider most significant in the immediate cultural background of twentieth-century Americans?

## SELECTED REFERENCES

Addams, Jane, *Twenty Years of Hull House*
Brooks, Van Wyck, *New England Indian Summer*
Hall, Thomas, *Religious Background of American Culture*
Howard, J. T., *Our American Music*
Mumford, Lewis, *Brown Decades*
Parrington, V. L., *Beginnings of Critical Realism in America*
Quinn, A. H., *History of American Drama*
Slosson, E. E., *The American Spirit in Education*

CHAPTER XI

# THE ERA OF
# THEODORE ROOSEVELT

## THE SEARCH FOR SOCIAL JUSTICE

The significance of Theodore Roosevelt's influence is to be found in his ability to arouse his generation to an awareness of its civic duties rather than in any measurable progress made under his leadership toward the ideal of social justice.

**The Presidential Program.** The assassination of President McKinley by a crazed anarchist in the autumn of 1901 threw the conservative Republican leaders into a panic, for they feared the "radical" tendencies of Vice-President Roosevelt. The new President's first message to Congress, calculated to quiet the misgivings of his party associates, was nevertheless a blueprint of far-reaching reforms. It called for (1) greater control by the government of corporations; (2) large powers for the Interstate Commerce Commission; (3) creation of a federal department of commerce and industries; (4) construction of an isthmian canal; (5) conservation of natural resources; (6) extension of the merit system; (7) a vigorous colonial policy. Implicit in all of his recommendations was his theory that the President should be the leader in the formulation of governmental policies.

**The Coal Strike (1902).** In defining the government's relation to business enterprise, Roosevelt manifested a lively concern that there should be a "square deal" for all parties — capital, labor, and the public. This concern motivated his action in the anthracite coal strike.

THE MINERS' GRIEVANCES. For many years the miners in the anthracite districts of eastern Pennsylvania, unable to effect a satisfactory organization to protect their interests, had been exploited by the mine operators. Their grievances included: (1) long hours and low wages; (2) the policy of compelling them to live in company houses and to trade at company stores; (3) the compulsion to produce 3000 pounds to a "ton"; (4) the refusal of the operators to recognize the union and collective bargaining. When the mineowners refused to arbitrate, the miners went on strike (May 15, 1902).

THE WHITE HOUSE CONFERENCE. Waiving the question of his constitutional prerogative, President Roosevelt invited John Mitchell, president of the United Mine Workers, and the mineowners to confer with him. But the President's attempt to mediate failed completely.

THE STRIKE SETTLEMENT. Roosevelt quietly exerted pressure in financial circles and finally persuaded the operators to agree to his plan for an arbitral board to review the questions in dispute. The decision of this arbitral board became the basis of industrial peace in the anthracite districts for fifteen years.

**Handling the Trusts.** Although Roosevelt felt that governmental regulation of industry was preferable to any program of "smashing the trusts," he was determined to put teeth into the Sherman Antitrust Law, which had never been vigorously enforced.

THE NORTHERN SECURITIES CASE. The first gun in the fight against illegal combinations was fired when Attorney-General P. C. Knox filed suit against the Northern Securities Company, a holding company which controlled the Northern Pacific, Great Northern and Chicago, Burlington and Quincy railroads. The President, who announced that the largest corporation, like the humblest citizen, would be held to compliance with the law, was highly pleased that the government won its case in the lower federal courts and that the Supreme Court upheld the decision (1904).

CONGRESSIONAL LEGISLATION. Congress failed to undertake a comprehensive modification of the Sherman Act, which Roosevelt urged, but it passed several measures designed to facilitate enforcement of the antitrust laws. (1) The Expedition Act gave precedence on the dockets of the federal courts to cases arising from the Sherman Act or the Interstate Commerce Act. (2) The Department of Commerce and Labor with a Bureau of Corporations, empowered to conduct industrial investigations, was created. (3) A special fund of $500,000 was appropriated for prosecutions of business combinations.

FEDERAL PROSECUTIONS. During Roosevelt's administrations the Department of Justice obtained twenty-five indictments and brought eighteen bills in equity against the trusts. The most important of the judicial decisions were (1) the injunction forbidding the members of the Beef Trust to engage in certain practises designed to restrain competition (1905) ; (2) the suit which resulted in the dissolution of the Standard Oil Company of New Jersey, a holding company which had a monopoly of oil refining (1906-1911) ; the order dissolving the American Tobacco Company as an illegal combination (1907-1911).

**The Railroad Problem.** Extension of the powers of the Interstate Commerce Commission, which had been crippled by judicial limitation of its functions, was Roosevelt's constant recommendation in connection with the regulation of the railroads.

THE ELKINS ACT (1903). This struck at the continuance of the practice of secret rebates which had been declared illegal in 1887. The recipient as well as the grantor of the rebate was made liable to prosecution and the agent or official of the railroad was held liable for any deviation from regular published rates.

THE HEPBURN ACT (1906). This piece of legislation fell short of conferring upon the Interstate Commerce Commission the absolute power to fix rates, but it represented a great advance toward government regulation of the railroads. The act (1) increased the membership of the Commission from five to seven; (2) extended its authority over express companies, pipe lines, ferries, and terminals; (3) gave the Commission power to reduce unreasonable and discriminatory rates, subject to judicial review; (4) placed the burden of proof upon the carrier rather than the Commission in all legal disputes; (5) forbade the railroads to transport commodities in the production of which they were themselves interested; (6) established a uniform system of accounting to be used by the common carriers. The Hepburn Act made the Commission an effective agency for the first time since its creation in 1887.

JUDICIAL DECISIONS. After the passage of the Hepburn Act the federal courts showed an increasing disposition to strengthen the Commission. In 1910 the Supreme Court laid down the principle that the common carriers could expect protection from the courts only if they could prove "beyond any reasonable doubt" that their property was being confiscated. At the same time the judiciary refused to sanction extreme penalties imposed upon railroads or shippers found guilty of violating the law. In 1907 Judge K. M. Landis' decision imposing a fine of $29,240,000 on the Standard Oil Company of Indiana for accepting railroad rebates was set aside by the higher courts.

THE MANN-ELKINS ACT (1910). In 1910 the progressives in Congress succeeded in remedying certain defects of the Hepburn Act. The Mann-Elkins Bill, as finally signed by President Taft, (1) extended the Commission's authority to include telephone, telegraph, cable, and wireless companies; (2) empowered the Commission to institute proceedings on its own responsibility against carriers who violated the law; (3) authorized the Commission to suspend all new rates until it was satisfied of their reasonableness; (4) created a new Commerce Court (abolished in 1913) to expedite the handling of rate cases.

THE PHYSICAL VALUATION ACT (1913). The progressive Republicans, under the leadership of Senator La Follette, finally persuaded Congress to order the Interstate Commerce Commission to make a study of the physical valuation of the railroads in order to provide a basis for fixing rates which would represent a *reasonable return on actual investment*. The Commission's study of valuation was not completed until 1921.

**Conservation.** No part of Roosevelt's program was carried forward more energetically or more successfully than his campaign for the conservation of natural resources.

EXPOSING NATIONAL WASTE. Roosevelt's outstanding achievement in the conservation movement was the widespread public interest which he aroused by his efforts to stop the squandering of our natural resources. The generosity of the government in transferring the public domain to private ownership had resulted in wasteful exploitation of our riches of lumber, coal, petroleum, natural gas, and minerals. Roosevelt, aided by such associates as Gifford Pinchot and James R. Garfield, undertook to educate the electorate and thus to secure legislative action.

IRRIGATION. The Newlands Act (1902), recommended by
Roosevelt, appropriated most of the money received from the
sale of public lands in the West and Southwest for the construction of irrigation projects. By 1907 twenty-eight projects
in fourteen states were under way.

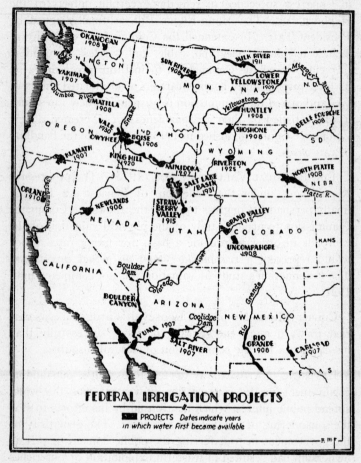

FORESTS AND NATIONAL PARKS. Roosevelt carried forward
the plans already outlined for the creation of forest reserves
and national parks. He set aside more than 148,000,000 acres
of timber lands, and withdrew from entry all public lands

containing mineral wealth until such time as Congress might safeguard the resources by proper forms of lease.

INTERNAL WATERWAYS. Conservation included also the utilization of our system of internal waterways in order to facilitate transportation, to promote irrigation projects, and to develop water power sites. The Internal Waterways Commission, appointed by Roosevelt, suggested that the President summon a conference of the governors of all the states to discuss the fundamental questions relating to conservation.

NATIONAL CONSERVATION COMMISSION (1908). The result of the White House Conference of 1908 was the appointment by Roosevelt of a National Conservation Commission, with Gifford Pinchot as chairman, and the creation of thirty-six state boards which co-operated with the national body.

**The "Muckrakers."** A group of enthusiastic young writers, whom Roosevelt named the "Muckrakers" because of their preoccupation with scandalous conditions in business and politics, exerted a powerful influence in stirring public opinion to the point of action. Roosevelt's crusade for social justice was benefited by the work of such journalists and novelists as Upton Sinclair, Ida Tarbell, Lincoln Steffens, Ray Stannard Baker, and Frank Norris, even if the President did not always recognize his indebtedness. One can trace to the "Muckrakers" and their efforts such legislation as the Meat Inspection Act and the Pure Food and Drugs Act and such prosecutions as the suit against the Beef Trust and the proceedings against the subsidiaries of the American Sugar Refining Company for defrauding the government of customs duties.

## AN AGGRESSIVE FOREIGN POLICY

Roosevelt's conspicuous and aggressive activity in the conduct of foreign relations increased the influence and prestige of the United States as a world power.

**In the Caribbean.** Our growing interests in the Caribbean, tremendously stimulated by the acquisition of the
Panama Canal Zone, caused the Roosevelt administration to
develop a theory of our responsibility for the preservation
of order in that area.

THE VENEZUELAN INCIDENT (1902). Great Britain and
Germany, endeavoring to collect debts owed to their citizens
by the government of Venezuela, established a blockade of
Venezuelan ports. Roosevelt feared that the debt question
might be made the pretext for a violation of the Monroe
Doctrine. His diplomatic pressure behind the scenes, particularly against Germany, probably helped both nations to
decide to grant Venezuela's plea for arbitration. Mixed commissions reviewed the claims against the South American republic and Venezuela agreed in 1903 to devote 30 per cent
of its customs receipts to pay the valid claims.

THE DRAGO DOCTRINE. The Venezuelan incident was the
occasion for the pronouncement by Luis Drago, Argentine
minister for foreign affairs, of the doctrine that no state
has a right to make the pecuniary claims of its citizens against
another state the pretext for military intervention. Our State
Department gave its support to the Drago Doctrine and at
the Second Hague Conference (1907) the United States delegation secured the adoption of a resolution that no nation
should resort to armed force to recover the debts due its citizens "unless the debtor nation refused arbitration, or, having
accepted arbitration, failed to submit to the award."

THE ROOSEVELT COROLLARY. When France, Italy, and
Belgium threatened in 1904 to use force in collecting debts
owed their citizens by the Dominican Republic, Roosevelt announced that "chronic wrong-doing, or an impotence which
results in a general loosening of the ties of civilized society,
may in America" compel the United States to exercise "an
international police power." Under this corollary of the
Monroe Doctrine the administration negotiated a treaty with
the Dominican Republic providing for control of the collec-

tion of the Dominican customs by the United States. When the Senate refused to ratify the treaty, Roosevelt put the receivership into effect by executive order. This manifestation of our "police power" was widely criticized in the United States and aroused grave apprehension throughout Latin America.

**The Panama Canal.** The results of the Spanish-American War dramatically emphasized the desirability of a canal between the Atlantic and the Pacific under the exclusive control of the United States.

DIPLOMATIC BACKGROUND. Several diplomatic steps were necessary before our government could proceed with any isthmian canal project.

a. *Hay-Pauncefote Treaty (1901).* By the Clayton-Bulwer Treaty (1850) the United States had agreed that any isthmian canal should be under the joint guarantee of Great Britain and the United States. The abrogation of this agreement was secured by Secretary Hay in the Hay-Pauncefote Treaty, which provided that we might build the canal and have full control and policing of it if its use was accorded to all nations on equal terms.

b. *Hay-Herran Treaty (1903).* Meanwhile, Congress had decided to build the canal across Panama, rather than across Nicaragua, and had offered the New Panama Canal Company $40,000,000 for the rights of the old French company which had tried to construct a canal during the eighties. The Hay-Herran Treaty with Colombia was signed whereby Colombia granted the United States a ninety-nine year lease over a zone ten miles wide in the province of Panama in return for $10,000,000 in cash and an annual rental of $250,000 beginning nine years after the agreement was ratified. The Colombian Senate, much to the disgust of President Roosevelt, refused to ratify the treaty, probably hoping to get better terms.

REVOLUTION IN PANAMA. Colombia's rejection of the Hay-Herran Treaty not only irritated the United States government, but it alarmed those who were interested in the New Panama Canal Company and it aroused patriotic Panamanians who feared the canal would be built in Nicaragua. In the summer of 1903 it was no surprise to the American government when revolution was fomented in Panama. The revolutionists were successful because the United States, basing its action on a treaty of 1846 with Colombia, maintained "free and uninterrupted transit" across the isthmus. Actually, this action prevented the Colombian government from moving the necessary troops to quell the revolt.

HAY-BUNAU-VARILLA TREATY (1903). Two weeks after the revolution the United States concluded a treaty with the Republic of Panama, which Roosevelt had already recognized. The new agreement granted to the United States in perpetuity the use of a canal zone ten miles wide; transferred to our government the properties of the New Panama Canal Company and the Panama Railroad Company; awarded Panama $10,000,000 and an annuity of $250,000 for its concessions. In 1921 the United States quieted Colombian complaints by a treaty in which we agreed to pay the South American republic $25,000,000.

Canal Zone

COMPLETION OF THE CANAL. After several false starts the construction of the canal went forward rapidly under the supervision of Colonel G. W. Goethals. Colonel W. C. Gorgas conquered the difficulties of sanitation in the Canal Zone. The first steamer passed through the canal in August, 1914.

**The Far East.** Roosevelt supported and extended Hay's vigorous assertion of American interests in the Far East. At the outbreak of the Russo-Japanese War he persuaded both powers to recognize the neutrality of Chinese territory outside of Manchuria, and he warned France and Germany that if either power aided the Russians the United States would side with Japan. His successful mediation resulted in the Treaty of Portsmouth (September, 1905). At the same time he reached a secret understanding with Japan whereby the United States virtually became a party to the Anglo-Japanese alliance of 1902 in guaranteeing the maintenance of the peace of the Far East.

**Toward World Peace.** Roosevelt's efforts to promote the cause of international peace were of considerable moment.

ARBITRATION TREATIES. In January, 1905, he presented to the Senate identical arbitration treaties with seven European nations. The Senate amended them in a manner which the President deemed undesirable, but two years later Secretary Root, who had succeeded John Hay, had them ratified as amended.

TREATY OF PORTSMOUTH (1905). The termination of the Russo-Japanese War was largely Roosevelt's work. It is doubtful whether the Treaty of Portsmouth would have been signed had he not guided the deliberations between the wrangling delegates.

ALGECIRAS CONFERENCE (1906). The Franco-German conflict over the Moroccan crisis of 1905 was so ominous that Roosevelt exerted diplomatic pressure at both Paris and Berlin to secure agreement to the plan for an international conference. The subsequent meeting at Algeciras revealed the powerful influence of the United States as represented in the person of Henry White. The formula finally accepted by the conference for the regulation of police, banking, and trade in Morocco did not differ materially from the proposals of Roosevelt's Secretary of State, Elihu Root.

THE NOBEL PRIZE (1907). In recognition of his work for international peace both as publicist and statesman, President Roosevelt received the Nobel Prize in 1907.

## REPUBLICAN POLITICS

Popular support of Roosevelt's policies enabled him to wield unusual political power throughout his term of office.

**The Election of 1904.** Having served three and one-half years of McKinley's term, Roosevelt was eager for an election in his own right, which would enable him to go forward with the program already under way. For a time he feared that the reactionary Republicans would refuse him the nomination and would name Mark Hanna. But Hanna's death in the spring of 1904 removed all possibility of opposition and Roosevelt was nominated by acclamation at the Republican convention. The Democrats, turning aside from the "radicalism" of Bryan and ignoring the claims of William Randolph Hearst, selected a conservative New York jurist, Alton B. Parker, as their standard-bearer. The issue of the campaign was really the policies of Theodore Roosevelt. The President was re-elected by an electoral vote of 336 to 140 for Parker. He carried every state outside the Solid South.

**Choosing His Successor.** At the end of his second term Roosevelt could have been nominated again had he permitted his friends to carry out their plans. Instead he directed all his political power toward the selection of William H. Taft, Secretary of War, as his successor. The convention of 1908 was a Roosevelt convention. The delegates were wildly enthusiastic over the President, and at his behest nominated Taft and adopted a platform which had been written at the White House. Bryan, once more dominant in Democratic circles, was unable to make any headway in the campaign against Roosevelt's trusted lieutenant. Indeed there was much in the Republican platform which met with the approval of the Democratic leader. Bryan's electoral vote of 162 to 321 for

Taft indicated that the Nebraskan had regained some of the ground lost by Parker four years earlier.

## REVIEW QUESTIONS

1. Why was Theodore Roosevelt regarded as a leader in social reform during his presidency?
2. In what sense did Roosevelt break long-established precedents in his handling of the coal strike of 1902?
3. How did the "Muckrakers" forward the political and social reform of their day?
4. Discuss the weakness of the Hepburn Act of 1906.
5. Did Theodore Roosevelt deserve the nickname of "trust buster"? Explain.
6. How did Roosevelt justify his "corollary" to the Monroe Doctrine?
7. What were the objectives of Roosevelt's policies dealing with the Far East?

## SELECTED REFERENCES

Croly, Herbert, *The Promise of American Life*
Dennett, Tyler, *Theodore Roosevelt and the Russo-Japanese War*
Faulkner, H. U., *The Quest for Social Justice*
Hill, H. C., *Roosevelt and the Caribbean*
Howland, H., *Theodore Roosevelt and His Times*
Regier, C. C., *The Era of the Muckrakers*
Rhodes, J. F., *The McKinley and Roosevelt Administrations*
Roosevelt, Theodore, *Autobiography*

CHAPTER XII

# THE DAY OF
# THE PROGRESSIVES

## TOWARD A MORE POPULAR GOVERNMENT

The period which Theodore Roosevelt made memorable with his quest for social justice was also a time of vigorous effort to remodel the structure of government and to democratize its processes.

**Direct Government.** The accusation that our legislative bodies were unrepresentative and dominated by privileged interests led to a demand that the popular will be translated more directly into governmental action.

THE INITIATIVE AND REFERENDUM. These devices, first adopted by South Dakota in 1898, permit a certain percentage of the electorate to initiate by petition measures which the state legislature or the people may vote upon. Likewise, a certain percentage of the electorate may have a law, which has passed the legislature, referred to the voters for acceptance or rejection. Twenty-two states have at various times tested the initiative and referendum.

THE RECALL. This plan to make public officials more responsive to public opinion, first used in Los Angeles in 1903, permits the voters to remove an official from office before the expiration of the regular term for which he has been elected or appointed. Its use in connection with the recall of judges, as provided in Arizona's constitution, aroused bitter controversy, but there have been few examples of summary removal.

DIRECT PRIMARIES. The system of direct primaries, introduced in Wisconsin by Robert M. La Follette in 1903, represents an attempt to give the voters a chance to name candidates, as well as to choose between candidates, for public office. By 1933 some form of the direct primary was used in all but six of the states. But the promises of the reformers that the power of the political boss would be broken and that the character of candidates for public office would be improved have not been completely fulfilled.

POPULAR ELECTION OF SENATORS. The champions of direct government were particularly insistent in their demand for popular election of United States senators. Charging that election by the state legislatures was thoroughly undemocratic, and resulted in a Senate controlled by an alliance between predatory wealth and unscrupulous politicians, they persuaded state after state to permit the voters to express a senatorial preference at the polls which the legislature was bound to accept. At the same time the reformers worked hard to secure a constitutional amendment. Not until 1911 did the Senate finally capitulate and join the House in passing a resolution, which was ratified by three-fourths of the states in 1913 and became the Seventeenth Amendment, providing for direct popular election of the upper house of Congress.

**Municipal Reforms.** Probably no part of the program of the political progressives was more valuable than their attack upon the structure and administration of city government.

COMMISSION PLAN. The notorious failure of municipal government in the United States was attributed in part to the anachronistic mayor-and-council system. In 1900 Galveston, Texas, experimented with a new form of government — the commission plan. All municipal functions were vested in a small commission — usually five — each commissioner being responsible for the management of a department. By 1914 more than four hundred of the smaller cities of the country had tried the plan, some with such indifferent results that they abandoned it.

THE CITY MANAGER. In 1914 Dayton, Ohio, introduced the city-manager type of municipal organization, in which the politically responsible commission appoints a business manager to run the city as if it were a going business concern. As in the case of the commission plan, the results have not been uniformly satisfactory. Both new types, however, have done much to arouse the electorate to an appreciation of the problems of municipal government.

**Woman-Suffrage Movement.** The progressive era was marked by a notable extension of the suffrage, as state followed state in granting the ballot to women.

STATE ACTION. The pioneer advocates of women's rights in the decade of the forties had started a suffrage movement which began to bear fruit after the Civil War. The discussion of the civil and political status of the Negro, the equalitarian philosophy of the Far Western frontier, the entrance of women into factories, trades, and professions, and the opening of the doors of institutions of higher learning to women, all gave impetus to the campaign for sex equality and for woman suffrage. Wyoming, the first suffrage state, was admitted to the Union in 1890; by 1912 Colorado, Utah, Idaho,

Washington, Kansas, Arizona, California, and Oregon had granted the ballot to women.

THE NINETEENTH AMENDMENT (1920). Many of the feminists believed that an amendment to the constitution was the royal road to equal political privileges with men. Susan B. Anthony proposed such an amendment as early as 1869; nine years later it was introduced in Congress. There it languished for forty-one years, until 1919, when Congress passed the amendment and referred it to the states. Ratification came in August, 1920, in time to permit the women of the nation to vote in the presidential election of that year. This result was a testimonial to the effective work of such leaders as Susan B. Anthony, Elizabeth Cady Stanton, Anna Howard Shaw, and Carrie Chapman Catt.

**The Challenge of Socialism.** Although the history of Socialism in the United States dates from the formation of Marx's First International in 1864, the Socialists attracted little attention until the opening years of the present century.

SOCIALIST PARTY OF AMERICA (1901). The remnants of the Socialist Labor party, established in 1876, and the following of Eugene V. Debs in the Social Democratic party (1897) united to form the Socialist party. The party has set for its ultimate goal the Marxian principle of public ownership and control of the means of production and distribution, but it has also advocated such preliminary steps as reduction of the hours of labor, unemployment insurance, labor codes, government ownership of railroads, telegraph and telephone companies, and other public utilities, adoption of the initiative, referendum, recall, and proportional representation. It denounced the programs of the progressives as futile "bourgeois tinkering." The Socialist vote in presidential elections reached its peak in 1912, when Debs polled 897,011 votes. In 1920, with woman suffrage, he secured 919,799 votes. The party strength since 1928 under the leadership of Norman Thomas has been disappointing to ardent partisans.

THE I.W.W. (1905). The Industrial Workers of the World (I.W.W.) was sponsored by an extremist faction among the Socialists and leaders of the revolutionary labor unions. It insisted that the "workers of the world, organized as a class, take possession of the earth and the machinery of production and abolish the wage system." Spurning the middle-class reformers and moderate Socialists alike, the I.W.W. championed direct action — the mass strike, sabotage, and violence. Its appeal was chiefly to foreign-born migratory laborers in the mines, lumber camps, and harvest fields of the Far West. Various states proceeded against it, and the federal government in 1918 imprisoned its most influential leaders. By 1925 the membership, which never numbered more than 60,000, had disintegrated.

## TAFT AND THE REFORMERS

President Taft was in sympathy with the main objectives of the political reformers of his day, but he frequently questioned their methods and criticized the unseemly haste with which they sought to put their reforms into effect.

**Roosevelt's Successor.** Taft's task was two-fold: (1) to carry forward in his own right the policies which his predecessor had so effectively dramatized; (2) to reconcile the progressives (insurgents) and the conservatives (standpatters) within the Republican party. The President's legal training and judicial temperament made it impossible for him to assume the role which Roosevelt had played successfully in the reform movement. His official advisers, with two exceptions, were lawyers, who emphasized the legal limitations on the presidential prerogative and the difficulties of the progressive program. As a result, Taft seemed to be inclined to restrain the zealous reformers rather than to convert the conservatives to the cause of political reform.

**Payne-Aldrich Tariff (1909).** The first significant test of Taft's leadership came with the attempt to revise the tariff in the special session of 1909.

PROTESTS AGAINST PROTECTION. The protective duties of the Dingley Tariff, which had seemed reasonable in 1897, became the object of vigorous attack as the prices of manufactured goods advanced more rapidly than the wages of labor. In 1907 Roosevelt admitted that the tariff schedules needed revision, and the following year Taft promised that he would interpret the Republican platform on the tariff to mean downward revision of rates.

CONGRESSIONAL TARIFF-MAKING. Neither the Payne Bill, as it passed the House, nor the completed Payne-Aldrich Bill, with the Senate amendments, was a redemption of the party pledge. The measure was fought by the Republican insurgents, ably led by La Follette, Dolliver, Bristow, and Beveridge, but the schedules were not altered in any important particular. The levels of the Dingley Tariff were generally maintained.

TAFT'S ATTITUDE. The President, eager to preserve party harmony, tried to persuade the insurgents to accept the Payne-Aldrich Bill as a party measure. His assertion that the bill was "the best tariff ever passed by the Republican party" put the progressives immediately on their guard against the President.

**Ballinger-Pinchot Controversy.** This quarrel over the conservation program convinced many of Roosevelt's friends that Taft was not willing to continue the policies initiated by his predecessor.

BALLINGER'S PLANS. The ardent supporters of conservation were apprehensive over the plans of Richard A. Ballinger, whom Taft had promoted from Superintendent of the General Land Office to Secretary of the Interior. The new Secretary concluded that Roosevelt had exceeded his legal powers in reserving certain public lands and he opened them once more to private leasing. In addition he restored to private operation water-power sites in Wyoming and Montana, and approved the so-called Cunningham claims of the Guggenheim-Morgan syndicate to valuable coal lands in Alaska. For these acts he was severely criticized in published articles by L. R. Glavis of the Public Land Office and Gifford Pinchot, Chief Forester.

PINCHOT'S DISMISSAL. Taft, distressed by the publicity attending this quarrel in administration circles, dismissed Glavis immediately and removed Pinchot after the forestry official carried his charges to Congress. Pinchot was quick to rally Roosevelt's friends and persuade them that Taft was a traitor to the former president's conception of conservation. The accusation was unjust to Taft but he had to bear the brunt of the public antagonism to Ballinger, who was permitted to resign in 1911.

**Congressional Insurgents.** Although Taft was not directly involved in the warfare between conservatives and progressives in Congress, the revolt of the Republican insurgents against Speaker Cannon's rule clearly indicated the President's inability to control the party.

"CANNONISM." As Speaker of the House of Representatives, Joseph G. Cannon wielded enormous power in connection with the legislative process, for (1) he controlled the Committee on Rules, which determined the routine procedure of the House; (2) he appointed all committees and designated their chairmen; (3) he had the power to recognize members who desired to speak from the floor and therefore he could guide the course of debate. Cannon wielded these considerable powers in such fashion as to aid the conservatives and embarrass the progressives.

THE REVOLT OF 1910. The insurgent Republicans rose in revolt against Cannon's dictatorial tactics in the spring of 1910. Aided by the Democratic minority they passed a resolution, introduced by George W. Norris of Nebraska, which deprived the Speaker of his control over the Rules Committee. The following year the Democrats, now in the majority, denied the Speaker the right to appoint standing committees, thus establishing "representative government" in the House.

**Canadian Reciprocity.** The antagonism to President Taft on the part of the progressives, notably the Western insurgents, was accentuated by his ill-fated plan for reciprocity with Canada.

AGREEMENT OF 1911. A reciprocity agreement was negotiated with Canada which provided for (1) free trade in primary foodstuffs, such as grain, vegetables, and eggs; (2) mutual reduction of tariff duties on secondary food products, like flour and meats; and (3) slight decrease in the duties on manufactured goods. Despite the bitter opposition of the Western agrarian interests, who feared the competition of Canadian produce, the President succeeded in persuading Congress to approve the reciprocity agreement.

CANADA'S REACTION. Taft's victory was fruitless, for the reciprocity issue caused a dissolution of the Canadian Parliament and the overwhelming defeat of Sir Wilfred Laurier, who had negotiated the agreement. Many Canadians interpreted Taft's interest in reciprocity as the first move in an American policy to bring Canada within the political and economic control of the United States.

**Legislative Achievements.** The record of the Taft administration for progressive measures and policies compares favorably with that of the Roosevelt administration. In listing the achievements of Taft's four years in office his friends included: (1) the Mann-Elkins Act (see page 111); (2) the eight-hour day for workers on government contracts; (3) the establishment of the postal savings system and the parcels post; (4) the creation of the Department of Labor; (5) the passage of the Sixteenth and Seventeenth amendments to the Constitution; (6) the extension of the merit system to new branches of the civil service; (7) the vigorous prosecution of illegal combinations in restraint of trade; (8) legislation reserving additional public land from private exploitation.

### THE PROGRESSIVES

From the standpoint of party politics the battle of 1912 was of tremendous significance; from the standpoint of the crusade for social justice it was confusing and indecisive.

**The Preconvention Campaign.** Within both the Republican and Democratic parties the struggle to control the national nominating conventions was unusually spirited, as conservatives and progressives matched strength.

THE REPUBLICAN SCHISM. More than a year before the presidential election the insurgent Republicans tried to mobilize the progressive sentiment of the country.

a. *Progressive Republican League.* This organization, sponsored by several Republican senators in January, 1911, announced the political program of Progressivism: (1) direct election of United States senators; (2) direct primaries; (3) direct election of delegates to national nominating conventions; (4) state adoption of the initiative, referendum, and recall; (5) a national corrupt-practises act.

b. *Robert M. La Follette.* At first the League merely advocated progressive principles, but in October it indicated that Robert M. La Follette of Wisconsin was its candidate for the Republican nomination against President Taft. La Follette, who had won national fame by his successful battle against the power of the great corporations in his own state, promptly started a vigorous campaign to arouse the voters from their lethargy.

c. *Roosevelt's Attitude.* Although ex-President Roosevelt had been supporting progressive principles ever since his return from Africa in 1910, he refused to join the Progressive Republican League or to support La Follette. After weeks of indecision he agreed to become a candidate for the Republican nomination. Then came an unseemly scramble for delegates between Taft and Roosevelt, with La Follette trying to salvage something from the wreck of his high hopes.

TAFT'S NOMINATION. Wherever the Republican delegates were chosen by state conventions or were hand-picked by the "bosses," President Taft had the advantage, but in those states which permitted the voters to express their preference for the nominee, Roosevelt was clearly the choice. The national convention was controlled by the Administration forces and proceeded amidst great confusion to grant Taft another nomination.

THE FORMATION OF THE PROGRESSIVE PARTY. Roosevelt charged that the nomination had been "stolen" from him by irregular tactics. With evangelical fervor his followers undertook the task of forming a new party. On August 5, 1912, the Progressive party held its first convention in Chicago, where two months earlier its hero had been rejected by the Republicans. Roosevelt was nominated by acclamation, while Hiram Johnson of California was named for the vice-presidency. The schism in the Republican ranks was complete.

NOMINATION OF WOODROW WILSON. The Democrats meanwhile had been engaged in a spirited contest between the conservative and liberal forces within the party.

a. *The Democratic Convention.* As the delegates assembled at Baltimore it was evident that no candidate for the nomination could control the convention. Champ Clark, Speaker of the House, had both conservative and liberal delegates in his following. The extreme conservatives were kindly disposed toward Governor Judson Harmon of Ohio and Representative Oscar Underwood of Alabama. The liberals had rallied behind Governor Woodrow Wilson of New Jersey, who described himself as a "progressive with the brakes on."

b. *The Influence of Bryan.* Speaker Clark would probably have been nominated had it not been for the influence of William Jennings Bryan. Although one of the delegates instructed to vote for Clark, Bryan dramatically denounced the "sinister influences" supporting Clark and on the fourteenth ballot switched to Woodrow Wilson, who was finally nominated on the forty-sixth ballot.

**The Election of 1912.** The triangular contest of 1912 was not a clear-cut clash of principles. The fundamental issue was really the personalities of the three candidates — Taft, Roosevelt, and Wilson.

THREE PLATFORMS. The Progressive and Democratic platforms frankly invited the support of those who were willing to enlist in the warfare against political and economic privilege. Even the Republican pronouncement could not be regarded as ultraconservative. Roosevelt's "New Nationalism," which was an insistent demand for governmental regulation of economic activity, was not really distasteful to Wilson, though he presented his "New Freedom" in the lofty phrases of economic liberalism. Both candidates were eager to offer some program to meet the social unrest of the times, but Taft seemed anxious to avoid recognition of popular discontent.

DEMOCRATIC VICTORY. The overwhelming nature of the Democratic victory in November was largely due to the disruption of the Republican party. Roosevelt's popular following was amazing, for he had no regular organization and his most ardent supporters were amateurs in politics. He carried six states with eighty-eight electoral votes. Taft secured only the eight votes of Utah and Vermont; the remaining 435 went to Wilson. The House and Senate were Democratic by wide margins.

## REVIEW QUESTIONS

1. Show how the political reforms advocated by the progressives would have made the government of the United States more responsive to the popular will.
2. What were the fundamental defects of municipal government which the commission plan and the city-manager plan sought to remedy?
3. In what respect did Taft's attitude toward conservation of natural resources differ from that of Roosevelt?
4. How do you account for the growth of "insurgency" within the Republican ranks during Taft's administration?

5. Discuss the motives behind Roosevelt's decision to contest the nomination with Taft in 1912.
6. Compare the Republican, Progressive, and Democratic platforms on such issues as (*a*) protective tariff, (*b*) trust problem, (*c*) injunctions in labor disputes.
7. Do you find any fundamental difference between the economic philosophy of Theodore Roosevelt's "New Nationalism" and Woodrow Wilson's "New Freedom"?
8. Discuss the wisdom of Roosevelt's action in forming the Progressive party.

## SELECTED REFERENCES

Bowers, Claude, *Beveridge and the Progressive Era*
Bryan, W. J., *The Tale of Two Conventions*
Chamberlain, John, *Farewell to Reform*
Dewitt, P. B., *The Progressive Movement*
Howe, F. C., *Wisconsin, an Experiment in Democracy*
LaFollette, R. M., *Autobiography*
Oberholtzer, E. P., *The Referendum, Initiative and Recall*
Weyl, W. E., *The New Democracy*

CHAPTER XIII

# WILSONIAN LIBERALISM

## THE "NEW FREEDOM"

President Wilson carried forward relentlessly the legislative attack upon political and economic privilege which he had promised in his campaign speeches.

**Preparing for Leadership.** Wilson regarded his office as an instrument for guiding the course of national legislation in conformity with his interpretation of the will of the people.

THE INAUGURAL ADDRESS. The ringing challenge to "all forward-looking men" in the President's inaugural address indicated that executive leadership was to be something more than a pious wish. His lofty idealism was set forth in the phrases of the zealous and determined reformer.

THE CABINET. The selection of the cabinet advisers revealed some of the difficulties in the path of the new administration: (1) Wilson's contacts with the leaders of his own

132

party were limited; (2) he found it difficult to secure men trained in public office, for his party had long been out of power; (3) there were political debts which had to be paid; (4) the strength of the Democrats in the South tended to give that section undue influence with the administration. With the exception of W. J. Bryan (State), W. G. McAdoo (Treasury), and F. K. Lane (Interior) the cabinet appointees were not well known. Most of them, however, worked well under the President's aggressive leadership.

**Reducing Tariff Schedules.** Tariff revision, banking reform, and trust regulation were three cardinal points in Wilson's attack on the "invisible government" which he felt dominated the country.

PRESIDENTIAL GUIDANCE. Unlike Taft, Wilson constantly exerted pressure upon Congress, while the new tariff act was being framed, in order to secure the sort of schedules which he desired. When it seemed possible that the lobbyists would be able to block some of the reductions in rates, the President appealed to the country to aid him in obtaining satisfactory duties.

UNDERWOOD-SIMMONS BILL (1913). The completed bill contained features which contrasted sharply with the protective principles of Republican tariff laws. Its distinctive characteristics were: (1) an enlarged free list, which contained foodstuffs and other necessities of primary importance in the average citizen's living costs; (2) the reduction of duties on articles which no longer required protection against foreign competition; (3) increased rates on luxuries; (4) use of ad valorem rather than specific duties; (5) imposition of a graduated income tax to compensate for any loss in revenue which might result from decrease in customs. Before the effect of the measure either upon domestic and foreign trade or upon governmental finances could be determined, the First World War had ushered in an abnormal era.

**Creating a Banking System.** The Federal Reserve Act of 1913 was the culmination of protracted discussion of the defects of the currency and banking systems.

FINANCIAL PANIC OF 1907. This sharp, but brief, reversal in financial affairs was attributed by many to the inelasticity of our currency. which could not be expanded quickly to meet extraordinary needs, and to the rigidity of our bank reserves. As a temporary measure of relief, the Aldrich-Vreeland Act was passed (1908), permitting the Treasury Department to issue emergency currency to be loaned to banks in times of stress.

THE NATIONAL MONETARY COMMISSION. The Aldrich-Vreeland Act also created a congressional committee, known as the National Monetary Commission, with Nelson W. Aldrich of Rhode Island as chairman. The findings of the Commission after a three-year survey were incorporated in forty volumes and in the Aldrich Bill (1912), which called for the complete revision of American banking laws and the establishment of a central bank to dominate the system. Congress postponed all action until after Wilson's inauguration.

THE "MONEY TRUST." At the time the Aldrich Commission filed its report a special committee of the House, under the chairmanship of Representative Pujo of Louisiana, was investigating the structure of private control of money and credit. Its conclusions, published early in 1913, pointed toward the existence of a "money trust," dominated by a few of the great banking houses in New York City, which had its ramifications throughout the transportation, industrial, and commercial establishments of the nation. This reputed concentration of credit resources in the hands of a few gave point to the demand for monetary and banking reform.

THE FEDERAL RESERVE ACT. Rejecting the idea of a central bank, President Wilson participated actively in the discussions which resulted in the framing of the Federal Reserve Act, and in the legislative maneuvering which secured its

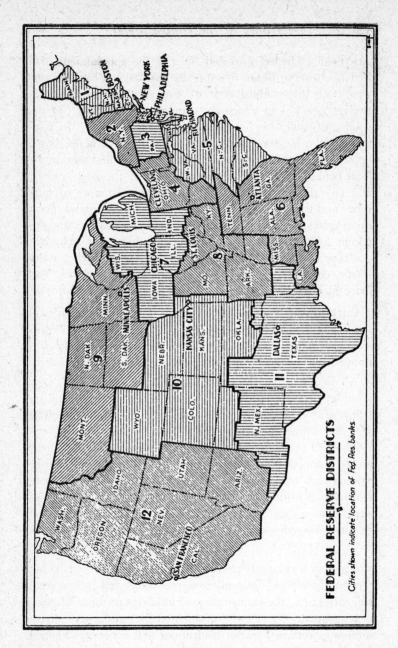

**FEDERAL RESERVE DISTRICTS**

Cities shown indicate location of Fed. Res. banks.

enactment. The act provided for (1) the appointment of a Federal Reserve Board to supervise the national banking system; (2) the establishment of Federal Reserve banks in twelve regions into which the country was divided; (3) the pooling of bank reserves in these regional banks; (4) the issuance by the Reserve banks of Federal Reserve notes, based upon commercial paper and agricultural credits sent in by local banks which had become members of the new system; and (5) the elimination of intersectional transfers of currency and the reduction of collection charges through a great clearing system. Despite numerous defects which became apparent as the act was put into effect, there was abundant evidence that the Federal Reserve gave the country a more elastic currency, greater flexibility in bank reserves, and more adequate credit facilities than it had ever before enjoyed.

**Curbing the Trusts.** Having laid down the proposition that "private monopoly is indefensible and intolerable," Wilson urged Congress to undertake the clarification and elaboration of the Sherman Antitrust Law. Two measures resulted.

1. FEDERAL TRADE COMMISSION. The Bureau of Corporations was replaced by a commission of five members which was empowered to promote equitable trade practises between competitive enterprises. The Commission was authorized (1) to conduct investigations whenever unfair methods of competition came to its attention; (2) to issue orders against such trade practises as it disapproved; (3) to apply for judicial injunctions to enforce its orders. The commission's findings as to the facts were regarded as final in all judicial proceedings which arose out of its investigations.

2. CLAYTON ACT. Whereas the Federal Trade Commission's work was largely preventive, the purpose of the Clayton Act was punitive. Its numerous provisions fell into several categories: (1) the enumeration of unlawful methods of business competition; (2) the prohibition of interlocking directorates in certain banking institutions and concerns engaged in interstate commerce; (3) the listing of various means of

securing relief from illegal trade practises; (4) the labor clause, which exempted labor unions and agricultural associations from the antitrust laws, prohibited the use of injunctions, except in certain instances, in labor disputes, and provided that strikes, boycotts, and peaceful picketing were not violations of the federal laws.

**Aiding Agriculture.** Two attempts were made by the Wilson administration to meet the needs of the farmers for adequate credit at reasonable rates.

1. SHORT-TERM CREDITS. Provisions in the Federal Reserve Act permitted national banks to loan money on farm mortgages, and authorized the rediscount of agricultural paper which was payable within six months. Neither of these provisions actually met the farmer's demand for long-term credits.

2. FEDERAL FARM LOAN ACT (1916). This measure created twelve Federal Land banks which were empowered to make loans at reasonable rates to co-operative farm loan associations composed solely of farmers wishing to borrow on long-term farm mortgages. In 1930 there were more than 4600 such farm loan associations.

**Protecting Labor's Interests.** During Wilson's administration the conservative leaders of American labor exercised a political influence which was reflected in several important pieces of legislation. In addition to the features of the Clayton Act, which were designed to protect union labor, the following acts should be noted: (1) the La Follette Seamen's Act (1915), which prescribed the minimum wages, food, and accommodation to be accorded seamen employed on ships under American registry; (2) the Keating-Owen Act (1915), forbidding the transit in interstate commerce of products manufactured in establishments using child labor; (3) the Adamson Act (1916), establishing the eight-hour day for employees of common carriers engaged in interstate commerce.

## PROBLEMS OF FOREIGN POLICY

At the beginning of his presidency Wilson was little concerned with foreign policy, but the trend of events compelled him finally to subordinate domestic issues to foreign affairs.

**Friction with Japan.** The anti-Japanese feeling on the Pacific Coast, which had become evident during the early years of the century, became acute during Wilson's administration.

THE ROOT-TAKAHIRA AGREEMENT (1908). Japanese resentment had been aroused in 1906 by California's demand that all Japanese immigration be forbidden by Congress, and by the action of the San Francisco Board of Education in segregating all Oriental students in special schools. After considerable discussion in the press of both nations, the Root-Takahira Agreement was concluded, in which Japan promised to restrict the emigration of laborers to the United States while the California school officials modified their rulings concerning Japanese pupils.

CALIFORNIA LANDHOLDING ACT (1913). In 1913 the Japanese question again became serious when the Tokio government protested against the Webb Act, whereby California denied to aliens, ineligible for naturalization, the right to own agricultural lands or to acquire leaseholds running more than three years. Japan claimed violation of her treaty rights, but the federal government insisted the legislation affected state matters over which it had no control. Tension was somewhat relieved during the period of the First World War.

JAPANESE IMMIGRATION. The "gentlemen's agreement" concerning immigration, which was implicit in the Root-Takahira Agreement, was rudely brushed aside by the United States in 1924 when Congress forbade immigration from Oriental countries. Japan, regarding this as an unfriendly act of discrimination, was never afterwards willing to accept our immigration policy as final.

**Canal Tolls Controversy.** Reversing his earlier attitude, President Wilson in 1914 urged Congress to meet the British objections to our policy concerning Panama Canal tolls.

THE TOLLS ACT OF 1912. This act had imposed a schedule of tolls upon all foreign vessels using the completed canal, but had provided that vessels of United States registry engaged in the coastwise trade should be exempt from toll payment. Great Britain contended that this was a violation of the "equality of treatment" for the vessels of all nations which our government had promised in the Hay-Pauncefote Treaty.

REPEAL. Wilson strongly urged repeal of the act on the ground that the British interpretation of the treaty was correct. His attitude was probably determined by (1) his desire to avoid trouble with the British at the moment that our relations with Japan were disturbed; (2) his feeling that cordial Anglo-American relations were a necessary prelude to Colonel House's mission to promote European peace; and (3) his hope that in return for repeal of the Tolls Act, Great Britain would support the American policy in Mexico. The Act was repealed on June 15, 1914.

**The Mexican Situation.** President Wilson's determination to "cultivate the friendship and deserve the confidence of our sister republics of Central and South America" was the basis of his well-intentioned, if not highly successful, policy in dealing with Mexico.

THE OVERTHROW OF DIAZ. The despotic regime of Porfirio Diaz (1876-1910) was brought to a sudden close by the revolt of wealthy liberals and landless peons, under the leadership of Francisco Madero. From 1910 to 1913 Madero worked in vain to establish his program of reforms — the allotment of land to landless peons, the nationalization of the railroads, the extension of the suffrage, and the grant of provincial autonomy. His efforts were ended by the revolt of one of his military supporters, General Victoriano Huerta.

THE QUARREL WITH HUERTA. Although twenty-five nations recognized Huerta as the *de facto* president of Mexico, Wilson refused to recognize the new regime, charging that it was responsible for the murder of Madero. Huerta retaliated with acts of reprisal on American citizens, culminating in the arrest of a squad of American marines at Tampico in April, 1914. When the United States promptly seized Vera Cruz in order to prevent a shipment of arms from reaching Huerta, war seemed imminent.

THE "ABC" MEDIATION. To avert the possibility of war Argentina, Brazil, and Chile (the "ABC" powers) offered their good offices which were accepted. But the several weeks of deliberations were fruitless, since Venustiano Carranza, in revolt against Huerta, refused to sign the protocol to maintain peace and order.

CARRANZA AND VILLA. When Carranza, having seized power, gave promise of establishing an orderly government, President Wilson abandoned "watchful waiting" and accorded the new regime *de facto* recognition. But Carranza failed to refrain the swashbuckling Pancho Villa, who attacked foreigners and finally led a raid against Columbus, New Mexico. The United States, with Carranza's permission, sent a punitive expedition, under General John J. Pershing, into Mexico (1916). It failed to capture Villa and was withdrawn as war with Germany loomed in 1917.

RECOGNITION OF OBREGON. A military clique drove Carranza from office in 1920 and elevated General Obregon to the presidency. For three years our State Department and the Mexican authorities argued over the possibility of recognition. Finally an agreement was reached whereby Mexico promised to meet her foreign obligations and to refrain from interpreting the Constitution of 1917 in such a way as to prejudice the concessions and property rights of foreigners. Obregon was promptly recognized (1923).

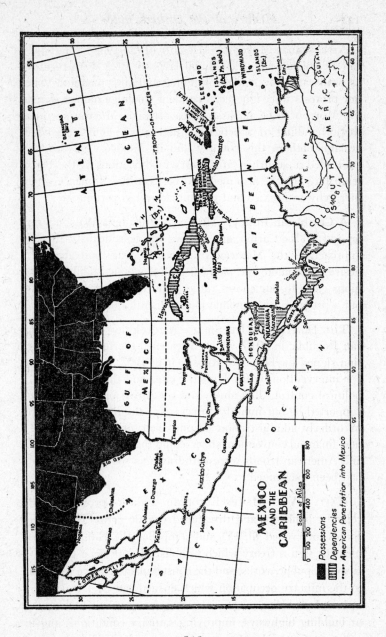

MEXICO
AND THE
CARIBBEAN

Scale of Miles

0   100  200  400  600  800

▮ Possessions

▦ Dependencies

•••• American Penetration into Mexico

AMBASSADOR MORROW'S MISSION (1927-1930). The Mexican Petroleum and Alien Land laws of 1925 were regarded as confiscatory by American mining and oil companies. When our protests were ignored, President Coolidge named Dwight W. Morrow to be ambassador to Mexico. Morrow's sympathetic handling of a delicate situation won him tremendous acclaim both in this country and in Mexico. He not only succeeded in securing satisfactory modifications of the Petroleum Law, but he also mediated between the Roman Catholic hierarchy in Mexico and the anticlerical government.

**A Caribbean Policy.** Although President Wilson's policy toward the Caribbean countries was less idealistic than his approach to the Mexican situation, he was motivated by a desire to promote the political and economic stability of regions close to our shores rather than by any desire to carry out a program of economic imperialism.

THE DOMINICAN REPUBLIC. A revolution in the Dominican Republic in 1916, which threatened the financial convention signed by Theodore Roosevelt in 1907, was the occasion for intervention by the United States and the assumption of political control. For nine years the provisional government, supported by our military forces, gave the natives the benefit of orderly administration despite their protests. In 1924 a new financial convention, superseding that of 1907, was signed and American troops were withdrawn as soon as ratifications had been exchanged.

HAITI. When Haiti's European creditors pronounced the republic bankrupt and threatened drastic action, the United States intervened (1915) and compelled the Haitian government to sign a treaty which established American control of customs, public works, and the constabulary. Native resistance to the military occupation which ensued caused frequent disorders, but American officials went forward with their work of building highways, improving sanitary conditions, and instituting financial reforms. Not until 1930 did the State

Department announce that military evacuation would be completed just as soon as political conditions warranted.

NICARAGUA. From 1912 to 1925 American marines were in Nicaragua to protect our administration of Nicaraguan finances and to maintain political tranquillity in the country. During this occupation the Bryan-Chamorro Treaty was negotiated (1916), by which we acquired a ninety-nine year lease to the Corn Islands and permission to establish a naval base on the Gulf of Fonseca. The withdrawal of marines in 1925 was followed by political insurrection, and two years later President Coolidge sanctioned another intervention for the purpose of (1) protecting the lives and property of our citizens; (2) defending our canal rights in Nicaragua; (3) enforcing the Central American treaty (1923) which pledged the Central American republics to deny recognition to any government which seized power by force. Having successfully supervised new elections, the marines were withdrawn in 1929, save for a legation guard which left the country in 1933.

THE VIRGIN ISLANDS. The Wilson administration acquired the Virgin Islands (Danish West Indies), which we had been endeavoring to purchase from Denmark for more than a decade. The chief motive behind the purchase seems to have been the desire to use the islands as a necessary naval defense for the Panama Canal and the proposed canal through Nicaragua.

THE FRUITS OF INTERVENTION. One of the results of our policy of intervention, which has gone far toward converting the Caribbean into an American lake, is the widespread distrust of the United States in Latin America. Whether our acts are based upon a logical application of the Monroe Doctrine or are merely a manifestation of national self-interest, they are regarded by many publicists in South America as proof that we desire to establish our hegemony of the two Americas. In the decade after the First World War we were but slowly beginning to appreciate both the changed status of the Latin American republics and our new relations to them.

## REVIEW QUESTIONS

1. Why did President Wilson give tariff revision so important a place in his program of reform?
2. How did the fundamental principles of the Underwood-Simmons Tariff differ from those of the Payne-Aldrich Tariff?
3. What connection, if any, do you establish between the Federal Reserve Act of 1913 and each of the following:
   a. Aldrich Bill (1912)
   b. Panic of 1907
   c. Pujo Committee Investigation?
4. In what way did the Federal Reserve System provide for greater elasticity in our currency system?
5. Discuss the reasons which impelled Wilson to urge upon Congress a redefinition of the Antitrust laws.
6. How do you account for the difficulties which Wilson encountered in the application of his Mexican policy?
7. What have been the stakes of American diplomacy in the Caribbean in the last quarter-century?
8. Discuss the relation of the Monroe Doctrine to our present position in the Caribbean.

## SELECTED REFERENCES

Dodd, W. E., *Woodrow Wilson and His Work*
Glass, Carter, *An Adventure in Constructive Finance*
Hackett, C. W., *The Mexican Revolution and the United States*
Houston, D. F., *Eight Years with Wilson's Cabinet*
Jones, C. L., *Caribbean Interests of the United States*
McAdoo, W. G., *Crowded Years*
Willis, H. P., *The Federal Reserve System*
Wilson, Woodrow, *The New Freedom*

## Significant Dates

Sinking of the *Lusitania* . . . 1915

*Sussex* Pledge . . . . . . . 1916

United States Enters the War 1917

The Armistice . . . . . . 1918

Treaty of Versailles . . . . . 1919

## Chapter XIV

# THE UNITED STATES AND THE FIRST WORLD WAR

## THE DIFFICULTIES OF NEUTRALITY

The efforts of the Wilson administration to maintain American neutrality, which inspired the hope that the United States might find a way to mediate in the great European conflict, were finally abandoned in 1917, when Germany decided to resume her program of unrestricted submarine warfare.

**Wilson's Neutrality Proclamation.** With the outbreak of war between the Triple Entente and the Central Powers, President Wilson issued a formal proclamation of the neutrality of the United States (August 4, 1914). He was not able, however, to prevent the American people, who were heavily bombarded with propaganda by both belligerent groups, from displaying partisan preferences in the conflict.

**Great Britain's Maritime Policy.** Our first difficulties over our rights as a neutral were with the British government, which was using its control of the seas to starve Germany into submission. Our State Department protested (1) that the British method of enforcing the blockade against the Central Powers was not recognized in international law; (2) that the definition of contraband goods included more commodities than had been listed in the Declaration of London (1909) ; and (3) that British ships were interfering with our shipments to other neutral nations. The British insisted (1) that their definition of contraband could not be restricted by the Declaration of London, which they had never ratified; (2) that their application of the doctrine of "continuous voyage," which had been upheld in American courts during the Civil War, was designed to stop shipments from the United States to neutral countries when it was clear that the ultimate destination was Germany; and (3) that the British government would compensate our nationals for noncontraband goods seized on the high seas.

**The Menace of the Submarine.** Our mild dispute with Great Britain was overshadowed by the implication of Germany's submarine policy, which threatened the lives, as well as the property, of our citizens.

GERMANY'S ATTEMPT TO BREAK THE BLOCKADE. On February 4, 1915, Germany declared that the waters surrounding Great Britain and Ireland constituted a "war zone" in which German submarines would destroy all enemy vessels. To avoid "unfortunate mistakes" the German government warned neutral ships to remain outside the zone and advised citizens of neutral countries to refrain from traveling on the Allies' ships. To the spirited protests of the United States against the use of the submarine without observing the rule of visit and search, Germany (1) complained that we were permitting the British to violate our rights with impunity; (2) urged us to compel Great Britain to abide by the Declaration of London; and (3) suggested that unrestricted submarine warfare would be abandoned if the United States would cease to furnish the Allies with supplies and munitions.

THE SINKING OF THE "LUSITANIA." The potential threat of the sumarine became actual in the sinking of the Cunard liner *Lusitania* (May 7, 1915) off the Irish coast with the loss of 1,153 passengers and crew, 114 of whom were American citizens. Avoiding the pressure of the war party in the United States, President Wilson strove by diplomatic pressure to persuade Germany to abandon unrestricted use of the submarine. In September, 1915, Von Bernstorff, the German ambassador, informed the State Department that liners would not be sunk without protection of the lives of noncombatants.

THE "SUSSEX" PLEDGE (MAY, 1916). Despite this assurance miscellaneous reports of submarine tactics caused misgivings. The sinking of the unarmed channel steamer *Sussex*, without warning and with the loss of two Americans, caused Wilson to send an ultimatum to Germany. The official reply reaffirmed Germany's decision not to sink merchant vessels "without warning and without saving human lives." For the next nine months there was little cause for complaint on the score of submarine activities.

**Pacifism and Preparedness.** The struggle to defend neutral rights was paralleled by the contest between those who desired to avoid every possibility of war and those who wished to prepare effectively for the probability of armed conflict.

ANTIWAR ORGANIZATIONS. The conflict in Europe emphasized the unprepared condition of the United States for any war of considerable proportions, and increased the pressure for an increase in armaments and military forces. To counteract this tendency such peace organizations as the American Union against Militarism, the American League to Limit Armaments, the American Neutrality League, and the Woman's Peace Party labored valiantly. Secretary Bryan and President Wilson were both sympathetic with the aspirations of the antimilitarists in the first years of the administration.

THE PREPAREDNESS CAMPAIGN. General Leonard Wood and ex-President Theodore Roosevelt campaigned vigorously for a comprehensive program of military preparedness. Their pleas were reinforced by the work of the National Security League, the Navy League, and the American Rights Committee in molding public opinion. As the German submarine warfare developed, and the likelihood of war became more apparent, the preparedness movement gained force. In the spring of 1916 President Wilson abandoned his earlier position and appealed to the electorate to support an increase in the military and naval establishments.

NATIONAL DEFENSE LEGISLATION (1916). The drive for preparedness brought tangible results in the form of congressional legislation. (1) A Shipping Board was created and authorized to build or buy ships which might be transferred to private concerns or operated by government corporations. (2) A Council of National Defense was empowered to formulate plans for the efficient use of the nation's material resources in the event of war. (3) The Naval Appropriation Bill provided for the construction of dreadnaughts, battle cruisers, and other ships at a cost of $500,000,000. (4) The National Defense Act increased the regular army to 223,000 men and the national guard units to 425,000. The Act did not meet Secretary of War Garrison's ideas concerning the regular army and he resigned. President Wilson appointed Newton D. Baker of Ohio in his place.

**The Campaign of 1916.** In a close, but unexciting, contest the voters endorsed the progressive legislation and pacific foreign policy of Woodrow Wilson. The President was stronger than his party in all parts of the country.

HUGHES AND THE REPUBLICANS. In an effort to unite their scattered forces the Republicans nominated Justice Charles Evans Hughes of the Supreme Court, who had been far removed from the turmoil of the battle of 1912. Theodore Roosevelt, determined to defeat Woodrow Wilson, refused the Progressive nomination and urged his followers to support Hughes. The Republicans criticized the domestic policies of the Democrats and denounced the Wilson administration for its indecision in Mexico and its bungling of the submarine question. It was soon apparent, however, that Hughes had only generalities to offer in place of the Wilsonian record. Furthermore he failed to reconcile the former Progressives.

"He Kept Us out of War." This slogan represented the chief appeal of the Democratic campaign. By implication it endeavored to stress the fact that the war party in the United States was supporting the Hughes candidacy.

Wilson's Victory. Hughes carried the sixteen Northeastern states with the exception of New Hampshire and Ohio, while Wilson carried the Solid South and the trans-Mississippi West, except South Dakota and Oregon. The old Bryan country rallied to the President's support. The vote in the electoral college was 277 to 254.

"Peace without Victory." Wilson interpreted his reelection as a mandate to use American influence to end the European war by a negotiated peace. This he had tried to do by sending Colonel House to London and Paris in January, 1916. After the failure of House's mission he bided his time. In December, 1916, he called upon the belligerents to state their war aims. Germany agreed to discuss peace around the conference table; the Allies defined their aims in terms which Germany spurned. Late in January, 1917, Wilson addressed the Senate pleading for a speedy peace settlement which should include (1) abandonment of secret alliances and the balance of power in Europe; (2) recognition of the equality of all nations; (3) the protection of oppressed minorities; (4) the limitation of land and naval armaments; (5) freedom of the seas. This "peace without victory" proposal found no favor with the belligerents.

The Resort to Arms. The announcement on January 31, 1917, that the German government would resume unrestricted submarine warfare caused the United States to sever diplomatic relations with Germany and within two months to enter the war against the Central Powers. The decision for war probably was based on numerous considerations: (1) the widespread sympathy for the Allies engendered by the effective propaganda of the British and the French; (2) the hostility to the Central Powers aroused by their crude attempts to prevent American mills and munition plants from supplying the Allies; (3) the financial stake in the cause of the Allies held by American manufacturers and private bankers; (4) the determination of President Wilson that the United States should have a voice in the peace settlement; (5) the immediate resentment occasioned by Germany's violation of the *Sussex* pledge and by the publication of the "Zimmerman Note," in which an effort was made to enlist Mexico and Japan in a joint attack upon the United States, if the American government declared war against Germany.

## MOBILIZING THE NATION'S STRENGTH

During the war years the majority of our citizens, and their representatives in Congress, rose above the limitations of partisanship, conferring upon the President the powers which he requested and co-operating in numerous ways to insure victory on the field of battle.

**The War Machine.** Congressional legislation in 1917 dealt with the reorganization of the army and navy, the mobilization of money and material, and the molding of public opinion in support of the war.

THE ARMY. The regular army and the National Guard units were increased by voluntary enlistment to 750,000 men. The Selective Service Act of 1917, based on the principle of universal conscription, compelled all young men between the ages of twenty-one and thirty to register with their local draft boards. Subsequently the age limits were fixed at eighteen to forty-five. More than 24,234,000 persons were enrolled, of whom 2,810,000 were inducted into the federal service. They were trained in thirty-two great cantonments located in various sections of the country.

THE NAVY. Our naval force in European waters numbered 5000 officers and 70,000 enlisted men. It co-operated with the British and the French in convoying merchantmen and troopships, combating submarines, and laying down a mine barrage in the North Sea. The merchant marine, likewise, was greatly expanded. By the autumn of 1918 the Shipping Board had a fleet of 2600 vessels and 10,000,000 tons.

THE TREASURY. Between April, 1917, and October, 1919, governmental appropriations totaled $35,400,000,000. Of this stupendous sum $11,280,000,000 was raised by taxation. Income tax rates were increased; new levies were imposed on the excess profits of corporations; and a sales tax was placed upon numerous commodities. The bulk of the war expenses was met by borrowing from the public. Four Liberty Loan "drives" and a final Victory Loan brought $21,448,000,000 into the treasury from the sale of bonds.

MATERIAL RESOURCES. Private business co-operated with the government in numerous ways to insure success in the war. Representatives of organized labor, as well as distinguished industrialists, served upon the boards and commissions created in order to co-ordinate the economic life of the nation in one great war machine. The work of the Council of National Defense was supplemented by a War Industries Board, a War Labor Board, a General Munitions Board, the Federal Food Administration, and the Federal Fuel Administration. The stream of munitions, military supplies, and food to Europe never failed.

TRANSPORTATION. The extraordinary demands of war proved to be a problem greater than the railroads could solve through voluntary co-operation. Therefore in December, 1917, President Wilson assumed control of the roads and named Secretary McAdoo as director-general to operate them as a unified system. Passenger service was curtailed to facilitate freight in transit; terminals and equipment were improved; wages were raised to spur employees to greater efforts; rates were increased.

THE PUBLIC MORALE. The government manifested considerable concern to "sell the war" to the country. A Committee on Public Information published an *Official Bulletin* and furnished governmentally inspired material to the press. Under the terms of the Espionage Act (June, 1917) and the Sedition Act (May, 1918), the government was able to suppress any form of dissent from its policy which it deemed a hindrance to the winning of the war. The Department of Justice acted vigorously in ferreting out obstructionists and bringing them to trial, while the postal authorities exercised a rigorous censorship over publications sent through the mails.

**The A.E.F.** In answer to the pleas of the statesmen and military leaders of the Allies, the United States government pushed forward rapidly its plans for an American Expeditionary Force.

"OVER THERE." General John J. Pershing, who had commanded the punitive expedition into Mexico in 1916 (see page 140), was given command of the A.E.F. He recommended steps to prepare an army of 3,000,000 men for service overseas. By December, 1917, there were 176,000 American troops in France and one division was holding the quiet sector near Belfort. The training and maintenance of an American army on French soil required the construction of extensive transportation and communication facilities, the establishment of huge depots for the commissary and quartermaster departments, and the erection of cantonments and training schools behind the combat lines. The following table illustrates the acceleration with which our troops were transported overseas during the six months from June to November, 1918.

| Months (1918) | Strength of United States Army | In A.E.F. | Percentage |
|---|---|---|---|
| June | 2,112,000 | 722,000 | 34 |
| July | 2,380,000 | 996,000 | 42 |
| August | 2,658,000 | 1,293,000 | 49 |
| September | 3,001,000 | 1.576,000 | 52 |
| October | 3,433,000 | 1,843,000 | 54 |
| November | 3,634,000 | 1,971,000 | 55 |

THE WESTERN FRONT. Although Pershing was resolute in his decision to create an American army, rather than to brigade his troops with the British and French, he postponed the realization of his complete program in order to meet the challenge of the Germans in the spring of 1918 as they stood before Amiens, Ypres, and Chateau-Thierry. American troops participated in the counteroffensives at Montdidier, Cantigny, Belleau Wood, Bouresches, and Vaux. In July, 1918, more than 85,000 fought in the Marne-Champagne battles and the assault against the German lines between Soissons and Chateau-Thierry. By October two American armies had been formed, one commanded by General Hunter Liggett and the other by General Robert L. Bullard. The September-October campaigns of these armies were marked by two signal achievements—the reduction of the St. Mihiel salient and the Meuse-Argonne drive, which broke the German lines from Metz to Sedan.

THE ARMISTICE. The Meuse-Argonne offensive was a small part of the general forward movement launched by Marshal Ferdinand Foch, commander-in-chief of the Allied forces. It started the Germans on their last retreat. As it became evident that the Allies were headed for German territory, resistance collapsed and a provisional German government signed the terms of an armistice, dictated by Foch at his headquarters in the forest of Compiegne, on November 11, 1918.

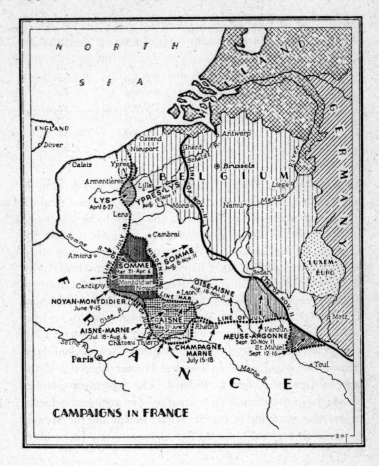

CAMPAIGNS IN FRANCE

## FROM WAR TO PEACE

The greatest tragedy of the war was the fact that the mood and manner of the peace conference, and the terms of the Treaty of Versailles, were far removed from the high idealism which President Wilson had voiced during the momentous years of the conflict.

**The Background of the Peace.** After the entrance of the United States into the war President Wilson became by general consent the spokesman for the cause of the Allies. While his pleas for a "war to make the world safe for democracy" and for a "peace founded upon honor and justice" stirred liberals everywhere, he did not succeed in exorcising the spirit of selfish nationalism.

THE "FOURTEEN POINTS." The most significant statement of Wilsonian war aims was contained in the President's address to Congress on January 8, 1918. His fourteen-point program included political and territorial readjustments dealing with Alsace-Lorraine, Belgium, Italy, Austria-Hungary, Poland, Russia, the Balkan states, and the Turkish Empire, but the important features were (1) abolition of secret diplomacy, (2) freedom of the seas, (3) removal of international economic barriers, (4) reduction of armaments, (5) impartial adjustment of colonial claims, (6) establishment of a general association of nations.

THE "SECRET TREATIES." The European statesmen who accepted these high aspirations of President Wilson were well aware that they had already entered into secret treaties whereby they had in prospect divided the spoils which would result from their victory over the Central Powers. These secret agreements were specific pledges of the precise gains to be realized by Great Britain, France, and Russia, and were promises made to Italy, Japan, Roumania, and Greece in order to win their support for the Allied cause.

FRENCH REVENGE. The French, led by Clemenceau, were determined to destroy Germany's military power and economic strength. French security, they insisted, meant a permanently crippled Germany.

THE BRITISH ATTITUDE. In the autumn elections of 1918 British liberalism had succumbed to the leadership of a Lloyd George, who demanded that the Kaiser be hanged and the Germans compelled to pay to the last shilling the total costs of the war. Neither in Great Britain nor France was the official atmosphere congenial for the Wilsonian idealism.

**The Paris Conference (1919).** The conference of more than sixty delegates from tweny-seven nations, which met at Paris on January 18, 1919, completed the Treaty of Versailles on May 7. It was signed by German representatives on June 28, 1919.

ORGANIZATION OF THE CONFERENCE. The representatives of the Central Powers were denied a place at the conference table. So numerous were the delegates accredited to the conference that it was utterly impossible to transact business in plenary sessions. The steering committee was the Council of Ten, consisting of two representatives from each of the five powers — Great Britain, France, the United States, Italy, and Japan. Finally, most important questions were settled by the "Big Four," Wilson, Lloyd George, Clemenceau, and Orlando. The committee of experts filed multitudinous reports for the guidance of the negotiators, though they could not be sure that the memoranda would be used.

WILSON'S DIFFICULTIES. The people of Europe to an astounding degree relied upon the President of the United States to satisfy their nationalistic aspirations and to meet their economic needs. Confronted by the most vexing problems, Wilson was handicapped from the very beginning of the conference. (1) His party had been repudiated at the polls in the congressional elections on the eve of his departure for Paris; (2) his choice of the American delegation — Lansing, House, White, and Bliss — had not increased his influence with the Senate, which was disquieted by his plans for a League of Nations; (3) his relations with the press at Paris were unfortunate, when he most needed favorable publicity; (4) his failure to thresh out the question of the secret treaties before the conference was a major blunder.

THE FIGHT FOR THE LEAGUE. Wilson's greatest victory at the conference was the writing of the covenant of the League of Nations as an integral part of the Treaty of Versailles. In the course of this victory he was compelled to compromise with the British, French, Italians, and Japanese to secure support. Although Wilson was the chief architect of the League, he received valuable aid from Lord Robert Cecil of England, General Jan Smuts of South Africa, and Leon Bourgeois of France, and he incorporated several suggestions made by Taft, Root, and Hughes. The final draft of the Covenant provided for (1) an Assembly consisting of delegates from all the member states, each of which was entitled to one vote in the periodic meetings at Geneva, Switzerland; (2) a Council of Nine, representing the five great powers and four nations elected by the Assembly; (3) a secretariat composed of a Secretary-General and assistants to handle routine work of the League. The purposes of the League were to respect and preserve the territorial integrity and political independence of its members, to minimize the possibilities of international strife, to formulate plans for the reduction of armaments, and to provide for the registration of all international agreements. A Permanent Court of International Justice was to be established to facilitate the settlement of serious international disputes.

**The Treaty of Versailles.** This document of 80,000 words was a punitive settlement imposed by the victors upon a vanquished Germany. It compelled the Central Powers to assume responsibility for the outbreak of the war. By its provisions Germany lost 1,000,000 square miles of colonial possessions and 50,000 square miles of European territory, reduced her army to 100,000 men, surrendered all warships, submarines, airplanes, and other military equipment, and agreed to pay to the Reparations Commission the total costs of the war, which were finally fixed at approximately $56,-500,000,000 in gold. The furious protests of German statesmen and publicists brought no modification in the treaty provisions, and on June 28, 1919, the German delegation in sullen mood signed the document. Though the burden imposed on Germany was heavy, it was by no means crushing.

**The Senate and the Treaty.** Having won his fight at Paris to incorporate the League Covenant as an integral part of the treaty, Wilson lost his struggle with the American Senate over ratification.

SENATORIAL HOSTILITY. On July 10, 1919, President Wilson presented the treaty to the Senate, which had previously secured a copy through newspaper channels and had been debating its provisions acrimoniously. The hostility to the document arose chiefly from the League provisions, but there were criticisms of the sections which dismembered the Austro-Hungarian monarchy, which granted Japan rights in the Shantung peninsula in China, and which allotted most of the German colonies under the mandate system to Great Britain and the Dominions. The enemies of the League centered their attack on (1) the probability that Article X would compel Congress at the dictates of the League Council to defend the territorial integrity and political independence of any member state which was attacked; (2) the fact that the British Commonwealth of Nations had six votes in the Assembly, since all the Dominions were regarded as independent nations; (3) the possibility that the League might interfere in cases arising out of our interpretation of the Monroe Doctrine, or in cases of purely domestic concern; (4) the danger that the League might develop into a supergovernment, impairing the sovereign powers of its members.

WILSON'S APPEAL TO THE COUNTRY. Having failed to persuade the Senate Committee on Foreign Relations, of which Henry Cabot Lodge was chairman, to recommend ratification of the treaty, President Wilson carried his case to the country, speaking to enthusiastic audiences in the Middle and Far West during September, 1919. His tour ended in failure, however, when his health broke, and he was compelled to return to Washington, suffering from a cerebral thrombosis which partially paralyzed his left side. There was no indication that his appeal had aroused the electorate to demand ratification.

THE LODGE RESERVATIONS. On September 10 the Committee on Foreign Relations reported the treaty, with more than forty amendments and four reservations to the League Covenant. After weeks of debate the Senate passed fifteen reservations (the Lodge Reservations) but refused to ratify the treaty either with or without the reservations. Sentiment among the Senators seemed to fall into four categories: (1) the fifteen "irreconcilables," (2) the supporters of the Lodge Reservations; (3) the "mild reservationists," who were willing to accept the treaty with minor changes; and (4) the Wilsonians, who demanded that the treaty be ratified without change.

THE REJECTION OF THE TREATY. In the spring of 1920 the Senate returned to a consideration of the treaty and the Lodge Reservations. The final test came on March 19 when the treaty with reservations received fifty-seven ayes and thirty-nine nays, less than the two-thirds necessary for ratification. In May President Wilson vetoed the joint resolution declaring the war with Germany at an end, but President Harding signed a similar resolution on July 2, 1921. Subsequently treaties were negotiated with Germany, Austria, and Hungary, and were promptly ratified by the Senate.

## REVIEW QUESTIONS

1. Why did the United States government protest more vigorously against the German violations than the British infringements of our neutral rights?
2. Was Germany justified in demanding that we make our neutrality real by refusing to sell munitions and supplies to the Allies?
3. Do you regard the resumption of submarine warfare in January, 1917, as the sole reason for the entrance of the United States into the First World War? Why?
4. How do you explain the victory of President Wilson in the presidential election of 1916?
5. In what ways were the "secret treaties" and the "Fourteen Points" irreconcilable?
6. Why was President Wilson so determined to write the Covenant of the League of Nations into the Treaty of Versailles?
7. Discuss the opposition to the treaty which developed in the United States Senate.
8. Who was to blame for the failure of the Senate to ratify the treaty? Discuss fully.
9. Why did the economic provisions of the treaty prove to be so difficult to enforce?

## SELECTED REFERENCES

Bullard, Arthur, *Mobilizing America*

Creel, George, *How We Advertized America*

Fleming, D. F., *The United States and the League of Nations*

Grattan, C. H., *Why We Fought*

Hendrick, B. J., *Life and Letters of Walter Hines Page*

House, E. M., and Seymour, Charles, *What Actually Happened at Paris*

Pershing, J. J., *My Experiences in the World War*

Seymour, Charles, *Woodrow Wilson and the World War*

CHAPTER XV

# WAR'S AFTERMATH

## PEACETIME RECONSTRUCTION

The period of liquidating war organizations and activities was characterized by governmental indecision, industrial strife, and social unrest.

**Military Demobilization.** The return to civilian status of 4,000,000 soldiers and sailors and more than 11,000,000 war workers was speedily accomplished as industry was able to absorb an increasing labor force during the first half of the year 1919.

REORGANIZING THE ARMY. An Army Act of 1920 placed the peacetime strength of the regular army at 300,000 men and provided for closer contact between the representatives of the federal government and the National Guard units in the various states.

CARING FOR THE VETERANS. The Bureau of War Risk Insurance, reorganized in 1921 as the Veterans' Bureau, was authorized to supervise insurance claims and payments, the hospitalization of wounded veterans, and the vocational training of the partially incapacitated. In 1920 the American Legion, formed by World War veterans the previous year, championed a demand for "adjusted compensation," or bonus, to be granted by the government to all ex-soldiers. After President Harding had vetoed a bonus bill in 1922, Congress passed an act in 1924 over President Coolidge's veto, which authorized the Treasury to issue twenty-year paid-up certificates against which the veterans might borrow money from the government at 6 per cent interest. Seven years later Congress refused to yield to the demand for immediate cash redemption of the certificates but increased the loan value of the certificates at the same time that it reduced the interest rates. In 1936 the veterans' certificates were paid off in 3 per cent bonds, which could be redeemed for cash on demand.

**Scrapping the War Machine.** The government followed no consistent program in liquidating the vast and complicated administrative organization of the war years; in some instances boards and commissions merely ceased to function, but in most cases executive orders transferred power to the regular governmental departments.

SCRAPPING MATERIALS. Governmental losses were heavy in disposing of surplus materials and in canceling contracts for goods and services no longer needed. The construction projects in France, and the mobile supplies, were sold to European buyers at approximately half their cost. The Board of War Claims and the Liquidation Commission (1919) managed to salvage about $7,000,000,000 through the adjustment of war contracts.

THE MERCHANT MARINE. The heaviest financial loss was suffered by the government in its efforts to dispose of the ship tonnage, built during the war, which it could neither use nor sell. The Merchant Marine Act of 1920 enabled the Shipping Board to sell about 40 per cent of its fleet at bargain prices, but it was not until the Jones-White Act of 1928 that an indirect subsidy grant in the form of construction loans and mail contracts stimulated the sale of old ships and the building of a more modern merchant fleet. In 1931 the percentage of our foreign trade carried in American bottoms had tripled as compared with the prewar years.

**The Railroads.** The operation of the railroads by the government as a war measure stimulated the demand in certain quarters for government ownership and operation, but President Wilson recommended the return of the roads to private operation, warning against the re-establishment of "the old conditions unmodified."

THE PLUMB PLAN. A plan formulated by Glenn E. Plumb of Chicago had the support of the railroad brotherhoods and the American Federation of Labor. It provided for (1) the purchase of the railroads by the government; (2) the operation of the lines by a National Railway Operating Corporation composed of all railroad officials and employees; (3) the direction of the Operating Corporation by a board of fifteen, five chosen by the officials, five by the workers, and five by the government; (4) the establishment by the board of directors of a wage scale and a schedule of rates, subject to review by the Interstate Commerce Commission. Although the Plumb plan was widely debated, hostility in Congress prevented its serious consideration.

THE ESCH-CUMMINS BILL. Congressional discussion of numerous proposals for the revamping of the transportation system finally resulted in the passage of the Esch-Cummins Bill, or Railroad Transportation Act, in February, 1920. Its salient features were (1) increased regulation of the railroads by the Interstate Commerce Commission, which was granted control of security issues, traffic regulations, and consolidation of lines for the purpose of eliminating unnecessary competition; (2) the guarantee by the government of a fair return (5½ per cent) to the owners for a period of two years; (3) the creation of a revolving fund by the government to facilitate railroad loans for improvements; (4) the compulsory arbitration of labor disputes by a Railway Labor Board composed of three from the owners, three from the workers, and three from the public.

**Industrial Disturbances.** The period immediately following the war was marked by excessive profiteering in commodity prices, bitter strife between employers and employees over wage scales, and costly strikes and lockouts in numerous industries.

HIGH PRICES AND PROFITEERING. The upward trend of prices, which began with the extraordinary demand for commodities as a result of the European war, and which was accentuated by the inflationary financial policy of the war years, caused an investigation by the Federal Trade Commission in 1919. The evidence of unscrupulous profiteering by manufacturers and middlemen resulted in a series of ineffective prosecutions by the Department of Justice against illegal trade practises. Much more significant was the spontaneous but widespread "buyers' strike" in the summer of 1920 which sent prices rapidly downward from the peak.

INDUSTRIAL CONFERENCE. In 1919 the government was much more concerned with foreign affairs than with domestic problems, but it could not continue to ignore the devastating effect of the warfare between capital and labor. President Wilson summoned representatives of employers, employees, and the public to meet at Washington in October, 1919. These deliberations ended in failure as did a later attempt by industrialists and government officials to create regional tribunals to settle labor disputes.

STEEL STRIKE (1919). One of the most serious of the numerous strikes was that of 370,000 steel workers, growing out of the efforts of the A.F. of L. to unionize the steel industry. The report filed by an investigating committee of the Interchurch World Movement indicated that the workers' demands were not unjustified, but the strike was associated with bolshevism and anarchism in the minds of many, and the employers broke it with nonunion labor.

COAL STRIKE (1919). The strongly unionized miners in the bituminous coal fields went out on strike (November 1, 1919) for higher wages. The government branded the strike as "not only unjustifiable, but unlawful," and secured an injunction forbidding the officials of the United Mine Workers from directing the strikers' activities. When a second injunction demanded the speedy recall of the general strike order, the United Mine Workers agreed to confer with representatives of the government and the operators. A special commission formulated a new wage agreement which was made effective in April, 1920.

**The "Red Scare."** As a result of the industrial strife and the activities of extreme radicals who openly avowed their sympathy with communism, many citizens were convinced that an organized attack on the government and the capitalistic system was under way. The "red scare" was marked by the deportation of "undesirable aliens," the expulsion of Socialists from legislative bodies to which they had been elected, the campaign of the Department of Justice against all radicals, and the passage of laws in several states to suppress communism and syndicalism.

## REPUBLICAN DOMINANCE AND DEMOCRATIC REVIVAL

For a dozen years after the war the political scene was dominated by the Republican party, which gained great partisan advantage from the nation's prosperity, only to suffer defeat as soon as prosperous times were succeeded by panic and depression.

**The "Return to Normalcy."** Warren Gamaliel Harding was swept into office by a multitude of voters who desired to escape from the disturbing challenge of Wilsonian idealism and from the nervous strain of war activities and peacetime readjustments. They believed that they were taking the road back to the normal conditions of the prewar years.

THE ELECTION OF 1920. The Republican convention, which gave evidence that the party was united for the first time since the Progressive bolt of 1912, nominated a "dark horse," Senator Warren G. Harding of Ohio, in order to avert a deadlock between the followers of General Leonard Wood and Governor Frank Lowden of Illinois. The platform, designed to be all things to all men, was chiefly concerned with a denunciation of Wilsonian domestic and foreign policies. The Democrats, dispirited and disorganized, finally named Governor James M. Cox of Ohio as their nominee and drafted a platform acceptable to President Wilson. The ensuing test at the polls was not a solemn referendum on the League of Nations, as the President wished, but a mass protest which arose out of the animosities engendered by the war and the disappointments occasioned by the period of reconstruction. Harding received 16,152,220 votes, Cox 9,147,000, Debs (Socialist) 919,800, and Christensen (Farmer-Labor) 265,400. The Senate and House were overwhelmingly Republican.

HARDING'S ADVISERS. President Harding was eager to cooperate with the Republican chieftains in formulating policies. His choice of "best minds" for the cabinet included Charles E. Hughes (State), Andrew W. Mellon (Treasury), and Herbert Hoover (Commerce). Less distinguished, but probably more influential in the administration, were Harry M. Daugherty (Attorney-General), Albert B. Fall (Interior), and Will H. Hays (Postmaster-General).

BUDGETARY REFORM. Prompted by Secretary Mellon, Harding vigorously championed a financial program which included reduction of federal taxes, especially income, inheritance, and internal revenue levies, retrenchment in governmental expenditures, and the adoption of a budget system. Under the Budget and Accounting Act (1921) General Charles G. Dawes became supervisor of the government's economy campaign. Events proved, however, that the administration was less successful in curtailing expenses than in reducing tax rates. President Harding and Secretary Mellon won the acclaim of the industrialists by their efforts to relieve business from governmental restrictions and to lighten the income tax burden in the higher brackets.

POLITICAL DISSENT. Mellon's tax program was not entirely successful in Congress, where a combination of Democrats and insurgent Republicans compelled the administration to accept higher rates on large incomes than the Treasury proposed. This political dissent centered in the so-called "farm bloc," which represented the constituencies of the "corn belt," who were insistent that agriculture receive governmental favors equivalent to those conferred upon industry.

ADMINISTRATIVE SCANDALS. The last months of President Harding's life were darkened by his knowledge that some of his trusted advisers had betrayed him and that shocking revelations of graft and political corruption could not long be kept from the public. The major scandals were concerned with (1) Charles R. Forbes's dishonesty in handling the funds of the Veterans' Bureau, for which he was sentenced in federal court; (2) the conspiracy to defraud the government in the office of the Alien Property Custodian, for which Attorney-General Daugherty and Thomas W. Miller were tried, Miller being sentenced to federal prison; (3) the notorious "oil scandals" growing out of the fraudulent leasing by Secretary Fall of certain reserves in Wyoming and California to prominent oil companies.

**Coolidge and Prosperity.** Calvin Coolidge, who succeeded to the presidency at Harding's death, quickly won the confidence of the country, and achieved widespread popularity as a result of the prosperity which enriched the nation during his years in office.

ELECTION OF 1924. Within ten months of Coolidge's induction into office the presidential campaign of 1924 was in full swing.

a. *Republican Convention.* So successful had the new President been in removing the stigma of corruption from his party and in winning the favor of the business interests of the country, that he was the unanimous choice of the delegates to the Republican national convention. The platform was an appeal to the conservative business interests, already feeling the quickening influence of more prosperous times.

b. *Democratic Confusion.* Trouble developed in the Democratic ranks over the platform. After prolonged and acrimonious debate the delegates rejected (1) a plank demanding American membership in the League of Nations; and (2) a resolution denouncing by name the Ku-Klux Klan, an organization designed to maintain the political supremacy of native-born, white, Protestant citizens. The contest for the nomination broke all records. The followers of Alfred E. Smith of New York and William G. McAdoo prevented a choice until the 103rd ballot, when the delegates stampeded to John W. Davis of West Virginia and New York.

c. *La Follette's Candidacy.* The dissatisfaction of the Western farmers and organized labor with the two major parties resulted in the formation of a third party, which nominated Robert M. La Follette of Wisconsin. The new group had the endorsement of the Conference for Progressive Political Action, sponsored by the railroad brotherhoods, the American Federation of Labor, and the Socialist party. The platform, drafted by Senator La Follette, was largely an expression of agrarian discontent and labor unrest.

d. *The Campaign.* La Follette provided the action in a rather listless campaign. Davis tried unsuccessfully to raise the cry of corruption against the Republicans. The Republican strategy was to frighten the voters with the charge that La Follette was a dangerous radical and the best way to defeat him was to vote for Coolidge. The result revealed the drift away from the Democrats. Coolidge received 15,725,000 votes against 8,386,000 for Davis and 4,822,000 for La Follette. Davis secured the Solid South and Oklahoma, while La Follette won his own state, Wisconsin.

ECONOMY AND TAXATION. Coolidge, like Harding, supported enthusiastically the financial policies of Secretary Mellon. Despite the repeated assurances that the White House was directing an energetic economy campaign, the federal budget did not shrink appreciably during the Coolidge administration. Instead, the increasing prosperity of the country enabled the Treasury at the same time to reduce tax rates, to collect more than enough revenue to meet current expenses, and to apply the surplus to the steady reduction of the national debt. No wonder that Mellon was hailed as the greatest Secretary of the Treasury since Hamilton.

CONGRESSIONAL INSURGENTS. Although President Coolidge was immensely popular and had Republican majorities in both houses of Congress, his administration was characterized by considerable friction between the White House and the Capitol. An examination of the record proves that the President was compelled to modify his proposals or to abandon his recommendations more frequently than many Presidents less favored with the confidence of the voters.

**Herbert Clark Hoover.** Coolidge's cryptic statement that he did not "choose to run in 1928" opened the way for the candidacy of Secretary of Commerce Hoover, who was presented by his friends as a successful engineer qualified to manage the complicated mechanism of the national government.

ELECTION OF 1928. The chief significance of this campaign was the emphatic decision of the electorate that it wanted a continuance of prosperity under Republican auspices.

a. *The Platforms.* On such issues as the tariff, farm relief, and prohibition the pronouncements of both parties were either platitudinous or evasive. On many other public questions the difference between the platforms was negligible.

b. *The Candidates.* Between Herbert C. Hoover, who was nominated by the Republicans on the first ballot, and Alfred

E. Smith, who was named with equal facility by the Democrats, there was no fundamental conflict over social and economic theories. In background, temperament, and training they were strikingly dissimilar. Hoover appealed to the rural, "dry," and Protestant constituencies, while Smith's greatest strength was in the cities among the "wet," foreign-born, and Catholic voters.

c. *The Result*. Governor Smith's aggressive campaign was doomed from the outset. He was handicapped in the South and Middle West by his antiprohibition views, his religious faith, and his affiliation with Tammany Hall. Most important of all, the country was prosperous and in no mood to break the spell which seemed to have been induced by Republican rule. The Democrats carried only eight states and lost such strongholds in the Solid South as Texas, Florida, North Carolina, and Virginia.

POLITICAL DIFFICULTIES. Little versed in the ways of the practical politician, President Hoover had difficulty from the start in handling the party "bosses" and their office-seeking followers. With the exception of Henry L. Stimson (State), Andrew Mellon (Treasury), and James J. Davis (Labor), his cabinet appointments seemed to indicate he had been swayed by purely personal or political considerations.

RECALCITRANT CONGRESS. President Hoover's relations with Congress were far from happy. During the first two years of his administration he failed on numerous occasions to win the support of the Republicans in the Senate, and only the skillful parliamentary tactics of Speaker Longworth saved him from defeat in the House. After the congressional election of 1930 the Democrats controlled the House by a scant majority.

ECONOMIC DEPRESSION. It was President Hoover's misfortune that his years in the presidency were marked by a disastrous crash in the securities markets and a prolonged business reversal. The administration program to combat the depression did not produce results quickly enough to save the President from repudiation at the polls.

**The Democratic Landslide (1932).** The tremendous victory of the Democrats in the presidential election of 1932 was not so much a vote of confidence in the Democratic party and its leaders as a measure of the resentment, inspired in large part by the economic depression, against the Hoover administration.

THE REPUBLICAN CONVENTION. The President controlled the proceedings of the Republican convention. The platform, which was drafted in the White House, was adopted after a spirited battle over the prohibition plank. Hoover's nomination on the first ballot was quickly made unanimous, and in accordance with the President's wishes, Charles Curtis was renominated for Vice-President.

THE DEMOCRATIC CONVENTION. The preconvention campaign of Governor Franklin D. Roosevelt of New York had made such headway that the only question in the minds of the delegates was whether a combination could be effected to prevent him from securing the necessary two-thirds vote. When the "stop Roosevelt" movement, led by Alfred E. Smith, collapsed, the New York governor was nominated on the fourth ballot. The platform, which was unusually brief and specific, committed the party to repeal of the Eighteenth Amendment.

ROOSEVELT'S ELECTION. Both President Hoover and Governor Roosevelt carried out extensive programs of speech-making, the President defending his protective tariff, farm relief, and economic recovery policies and denouncing the proposals of the opposition as demagogic appeals. Roosevelt stressed the "new deal" for the "forgotten man" without clearly indicating the specific measures of his program. He accused the Republicans of seeking prosperity by conferring favors on the "special interests," and stressed the government's responsibility to promote the well-being of the great masses of its citizens. The result at the polls was a Demo-

cratic landslide, President Hoover carrying only six states —
Maine, New Hampshire, Vermont, Connecticut, Pennsylvania, and Delaware — with fifty-nine electoral votes.

CONGRESSIONAL ELECTIONS (1934). At the mid-term elections the Roosevelt administration not only maintained its
dominant position, but also increased its strength in both
houses of Congress. The number of Democrats in the House
rose from 309 to 322, while in the Senate the Republican
opposition was reduced to twenty-five members. Although
the administration leaders experienced difficulty in maintaining unity of action among the Democrats, they met with no
serious reversals in guiding the presidential program of legislation through the Seventy-fourth Congress.

REPUBLICAN REVIVAL. As soon as the results of the 1934
elections were known the Republicans began to formulate
plans for the revival of party strength throughout the nation.
In the spring and early summer of 1935 regional conventions
were held to discuss possible issues for the presidential campaign of 1936. It was evident that the differences of opinion
between the progressive and conservative wings of the party
would make it difficult to secure agreement on the extent to
which the policies of the "New Deal" should be condemned.

**Roosevelt's Re-election (1936).** In a campaign marked
by his vigorous defense of New Deal objectives and achievements, President Roosevelt was returned to office by a popular
majority of more than ten million, and by the electoral vote
of every state except Maine and Vermont.

THE ISSUES. The voters had little opportunity to register
their opinions on such issues as the philosophy underlying the
system of unemployment relief, the subsidizing of special
economic interests, the centralization of power in the federal
government, the delegation of unusual authority to the president, the reconciliation of individual liberty with economic
security, the relation of an unbalanced budget to the financial
structure of the nation. The Democrats were content to de-

fend their record, which, they insisted, was responsible for the return of prosperity, while the Republicans denounced the administration for its reckless experimentation, its extravagant spending, its use of the spoils system, and its failure to suppress communism.

CAMPAIGN STRATEGY. The conduct of the campaign by the Republicans was hesitant and inept, sharply contrasting with the assurance and skill of the politicians who managed the Democratic machine. President Roosevelt carried the brunt of the battle for his party, while Governor Landon of Kansas, nominated by the Republicans, proved to be a poor campaigner both in his direct appeals and in his radio speeches.

THE DEMOCRATIC VICTORY. The popular vote for President Roosevelt cut across party lines. The overwhelming character of his victory was bound to be embarrassing. The followers of Father Coughlin, Dr. Townsend, and the late Huey Long had apparently been relegated to obscurity, but within the Democratic ranks, for the time being, were many who had no interest in the perpetuation of the Democratic party. Some there were who prophesied the disruption of both major parties and a political realignment on the basis of economic attitudes.

## ECONOMIC AND SOCIAL PROBLEMS

Many important social and economic problems of the postwar decade remained unsolved and were emphasized anew by the impact of the Second World War.

**Economic Nationalism.** Despite the growing realization of the interdependence of industry and commerce throughout the world, there had been a significant increase in tariff barriers and trade discriminations after the First World War.

FORDNEY-MCCUMBER TARIFF (1922). This bill represented a return to protectionist principles. An elaboration of the emergency act of 1921, which had superseded the Underwood Tariff, it (1) reduced the commodities on the free list;

(2) increased the rates on agricultural products; (3) created a Tariff Commission to investigate and compare costs of production here and abroad; (4) authorized the President to revise rates whenever it seemed advisable on the basis of the Commission's reports. In general the act restored the levels of the Payne-Aldrich Tariff of 1909.

THE HAWLEY-SMOOT BILL (1930). This bill, which President Hoover rather reluctantly signed on June 14, 1930, contained rates which in one-quarter of the schedules were higher than the Fordney-McCumber Tariff. The Tariff Commission was made more effective and the principle of flexible rates was retained.

DEMAND FOR TARIFF REVISION. The act of 1930 did not receive universal acclaim. Many academic economists denounced it as an outrageous evidence of economic nationalism which would cause unjustifiable increases in the cost of living; importers, exporters, and international bankers feared its effect upon foreign trade and American investments abroad; the peace propagandists regretted its unfortunate effect upon international relations. By 1932 more than twenty nations had revised their tariffs as measures of reprisal against the United States. Secretary of State Cordell Hull at the World Economic Conference in London (1933) worked for mutual trade concessions, but did not receive the support of President Roosevelt and his close advisers.

**Agricultural Surpluses and the Farmer.** The perennial problem of the relation of agriculture to the new industrial order became acute after the First World War, for the farmer did not share with the manufacturer, merchant, and banker the prosperity of the third decade of the twentieth century.

THE GOLDEN HARVEST. The First World War brought unprecedented good times to American farmers, who were tempted by the phenomenal rise in the prices of their staples to buy more acres and to strive for an increase in the productivity of the acreage already under cultivation. The mechanization of agriculture, which went forward rapidly in response to the needs of the warring nations, brought increasing returns to progressive farmers.

THE AGRARIAN REVERSAL. The farmer's prosperous years were few. Peace brought a quick descent to the prewar price level. Between 1919 and 1921 the value of farm products was cut in half, though production had slightly increased. The farmer's plight, to which abandoned farms and foreclosed mortgages bore mute witness, was the result of (1) the excessive expansion of agricultural lands, many of them submarginal; (2) the increased productivity per acre due to improved machines and methods; (3) the decline of commodity prices in the great world markets where our agrarian surplus competed with the surplus of other nations.

LEGISLATIVE RELIEF. Like the Grangers and the Populists of other days the farmers turned to Congress for relief.

a. *The Farm Bloc.* The pressure exerted by the National Grange, the Farmers' Union, and the Farm Bureau Federation caused the formation in Congress of a bi-partisan "farm bloc" which worked for agrarian legislation. As a result Congress enacted a Futures Trading Act (1921) to curb speculation in grain prices; a Filled Milk Act (1922) to protect dairymen against dishonest competition; an Intermediate Credit Act (1923) to extend agricultural credit on easier terms; and a Co-operative Act (1924) to exempt agricultural co operatives from the antitrust laws.

b. *The McNary-Haugen Bill.* The basic problem of agricultural surpluses was attacked in the McNary-Haugen Bill which passed Congress in February, 1927, only to be vetoed by President Coolidge. Its sponsors modified some of its provisions and secured its passage in May, 1928, but again Coolidge vetoed the bill. The central feature of the scheme was the attempt to equalize the price of American farm surpluses in the world market with the price in the protected domestic market by the imposition of an "equalization fee" assessed against the farmers producing each staple. It was asserted that the fee would operate automatically to curb excessive production of any staple. A federal board was to handle the marketing of all surplus staples and to collect the equalization fee.

c. *Agricultural Marketing Act (1929)*. President Hoover followed President Coolidge's course in opposition to the principles of the McNary-Haugen Bill, but he supported a substitute measure, enacted June 15, 1929, creating a Federal Farm Board which was empowered to promote in various ways the marketing of agricultural commodities. The Board made extensive loans to co-operatives and through its subsidiaries, the Grain Stabilization Corporation and the Cotton Stabilization Corporation, purchased millions of dollars worth of agricultural crops in order to bolster up the price. The effort was a failure as farm prices continued down the toboggan and the grain and cotton holdings of the Farm Board could not be liquidated for fear of further decline.

**The Railroads.** Like the farmers the railroad operators, who had once been hostile to governmental regulation, now turned to the national government for relief.

New Form of Competition. After 1920 the railroads felt keenly the competition offered by (1) the barge canals and improved internal waterways; (2) the motor-transport companies; (3) the expanding pipe-line facilities; and (4) the airways. From the railroad executives came insistent demands that Congress place their competitors under governmental supervision.

Consolidation. The solution of the railroad problem which was implicit in the Railroad Transportation Act of 1920 was the unification of independent lines into great systems based upon a careful analysis of the country's needs. The Interstate Commerce Commission and the railroad executives alike studied the difficulties and possibilities of consolidation, but action was slow. Between 1920 and 1929 hundreds of short lines were acquired by the larger rail systems. Not until 1931 did the Northeastern roads submit a plan for unification which the Interstate Commerce Commission approved with certain changes in details. There were to be four great networks in the Northeast: (1) the New York Central, with 12,920 miles; (2) the Pennsylvania, with 16,548 miles; (3) the Baltimore and Ohio, with 11,156 miles; and (4) the unified Van Sweringen holdings, with 12,554 miles.

Co-ordination Bill (1933). The Reconstruction Finance Corporation helped many railroads by its generous loans during the depression. In June, 1933, Congress passed an act providing for a scheme of railroad co-ordination which would effect economies in the transportation system. Joseph B. Eastman was named Federal Co-ordinator of Railroads.

**The Power Issue.** During the postwar decade popular demand for governmental regulation of public utilities, especially those producing and distributing electric power, brought action from state and federal authorities.

State Regulation. The public-utilities companies, which had widely extended their activities through mergers and holding companies, were gradually brought under some sort of state supervision. By 1930 nearly every state had created a public-service commission, but the commissions were handicapped by the modest character of their powers and by the fact that the great utilities organizations were engaged in enterprises which crossed state lines.

Federal Water-Power Commission. Congress created this agency in 1920 and empowered it to license hydroelectric plants on the navigable rivers or on public lands and Indian reservations. Over its licensees the Commission had regulatory powers affecting rates whenever electricity was sold across state lines. After ten years only 5 per cent of the nation's hydroelectric power was produced under the Commission's supervision.

MUSCLE SHOALS. The champions of government ownership and operation of electric power facilities centered their
attack upon Muscle Shoals, the gigantic project on the Tennessee River which had been started under congressional appropriation as a nitrate-fixation plant in 1917. In 1928 Congress passed a bill, sponsored by Senator Norris of Nebraska,
providing for the creation of a government-owned corporation
to work the nitrate plants and to sell the surplus power gener-
ated at the hydroelectric station. President Coolidge vetoed
the bill. Two years later a similar measure, authorizing the
government to enlarge and operate the power station, was
vetoed by President Hoover, who denounced the entrance of
the federal government into the public-utilities field. The
Roosevelt administration, however, supported the Tennessee
Valley Development Act, which used Muscle Shoals as the
center of a plan for governmental control of power, fertilizer,
and explosives enterprises. The act was an elaboration of the
original Norris proposals.

**Immigration.** One of the direct consequences of the
First World War was the reversal by the United States of
its traditional immigration policy.

THE DEMAND FOR RESTRICTION. Prior to 1914 we permitted unrestricted European immigration, barring only such
aliens as seemed undesirable from considerations of public
health, safety, and morals. We were proud to be an asylum
for the oppressed of the Old World and we needed cheap
labor to exploit our abundant resources, build our railroads,
and expand our industries. Those who felt that foreign laborers were a menace to American standards of living, and
that we were no longer able to assimilate properly the millions
coming each decade to our shores, seemed to be in a minority.
Yet there was a growing demand for a restrictive and selective immigration policy.

ACT OF 1921. When it became apparent at the close of the
First World War that "the world was preparing to move to
the United States," Congress rather hastily adopted a policy

of restriction. The legislation of 1921 provided that no European country could send to the United States in any year more than 3 per cent of its nationals resident here at the time of the census of 1910.

QUOTA OF 1924. This legislation further restricted the number of immigrants and drastically reduced the quotas from the nations of southern and eastern Europe. It permitted each country to send 2 per cent of the number of its nationals who had resided here at the time of the census of 1890. The changing of the census base automatically increased the proportion of immigrants from northern and western Europe.

NATIONAL-ORIGINS PRINCIPLE. The quota of 1924 was to remain in effect three years when each country was to be accorded "that proportion of 150,000 which the number of persons of a given national origin residing in the United States in 1920 bears to the country's total population in 1920." So difficult did the determination of this base prove, that the new quotas were not made effective until 1929.

NONQUOTA GROUPS. The quota system does not apply to Canada or to the independent nations of Latin America. So wide is the latitude for administrative discretion under the law, however, that the officials of the State and Labor departments have been able to restrict selectively even nonquota groups by requiring property and other qualifications. Mexican immigration has been greatly reduced as a result of this administrative action.

**Labor.** The armies of labor emerged from the First World War in truculent mood, but most of them quickly succumbed to the pleasant features of the higher standard of living which the prosperous decade of the twenties made possible.

TRADE-UNIONISM. Prior to 1920 organized labor had grown steadily, but in the postwar decade it declined both in activity and in prestige. The American Federation of Labor, for example, reported 4,078,740 members in 1920; 2,961,096 in 1930; and 2,532,261 in 1932. Several circumstances explain this decline in conservative trade-unionism: (1) the Federation clung to craft distinctions which were rapidly becoming meaningless; (2) it failed to face the problem of "technological unemployment"; (3) it had nothing to offer the unskilled worker; (4) its affiliated unions ignored the entrance of the Negro into important trades and industries; (5) its organizers found it difficult to break the open-shop policy of employers who could rely upon the injunction to win labor disputes; (6) the company programs for health protection, sickness insurance, recreational facilities, and profit sharing made the union benefits less desirable to thousands of workers. The decline of organized labor was sharply accentuated by the industrial depression after 1929.

LEFT WING RADICALISM. The radical wing of American labor was temporarily curbed by the activities of state and national governments during the "red scare" of 1919 (see page 165). The I.W.W. never recovered from this onslaught and by 1924 it had virtually disappeared. Radical workers were responsible for the organization of the Communist party, the American section of the Third International, in 1919. Driven underground by the hostility of the government, it emerged as the Workers' party and frankly announced its affiliation with the Third International in 1928. It never polled more than 60,000 votes for its presidential candidate. In labor circles the Communists at first strove to capture conservative unions by a policy of "boring from within," but in 1929 they began a concerted movement to form industrial unions hostile to existing unions and committed to the accentuation of the class struggle.

INDUSTRIAL VERSUS CRAFT UNIONS. The activity of labor organizers, stimulated by the collective bargaining provisions of the National Industrial Recovery Act, raised anew the problem of the unskilled industrial worker. Within the A.F. of L. certain groups, notably the United Mine Workers, United Textile Workers, Amalgamated Clothing Workers,

International Clothing Workers, and International Typographical Union, sponsored industrial unionism against the more conservative representatives of the skilled craft unions. At the national convention of the Federation in 1935, President William Green blocked the attempt made by John L. Lewis of the United Mine Workers to commit the Federation to industrial unionism. Lewis promptly formed the Committee for Industrial Organization (CIO), defied the executive committee of the A.F. of L., and proceeded to organize the automobile and steel industries. By the spring of 1937 the CIO had secured partial recognition from the General Motors Corporation and several subsidiaries of the United States Steel Corporation. Two years later the A.F. of L. reported a dues-paying membership of slightly more then 3,600,000, while the CIO had reached 3,750,000.

**The Prohibition Experiment.** Probably no public question of the postwar period had been so widely debated over the years as the prohibition of the manufacture and sale of intoxicating beverages.

Prohibitory Movement. National prohibition was the culmination of a long campaign against the liquor traffic. From its inception early in the nineteenth century, the movement rested upon the conviction of an increasing portion of the American people that intoxicants (1) had an injurious effect upon the human body and mind; (2) contributed to poverty, vice, and crime; (3) were responsible for heavy taxes to support workhouses, asylums, and jails; (4) debauched the electorate and perpetuated evil influences in politics; (5) reduced the efficiency of workers and increased the problems of the employers; (6) constituted a menace to life and property in an industrialized society. Three organizations were particularly effective in the prohibitory movement: (1) the Prohibition party, formed in 1869, which placed the destruction of the liquor traffic above every other issue; (2) The Woman's Christian Temperance Union, which began an educational campaign in 1874; and (3) the Anti-

Saloon League, which mobilized the sentiment of evangelical Protestantism with great political astuteness after its organization in 1893.

The Eighteenth Amendment. So successful were the tactics of the Anti-Saloon League that by the autumn of 1917 the legislatures of more than half the states had banned the liquor traffic, and fully two-thirds of the people of the country were living in territory which was "dry" either by state or local legislation. It is not surprising that when the Eighteenth Amendment was passed by Congress (December, 1917) the list of ratifications by state legislatures was soon long enough to insure its incorporation in the Constitution (January, 1919).

Enforcing the Volstead Act. In September, 1919, Congress defined as intoxicating all beverages containing more than one-half of one per cent of alcohol and provided the machinery to make prohibition effective. The obstacles in the way of successful enforcement of the Volstead Act were many: (1) the fact that some communities, especially the larger cities, were opposed to national prohibition; (2) the lack of co-operation between federal and local authorities; (3) the interference of politicians with the work of the prohibition unit in the Treasury Department; (4) the faithlessness of enforcement agents who accepted bribes from "bootleggers," earning large profits in an illicit business; (5) the failure of the Treasury and Justice departments to centralize control of the enforcement service. The difficulties of making the Volstead Act effective caused the enemies of prohibition to denounce the Eighteenth Amendment as a failure, the chief fruits of which had been an increasing disrespect for all laws and the rise of the bootlegger, the hijacker, the racketeer, and the gangster.

The Wickersham Report. In 1929 President Hoover appointed a commission, headed by George W. Wickersham, to study the problem of law enforcement in general and its relation to the prohibition experiment in particular. The report submitted in January, 1931, was a confession of the breakdown of federal enforcement of the liquor laws, but the Commission advised further trial of the Volstead Act and the Eighteenth Amendment.

THE REPEAL MOVEMENT. By 1930 hostility to prohibition was well organized and generously financed. It had abandoned its agitation for the legalization of light wines and beer and was insisting upon repeal of the Eighteenth Amendment. Although politicians generally had avoided the issue and the platforms of the major parties had been models of evasion, some educators, publicists, and political leaders had openly championed the cause of repeal for a decade. In the campaign of 1932 the Democrats favored outright repeal, while the Republicans advocated reference of the question to the voters in their respective states. After the Democratic victory Congress passed a resolution repealing the Eighteenth Amendment, which was ratified by special conventions in three-fourths of the states. On December 5, 1933, the State Department announced that the Twenty-first Amendment to the constitution was in effect. Control of the liquor traffic reverted to the several states, but the President created a Federal Alcohol Control Administration (FACA), the duties of which were defined by an act of Congress in 1935.

**Prosperity, Panic, and Recovery.** The industrial expansion of the twenties, with its high wages and increased consumption of goods, culminated in an orgy of speculation which collapsed with disastrous results in 1929.

THE SPECULATIVE BOOM. A disquieting feature of the prosperous postwar years was the conversion of savings and earnings into speculative investments and the extension of credit for the purchase of land, buildings, stocks, and bonds at prices which were only fantastically related to earning power. The quotations of the stock market, rather than corporate earnings, became the barometer of investments for millions. Production far outran even prospective purchasing power. Never before had the country experienced such universal preoccupation with speculative ventures, yet the "boom" was pronounced sound by bankers, industrialists, economists, and government officials.

COLLAPSE OF THE STOCK MARKET. Late in October, 1929, panic developed in the great securities markets. Prices of stocks and bonds dropped with startling rapidity to low levels. At no previous period in their history had so many American people been directly interested in securities. The collapse of the financial markets, therefore, was but the prelude to widespread disaster.

COMBATTING THE DEPRESSION. One of the striking features of the economic depression was the alacrity with which all classes turned to the government for relief. The Hoover administration, which was at first inclined to believe that the business interests would work out their own salvation, finally attempted to check the lengthening statistics of bankruptcies, mortgage foreclosures, bank failures, and unemployment. The government offensive included (1) emergency appropriations for public works and farm relief; (2) formation of the National Credit Association (1931) to protect sound banks and assist in reopening those which had closed; (3) the Glass-Steagall Act, modifying the rules of the Federal Reserve System to grant more generous credit to farmers and businessmen; (4) the creation of the Reconstruction Finance Corporation with assets of $2,000,000,000 to make emergency loans to banks, insurance companies, railroads, and industrial enterprises. Despite these efforts the processes of liquidation and deflation which had started in 1929 went unchecked.

## COLLECTIVE SECURITY

Yielding to the trend toward economic nationalism and political isolation, the government of the United States found it increasingly difficult to co-operate with other nations in any system of collective security.

**War Debts and Reparations.** Relations with European nations in the decade after the First World War were constantly affected by efforts to collect the sums which we had loaned to the governments of the principal Allied powers during and immediately after the war.

FOREIGN DEBT COMMISSION (1922). Many Americans believed that for selfish, as well as sentimental, reasons the United States should cancel the war debts, but Congress created a World War Foreign Debt Commission which negotiated agreements with the various nations on the basis of each debtor's ability to pay. The total funded indebtedness of seventeen nations was fixed at $10,350,000,000, a considerable scaling down in the original loans and accrued interest. Payments were spread over a period of sixty-two years.

THE DAWES PLAN (1924). Although the United States refused to admit that payment of the war debts was contingent upon collection of reparations from Germany by the Allies, such was in reality the case. When Germany defaulted on reparations payments, the United States participated in formulating the Dawes plan whereby the German obligations were materially reduced and German industries were extended long-term credits.

THE YOUNG PLAN (1930). Revision of the reparations agreement became necessary in 1929 and a commission of experts, headed by Owen D. Young, arranged new terms partially contingent upon the American policy concerning inter-governmental debts, and set up a Bank for International Settlements to facilitate reparations payments and other processes of international finance.

THE MORATORIUM OF 1931. So alarming was the financial weakness of Germany and Austria in the spring of 1931 that President Hoover proposed "postponement during one year of all payments on inter-governmental debts, reparations, and relief debts, both principal and interest." This moratorium was not extended in 1932, but several nations failed to make payments on their debts to the United States, and the following year almost all of them defaulted.

**The Quest for World Peace.** After the First World War there was a spirited revival in the United States of the crusade against war.

DISARMAMENT. Four times after 1920 the United States participated in international conferences designed to effect a limitation of armaments.

a. *The Washington Conference (1921-1922).* At President Harding's invitation delegates from Great Britain, France, Italy, Japan, China, Belgium, the Netherlands, and Portugal met in Washington to discuss reduction of naval armaments and problems of the Pacific. The conference drafted nine treaties the most important of which were (1) a five-power treaty providing for a ten-year "naval holiday" in the construction of capital ships and fixing the relative tonnage of Great Britain, the United States, Japan, France, and Italy at $5:5:3:1.67:1.67$; (2) a four-power treaty binding the signatories (United States, Great Britain, Japan, and France) to respect one another's rights in the Pacific and to confer in the event that any question threatened to disrupt harmonious relations; (3) a nine-power treaty guaranteeing the political and territorial integrity of China and the "open door" for trade.

b. *The Geneva Conference (1927).* At President Coolidge's suggestion the signatories of the Washington naval treaty were invited to confer at Geneva in 1927. Delegates from Great Britain, the United States, and Japan spent six weeks in fruitless discussions.

c. *London Conference (1930).* The dangers of a new race in naval armaments caused Great Britain to invite the five powers to discuss naval armaments in 1930. France and Italy withdrew from the conference, but the United States, Great Britain, and Japan signed a treaty establishing naval parity between the United States and Great Britain, fixing ratios for the building of auxiliary craft, and extending the ban on battleship construction to 1936.

d. *General Disarmament Conference (1932).* President Hoover sent a distinguished delegation to the general disarmament conference of thirty-one nations which met at Geneva on February 5, 1932. Before its first recess in July it adopted a resolution setting forth certain principles which were regarded as basic in meeting concrete problems of disarmament. The prolonged deliberations were doomed when Japan, convinced that she could not secure satisfactory concessions from Great Britain and the United States, formally announced (December, 1934) that she would not renew the naval agreement originally signed at the Washington Conference of 1921. A new race to build naval armaments loomed on the horizon. Late in October, 1935, the Roosevelt administration accepted Great Britain's invitation to participate in another effort to forestall costly naval competition.

THE PACT OF PARIS (1928). Popularly known as the Kellogg-Briand Pact, this agreement signed by fifteen nations represented an attempt to outlaw war. Forty-four nations in addition to the original fifteen subscribed to the covenant which provided (1) that the signatory powers renounce war as an instrument of national policy and (2) that they agree to settle all international disputes by pacific means.

THE WORLD COURT. Three of our distinguished jurists have served upon this tribunal: John Bassett Moore (1921-1928); Charles Evans Hughes (1928-1930); and Frank B. Kellogg (1930-1935). On January 27, 1926, at the prompting of President Coolidge, the Senate accepted the protocol of membership with five reservations. Not all of these reservations were acceptable to the members of the Court, so our cooperation was delayed. Elihu Root participated in 1929 in the formulation of a revised protocol which seemed to be more satisfactory, but after long delay the Senate finally refused to ratify (January, 1935).

THE LEAGUE OF NATIONS. The United States gradually abandoned its earlier refusal to recognize the existence of the League of Nations. It co-operated constantly in the nonpolitical phases of the League's work; it participated in the preliminary plans for the League's general disarmament conference; and it indicated officially its willingness to act with the League in an effort to make effective the provisions of the Kellogg-Briand Pact.

## REVIEW QUESTIONS

1. What did President Harding's phrase "return to normalcy" imply?
2. Explain the economic factors which were responsible for the formation of the congressional "farm bloc."
3. What was the purpose of the government's immigration policy after the First World War? How was that purpose carried into effect?
4. How do you account for the rapid rise of the movement to repeal the Eighteenth Amendment?
5. Do you regard the policy of the Roosevelt administration as a deliberate abandonment of economic individualism? Why?
6. Would it have been wise from the standpoint of national self-interest for the United States to cancel the war debts?
7. Does economic nationalism as a factor in international relations seem more potent today than before the First World War? Explain.

## SELECTED REFERENCES

Adams, J. T., *Our Business Civilization*

Allen, F. T., *Only Yesterday*

Black, J. D., *Agricultural Reform in the United States*

Malin, J. C., *The United States After the World War*

Merz, Charles, *The Dry Decade*

Seldes, Gilbert, *The Years of the Locust*

Slosson, P. W., *The Great Crusade and After*

White, W. A., *Masks in a Pageant*

$$\left[\;\begin{array}{l}\textit{Significant Dates}\end{array}\;\right]$$

Creation of AAA and NRA . 1933
Gold Reserve Act . . . . . 1934
Social Security Act . . . . . 1935
National Labor Relations Act . 1935
Attempt to Reorganize Supreme
    Court . . . . . . . . . 1937
Wages and Hours Act . . . . 1938

CHAPTER XVI

# THE NEW DEAL IN ACTION

## ECONOMIC PLANNING

As Congress in the spring of 1933 enacted the measures which President Roosevelt deemed essential to the New Deal, it became apparent that the national government was moving away from traditional principles of *laissez faire* and was endeavoring to establish a planned economy.

**Theoretical Objectives.** Much of the new legislation rested upon the assumption that it would be possible to estab lish a balance in our economic system among conflicting interests and classes.

IMMEDIATE RELIEF FOR UNEMPLOYED AND NEEDY. Administration leaders argued that there was a public responsibility to aid those who had suffered most from the depression. Various agencies were created to distribute governmental relief in numerous forms. The Federal Emergency Relief Administration (FERA) was authorized to match funds with state and local governments; the Civil Works Administration (CWA) for one year created jobs of a temporary nature for 4,000,000 unemployed; the Public Works Administration (PWA) loaned money to public and quasi-public authorities to finance long-term construction projects; the Works Progress Administration (WPA) took care of needy employables through short-term improvements financed by the federal government; the Civilian Conservation Corps (CCC) provided work in national forests and conservation projects for more than 300,000 young men each year.

INCREASING PURCHASING POWER OF LABORERS. To maintain a satisfactory market for industry's goods and the farmers' produce the federal government undertook to protect the interests of the worker by recognizing his right to bargain collectively and by establishing minimum wages and maximum hours.

RAISING THE PRICE LEVEL. Reversal of the prolonged downward trend of prices was at the center of the New Deal philosophy. Price cutting was stopped by codes of fair competition. Mildly inflationary forces were encouraged by the devaluation of the dollar and the increase in the volume of paper currency.

REDUCTION OF PRIVATE INDEBTEDNESS. A vigorous attempt was made to scale down the sum total of private debts, commercial and personal. To this end, concessions were granted to mortgagors, and the federal bankruptcy law was modified to enable debtors to come to an accommodation with their creditors more quickly and more cheaply.

**Agriculture.** An elaborate program for the relief of American farmers was quickly formulated by Secretary Wallace and other administration advisers.

AGRICULTURAL ADJUSTMENT ACT. Passed in May, 1933, this act remained in operation until it was declared unconstitutional by the Supreme Court in January, 1936. It created an Agricultural Adjustment Administration (AAA) authorized (1) to control production of wheat, cotton, corn, rice, tobacco, hogs, and certain other crops by paying cash subsidies to farmers who voluntarily restricted acreage planted to such crops or reduced the numbers of their livestock; (2) to impose taxes upon the processors of agricultural commodities in order to secure the funds to pay these subsidies.

CROP CONTROL ACTS. Voluntary reduction of acreage proved unsatisfactory in the case of certain basic crops. Consequently, the Cotton Control Act (April, 1934) and the Tobacco Control Act (June, 1934) imposed an obligation on all growers to accept arbitrary production quotas. Along with this regimentation of producers went governmental attempts to help farmers market those crops which normally seemed to be adversely affected by market surpluses. In some instances the government bought up surpluses for distribution among the needy.

DOMESTIC ALLOTMENT ACT. After the AAA was declared unconstitutional, Congress passed the Soil Conservation and Domestic Allotment Act, whereby farmers were to receive grants from the federal government, distributed through state agencies, for their work in preventing soil erosion and in developing better methods of plowing, fertilizing, etc. Growers of such staples as wheat, cotton, tobacco, and corn were to receive outright subsidies.

THE AAA OF 1938. This act continued the soil conservation plans, but its chief feature was Secretary Wallace's idea of an "ever-normal granary." Through a system of benefit payments and crop loans an attempt was made to fix a point below which farm prices could not fall. In the case of wheat a crop insurance plan protected the growers against the effects of abnormally large harvests. In general, agriculture was accorded the position of a special interest, so important that the farmers were to be given governmental protection in storing and marketing crops and subsidies from the national revenues to help maintain their total income in normal relation to that of other persons in the country.

RURAL REHABILITATION. The problem of farmers, tenants, and agricultural laborers, trying to make a living on inferior and submarginal lands, became an important concern of the New Dealers. The Resettlement Administration (1935) took large areas of substandard land out of cultivation, made loans to needy families at low interest rates, and resettled families on new farmsteads. In four years more than 785,000 farm families received rehabilitation loans. The Farm Security Administration (1937) continued this work and in addition experimented with resettlement of rural groups on the basis of co-operative communities.

FARM CREDIT. The attempts to increase the farmer's income, and consequently his purchasing power, were supplemented by the Farm Mortgage Refinancing Act (1934) which (1) created the Farm Credit Administration (FCA) to supervise short-term as well as long-term loans to individual farmers and to co-operatives through the twelve federal land banks; (2) authorized the Farm Mortgage Corporation to help debt-burdened farmers to scale down their obligations and reduce their interest-payments. When the Farm Bankruptcy Act (1934) was declared unconstitutional, it was replaced by the Farm Mortgage Moratorium Act (August, 1935), under which farmers unable to meet interest obligations might, at court discretion, receive a three-year moratorium against foreclosure proceedings, thus enabling them to make an accommodation or refinancing arrangements.

**Industry.** To combat industrial unemployment and promote a revival of business activity, the Roosevelt Administration endeavored to raise commodity prices to the general level of 1926.

NATIONAL INDUSTRIAL RECOVERY ACT (NIRA). It was the purpose of this act to hasten the preparation by representatives of employers, employees, and the government of codes in each industry which would eliminate unfair competitive practices, abolish child labor and sweat shops, establish minimum wages and maximum hours, insure labor the right of collective bargaining, and create additional jobs for the unemployed. The National Recovery Administration (NRA) proceeded to draft and administer hundreds of these codes, though many of them fell short of the original objective. In the spring of 1935 President Roosevelt asked Congress to extend the duration of the NRA for two more years, but the legislators were unwilling to grant more than a ten-months extension. By unanimous decision the Supreme Court ruled (June, 1935) that the NIRA was unconstitutional.

MONOPOLY AND THE ANTITRUST LAWS. Under NRA the trend seemed to be toward monopoly prices in an increasing number of industries, and some insisted that small industries were being crushed by the power of bigger enterprises. Temporarily the government abstained from any attempt to compel competition. When the codes of NRA were abandoned, however, the administration indicated that a renewed attempt would be made to enforce fair competition in industry through the antitrust laws.

a. *National Economic Committee.* In June, 1938, Congress appropriated half a million dollars for the use of the Temporary National Economic Committee (TNEC) to investigate monopolistic trends in American business and the means necessary to combat them.

b. *Antitrust Activities.* At almost the same time President Roosevelt named Thurman Arnold an Assistant Attorney-General with especial responsibility for the vigorous enforcement of existing antitrust laws.

**Labor.** The New Deal gained some of its most substantial victories in the field of labor legislation.

THE NIRA AND ORGANIZED LABOR. Section 7(a) of the National Industrial Recovery Act provided that laborers under the various codes should have the right of collective bargaining, that they should choose their own representatives for such bargaining in free elections, and that employers should recognize such representatives. This "charter of liberties" stimulated the growth of trade-unions, greatly increasing the membership of the American Federation of Labor, and also led to many disputes over the way in which its provisions should be put into effect.

LABOR DISPUTES JOINT RESOLUTION. The task of settling these industrial disputes proved too difficult for the National Labor Board set up under NRA, and Congress passed (June, 1934) the Labor Disputes Joint Resolution which authorized the creation of special labor investigating boards to report on the causes of friction. These boards were finally co-ordinated under a National Labor Relations Board with power of final review in all disputed cases.

NATIONAL LABOR RELATIONS ACT. After NIRA was declared unconstitutional, Senator Wagner of New York sponsored a plan to protect effectively labor's right to organize. The National Labor Relations Act of July, 1935, created a National Labor Relations Board (NLRB) of three members empowered to determine suitable units for collective bargaining, to conduct elections for the choice of labor's representatives and to prevent interference with such elections. The Board's work was made difficult by the hostility of employers, who felt that the act was class legislation, and by the quarrel within the ranks of labor between the American Federation of Labor and the Committee for Industrial Organization.

INDUSTRIAL STRIFE. Although the CIO unions were suspended by the executive council of the American Federation of Labor, they promptly attempted to organize the automobile and steel industries. Against General Motors, Chrysler, Hudson, and other automobile companies they used the "sit-down strike," occupying the plants and refusing to leave so long as the dispute with the employers continued. During the nine months after September 1, 1936, nearly 500,000 workers were involved in such strikes. When the issue of their legality finally reached the Supreme Court (1939), the justices held that these "sit-downs" constituted unlawful seizures of property.

Meanwhile militant tactics had won recognition for the CIO from General Motors and had probably induced U. S. Steel to make an agreement before a strike of its workers was called. Despite the efforts of the NLRB, which reduced the number of strikes during 1938 and 1939, there were more than 1,170,000 persons involved in such disputes in the latter year.

INVESTIGATION OF NLRB. Although the Supreme Court upheld the NLRB in most of its interpretations of the scope of its own powers, there was widespread criticism both from industrial leaders and labor spokesmen during 1939. In December a special committee of the House of Representatives began an investigation of the Board's methods.

**Water Power.** Accepting the theory that hydroelectric power was as truly a natural resource as soil, the New Dealers were eager to demonstrate that public control could exploit this resource for the benefit of the American people.

THE TENNESSEE VALLEY AUTHORITY. In May, 1933, Congress created the TVA, which found its opportunity to experiment in the valley of the Tennessee River, an area embracing parts of seven states and including the power project at Muscle Shoals (see page 178). The plans of TVA were not confined to the generation of electricity, but were based upon the assumption that power development, prevention of floods, improvement of navigation, and manufacture of nitrates could be carried forward successfully as an interrelated public enterprise.

a. *Cheap Electricity.* Through governmental construction of dams, power plants, and transmission lines, more than forty thousand farms and homes in the Tennessee Valley were being supplied in 1939 with electric current at rates as low as one-half the average charged elsewhere in the country.

b. *The Electric "Yardstick."* The TVA believed that its rates for electricity could be used as a yardstick against which to check the rates of private utility companies. This

contention brought charges from the utility interests that
there was no sound basis for such a comparison in view of
the unorthodox accounting methods of TVA. A congressional investigation revealed great difference of opinion among
the experts, but a majority of the committee in 1939 declared
that TVA had set up a legitimate "yardstick" for purposes of
comparing rates.

Tennessee Valley Authority — Drainage area and dams

RURAL ELECTRIFICATION ADMINISTRATION. Created in
May, 1935, the Rural Electrification Administration was empowered to loan money for construction of power plants and
transmission lines in farming districts. During the first five
years of its operations it built almost 250,000 miles of lines in
more than forty states. Power for this program for rural
electrification was to come eventually from plants at Boulder
Dam (authorized in 1928) and at Bonneville and Grand
Coulee dams on the Columbia River.

REGULATION OF POWER COMPANIES. At the same time
that the government was encouraging public ownership of
power plants, Congress authorized the Securities and Exchange Commission and the Federal Power Commission to
tighten control over the corporate structure and the accounting practises of the private utilities companies. The legislation

was particularly designed to break up the holding companies which controlled the producing units and, in the opinion of the New Dealers, increased the cost to the consumer.

**Housing and Homes.** In its concern for the "forgotten man" the government endeavored to save the owners of small homes from foreclosure and eviction and to provide housing facilities for the underprivileged portion of the population.

HOME OWNERS' LOAN CORPORATION (HOLC). The act creating this corporation provided for the issuance of three billion dollars in bonds, principal and interest guaranteed by the government, to be used to refinance mortgages of home owners unable to pay off existing mortgages or about to lose their properties because their taxes were delinquent.

FEDERAL HOUSING ADMINISTRATION (FHA). An act of June 28, 1934, later amended, created the Federal Housing Administration for the purpose of guaranteeing mortgages on single-family houses and insuring loans made by banks and building and loan companies to persons interested in modernizing their homes. By the close of 1938 it had made more than $575,000,000 available in approximately 150 communities.

U. S. HOUSING AUTHORITY. Most of the governmental loans to promote construction of new houses and to encourage slum clearance were handled by the USHA. Created in 1937, it received 800 million dollars with which to make advances to communities that would co-operate with the federal government in building houses for the low-income families. It reported in December, 1940, that it had provided living accommodations for approximately 240,000 members of such families at reasonable rentals.

**Social Security.** One of the most important experiments made by the Roosevelt Administration was the attempt to give the country's workers a greater sense of security concerning wages, employment, and pensions for those forced to retire because of age.

SOCIAL SECURITY ACT. The Act passed in 1935, and amended in 1939, was in part an attempt to meet the demands of those who sponsored the Townsend plan and other schemes to provide pensions for the aged and insurance for the unemployed. Its numerous sections provided: (1) a federal program of old-age benefits, based on the workers' earnings before the age of sixty-five, to be paid out of funds derived from an income tax on employees and a payroll tax on employers; (2) a program of unemployment compensation administered by the states with federal grants approved by the Social Security Board; (3) federal aid to the states for maternal and child-health services, for medical work among crippled children, and for welfare services among the aged and the blind.

WAGES AND HOURS ACT. The Fair Labor Standards Act, which became effective in the autumn of 1938, was an attempt to reach a standard of minimum wages and maximum hours in the country's chief industries. Committees for each industry, representing employers and employees, were to recommend the highest minimum wage up to forty cents an hour which seemed compatible with economic conditions in the industry. Maximum hours per week were to be reduced gradually to forty. The statute was enforced by the Wage and Hour Division in the Department of Labor.

## FINANCIAL REFORMS

The New Deal program for economic recovery included drastic reforms in the management of financial institutions and a general revision of the nation's monetary system.

**Financial Institutions.** In response to what seemed to be a nationwide demand the government moved to protect the bank depositor and the investor.

BANKING. Following the bank holiday (March 5-9) in 1933, Congress enacted the Emergency Banking Law, which granted the President power to reorganize insolvent banks.

The Glass-Steagall Act went considerably farther in the direction of banking reform. It provided that a Federal Deposit Insurance Corporation should be created by the banks and the government to insure bank deposits up to $2500 each and to insure larger accounts on a partial basis, that all commercial banks must go out of the securities business, that member banks in the Federal Reserve System could not loan to any subsidiary or affiliate more than 10 per cent of their capital and surplus, and that member banks could not make loans to their own officers. National control of the banking system was further strengthened by the Banking Act of 1935, which provided (1) that all state banks with deposits of $1,000,000 or more must join the Federal Reserve System by 1942, if their deposits were to be insured by the government; (2) that control of open market transactions in federal bonds and other securities was to be vested in a special board on which were five members representing the regional Federal Reserve Banks and seven members nominated by the President.

SECURITIES EXCHANGES. To protect the investing public against fraudulent practices the Federal Securities Act of 1933 provided for federal registration and supervision of new issues, penalized issuing firms and dealers for sending out misleading information, and defined in somewhat general terms the responsibility of the seller in connection with fraudulent issues. This was supplemented in 1934 by an act putting the regulation of exchanges under a Securities and Exchange Commission of five members.

**Currency and Credit.** President Roosevelt early indicated that he favored a monetary policy which would induce a general rise in the price level and would minimize the fluctuations in prices characteristic of former periods of prosperity and depression.

THE GOLD POLICY. Congress, eager for an inflationary plan to raise prices, granted the President discretionary power. He was authorized (1) to issue legal-tender notes similar to the "greenbacks" of the Civil War years, (2) to establish free and unlimited coinage of silver at a fixed ratio with gold, (3) to reduce the gold content of the dollar by any amount up to 50 per cent. President Roosevelt chose dollar devaluation. After months of forcing up the price of gold through government purchases above the market price, Congress granted permission to stabilize the dollar within certain limits. This was done on January 31, 1934, by an executive order which fixed the gold content of the dollar at 59.06 per cent of its former value, transferred title to all gold in the Federal Reserve Banks to the government, and created a two-billion-dollar stabilization fund to maintain the dollar at a desired level in international exchange.

GOLD CLAUSE ACT. That the Roosevelt administration intended to retain its complete control over a managed currency was evident in the terms of the Gold Clause Act (1935), which denied to any person the right to sue the federal government in connection with gold clause contracts or claims arising out of changes in the metallic content of the dollar.

CREDIT EXPANSION. Through the Reconstruction Finance Corporation (RFC), created by the Hoover administration to fight the depression, direct loans were made to banks, railroads, building and loan companies, insurance companies, and agricultural credit corporations. From 1932 to 1937 the government made loans aggregating more than $6,500,000,000 in order to relieve the stringency in capital funds.

## FEDERAL FINANCES

The elaborate spending program, which characterized the government's efforts to promote recovery, and the extensive loans to private enterprise placed an extraordinary burden upon those responsible for federal finances.

**Taxation.** The Roosevelt administration was reluctant to embark upon a campaign of thorough tax revision, though it tried to increase the annual tax revenue.

REVENUE ACT OF 1935. Congress reluctantly yielded to presidential insistence in 1935 and passed a federal revenue act which increased the rates on individual incomes over $50,000, on gifts, on estates, on corporate earnings, and on excess profits.

REVENUE ACT OF 1936. Not satisfied that the larger corporations were being adequately assessed, the President urged Congress to modify the tax law so as to place a high levy against undistributed corporate profits and against all gains realized through the transfer of capital assets. Opposition to these two features was so widespread that in 1938 the rates in both instances were drastically revised in favor of the taxpayer.

**Deficit Financing.** Taxation did not provide sufficient revenue to pay for the experiments of the New Deal.

UNBALANCED BUDGETS. In five years after 1933 the accumulating annual deficits reached a sum slightly in excess of ten billion dollars.

THE PUBLIC DEBT. On June 30, 1933, the gross debt of the United States had stood at $22,500,000,000. Six years later it had increased to $40,439,000,000. The government claimed that it had some four billion dollars in recoverable enterprises to offset this. Deficit financing, however, had almost doubled the national debt in six years.

## THE SUPREME COURT AND THE "NEW DEAL"

Much of the legislation, passed by Congress and approved by the President during the first three years of the New Deal, was considered unconstitutional by a majority of the Supreme Court.

**Unconstitutional Legislation.** The Court, sometimes by five to four decisions, laid down certain principles limiting the Roosevelt program of recovery and reform.

CONSTITUTIONAL LIMITATIONS. The Court held that Congress could not use either the commerce clause or the taxing power as a pretext for regulation of industry or for social and economic reform. It furthermore ruled that Congress could not delegate its legislative function to administrative boards or to individuals.

DEFEATING CONGRESSIONAL ACTION. In applying these principles the Court held unconstitutional such important measures as (1) the National Industrial Recovery Act, (2) the Farm Mortgage Act, (3) the Agricultural Adjustment Act, (4) the Coal Stabilization Act, and (5) the Municipal Bankruptcy Act.

**Supreme Court Battle.** President Roosevelt attributed this "attack" upon New Deal legislation to the conservative judges, some of whom had served many years and were past the normal retirement age.

PACKING THE COURT. The presidential proposal to Congress (February 5, 1937) outlined a plan to appoint additional judges in the various federal courts, "where there are incumbent judges of retirement age who do not choose to resign." In the case of the Supreme Court the retirement age was to be seventy years, and the President was to appoint not more than six additional members to supplement nonretiring justices.

FAILURE AND VICTORY. The storm over the "Court Packing Bill" so impressed the members of the Senate that it was impossible for the administration forces to win in the upper house. The President reluctantly abandoned the contest after the death of Senator Robinson, who had directed the parliamentary tactics for him. In the end the President won, for resignation and death brought such a change in the Court's personnel after 1937 that a reversal in interpretation of the power of Congress over economic and social matters was clearly noticeable.

NEW PERSONNEL. By June, 1941, President Roosevelt had appointed seven of the nine members of the Court: Black, Reed, Frankfurter, Douglas, Murphy, Jackson, and Byrnes. With the retirement of Chief Justice Hughes, the President elevated Justice Stone to the vacant position.

## REVIEW QUESTIONS

1. Why did the Roosevelt administration make the agricultural program so important a part of its general recovery schemes?
2. Upon what economic theories did the New Dealers base their arguments in support of a "managed currency"?
3. How much justification was there for the charge that the recovery program constituted a denial of the American system of free enterprise?
4. What relation, if any, do you think should exist between our foreign policies and our expenditures for national defense?
5. What features of the New Deal seem to have contributed to the strength of organized labor in the United States?
6. If you had been a member of the Senate would you have supported Roosevelt's proposal for reorganization of the Supreme Court? Why?
7. Was the government wise in resorting to "deficit financing" after 1933? Give your reasons.

## SELECTED REFERENCES

Beard, C. A., *The Future Comes*
Brooks, Robert R. R., *Unions of Their Own Choosing*
Douglas, Paul H., *Social Security in the United States*
Jackson, R. H., *The Struggle for Judicial Supremacy*
Johnson, Gerald, *Roosevelt, Dictator or Democrat*
Lindley, E. K., *Halfway with Roosevelt*
Nourse, E. G., *Three Years of the Agricultural Adjustment Administration*
Wallace, Schuyler, *The New Deal in Action*

CHAPTER XVII

# FOREIGN POLICY AND WORLD POWER

## THE RESPONSIBILITIES OF POWER

Although Congress manifested an isolationist attitude on many questions of foreign policy, the Roosevelt administrations were marked by a wider participation of the United States in world affairs, political as well as economic.

**Foreign Trade.** The administration was not always consistent in its efforts to reconcile economic nationalism with the promotion of international trade through mutually profitable agreements.

WORLD ECONOMIC CONFERENCE. The most obvious example of the tendency to base our policies on national self-sufficiency was the refusal of President Roosevelt to accept the plans of the World Economic Conference (1933) for stabilization of gold currencies in the interest of freer international exchange.

EXPORT-IMPORT BANKS. For a time in 1934 the administration supported the ideas of George Peek concerning the possibility of selling American surpluses abroad through a system of barter agreements. Two Export-Import banks were created to extend loans to business interests which desired to push the sale of agricultural and industrial products, first in Russia and Cuba, and later in all foreign countries.

RECIPROCAL TRADE AGREEMENTS. Secretary Hull was the vigorous champion of reciprocal trade agreements with foreign nations, providing for a mutual lowering of trade barriers. Congress agreed (1934) that the President with the advice of certain qualified experts in the governmental service might negotiate such agreements without congressional approval in each instance, provided that the agreements did not modify the existing free list. By December, 1939, Secretary Hull had announced that twenty-one agreements were in effect with a list of nations which included Great Britain, France, Belgium, the Netherlands, and Canada.

**Relations with Latin America.** Administration spokesmen were insistent that Roosevelt's promise of a "good neighbor" policy in our foreign relations had greatly improved our economic interests in the countries of the Western Hemisphere.

CUBA. In 1934 the State Department announced the abrogation of the Platt Amendment so far as the intervention of the United States in the internal affairs of Cuba was concerned.

HAITI. By January, 1935, the last of our marines had been withdrawn from Haiti. Three years later, to forestall German financial interests, the United States through the Export-Import Bank virtually underwrote a loan of $5,000,000 to Haiti for a public works program.

DOMINICAN REPUBLIC. In 1940 President Roosevelt terminated the customs receivership which the United States had exercised in the Dominican Republic ever since 1905.

MEXICO. The experiments in state socialism, undertaken by the Mexican government after 1934, disturbed the United States, but our State Department refrained from interference. When Mexico expropriated foreign-owned properties in 1938, Secretary Hull admitted the right of a sovereign state so to do, and then reminded Mexico that she must compensate the dispossessed owners at "fair, assured, and effective values." Mexico refused Hull's suggestion of arbitration and insisted that she would reimburse the owners in her own way and at her own convenience.

SOUTH AMERICA. In the countries of South America the efforts of the United States were largely directed toward curbing the economic penetration of Germany and Italy. These efforts met with notable success in Brazil and bore fruit in improved commercial relations throughout South America. Between 1936 and 1938 our trade with Latin American countries increased from 40 to 90 per cent.

THE LIMA CONFERENCE (1938). The Eighth Pan-American Conference was held at Lima, Peru, late in December, 1938. The Conference endorsed the principles enunciated at the Inter-American Conference for the Maintenance of Peace which met at Buenos Aires in 1936. The twenty-one American republics affirmed their continental solidarity and announced that any threat to peace in the Western Hemisphere would lead to immediate consultation between all governments.

PANAMA DECLARATION. With the outbreak of war in Europe in September, 1939, the American states undertook to define their neutral position. The conference at Panama City in October, in harmony with the desire of the Roosevelt administration to keep the war out of the Americas, adopted a resolution establishing a 300-mile safety zone around the Western Hemisphere wherein belligerent activities were to be barred. There was no indication that the belligerents would recognize the declaration and little likelihood that the neutrals could enforce it.

**Uneasy Neutrality.** As a result of the unstable European situation following Hitler's rise to power in Germany, the Congress of the United States undertook to minimize, through legislation, the possibility of our becoming involved again in a war in Europe.

JOHNSON ACT (1934). Sponsored by Senator Hiram Johnson of California, this act forbade the sale in the United States of securities issued by any government which had defaulted in the payment of its obligations to this country. Since virtually every European nation except Finland belonged in the category of a defaulter, the law was regarded as an effective device to prevent the financial involvement of the United States or its people in the plans of any European nation seeking to finance war expenditures.

THE NEUTRALITY ACTS. Between August, 1935, and May, 1937, through joint resolutions, Congress wrote three Neutrality acts in an effort to meet all possible contingencies and insure our neutrality in the event of war anywhere in the world. The acts varied chiefly in the provisions affecting the discretionary powers of the President. Each succeeding act indicated a growing inclination on the part of Congress to keep control of foreign policy in its own hands. The Act of 1937, designed to be permanent, compelled the President to do certain things when a state of war existed. Among the compulsory prohibitions were: (1) travel by Americans on belligerent ships; (2) use of American merchantmen to transport implements of war to belligerents; (3) export of "arms, ammunition, and implements of war" to belligerents. The President might prohibit: (1) the use of American ports as supply bases for belligerent warships or armed merchant ships; (2) the transport of any commodities on an American ship to a belligerent; (3) the export of goods to a belligerent, unless title had first been transferred to a foreign government.

ARMS EMBARGO REPEAL. When war broke out over the Polish situation late in 1939, the administration urged Congress to reconsider certain of the mandatory features of the existing neutrality legislation. The point at issue was the compulsory embargo on "arms, ammunition, and implements of war." After spirited debate Congress modified the Neutrality Act so as to repeal the arms embargo, open the munitions trade to belligerents on a cash-and-carry basis, and bar our merchant shipping from war zones to be designated by presidential proclamation.

## RESISTANCE TO AGGRESSION

Despite our elaborate neutrality legislation, the Roosevelt administration moved steadily, though at times hesitantly, to prepare the nation for the impact of a second world war.

**Attitude toward the Axis Powers.** Many Americans believed that the Treaty of Versailles had been too severe in the penalties imposed upon Germany, but as they watched the rise of National Socialism under Hitler, they came to regard the Nazi regime as uncompromisingly dictatorial in its domestic policies and unjustifiably aggressive in its foreign relations.

PRESIDENTIAL POLICY. In 1937 Roosevelt suggested that the United States take the lead in persuading all peace-loving nations to "quarantine" the aggressor through economic boycott in the event of international strife. Finding little support in Congress, he undertook to persuade Germany and Italy that their just demands could be satisfied around the conference table rather than by military victories. When his pleas to the dictators brought no results, he advised Congress that there were means "short of war" to curb the spread of totalitarian power.

ISOLATIONISTS. The chief critics of the presidential policy came to be known as isolationists, for they recommended that the nation refrain from words as well as deeds which might involve us in any European or Asiatic struggle for power. By the spring of 1941 this group was devoting its efforts to keeping the United States out of the Second World War.

Its leaders in Congress were Senators Wheeler, Nye, Taft, Walsh, and Bennett Clark, while Charles A. Lindbergh, supported by General Robert E. Wood of the "America First" Committee, had won a considerable popular following by urging a negotiated peace between Great Britain and the Axis.

**The Far East.** With the Japanese invasion of China in July, 1937, American opinion, which had been aroused by China's loss of Manchuria in 1932, became strongly anti-Japanese.

BRUSSELS CONFERENCE. In November, 1937, representatives of the United States joined with delegates from eighteen other nations in denouncing Japan as a treaty-breaker and aggressor. No punitive action followed these sharp words, for the leaders were too much concerned over the European situation.

THE "OPEN DOOR." One year later Japan felt strong enough to warn the rest of the world that the "new order in Asia" would not be based upon the principle of the "open door" in trade and industry. The American State Department refused to accept any such unilateral abrogation of Japan's previous agreements.

THE "WAR OF NERVES." By 1939 Japan and the United States were carrying on a verbal war in which each was trying to wear down the other through nervous tension. In July of that year our State Department gave the necessary six-months' notice that we wished to terminate the reciprocal commercial treaty which had been negotiated in 1911. Japanese purchases of gasoline, scrap iron, and other war materials in the United States continued, but the control over them became increasingly rigorous.

AID TO CHINA. Resentment against Japan served to quicken American sympathy for China. Contributions to the relief of Chinese victims of the war were but one evidence of that sympathy. By 1940 our government had loaned almost $70,-000,000 to the Chinese government for the purchase of badly-needed supplies.

NETHERLANDS EAST INDIES. As soon as German troops had overrun the Netherlands in the spring of 1940, Japan began a drive to secure a larger portion of the products from the Netherlands colonial empire in the South Pacific. The British at Singapore and the American fleet at Pearl Harbor in the Hawaiian Islands probably prevented any overt act at that time, but Japanese desire to acquire the islands was obvious.

**The Arsenal of Democracy.** Though a large majority of Americans were anxious to avoid any involvement in the Second World War, which broke out with the German invasion of Poland in September, 1939, they were eager that Great Britain and France should win.

REPEAL OF ARMS EMBARGO. The revision of the Neutrality Act, late in 1939, enabled Great Britain and France to place orders for munitions and other war supplies in the United States. Delivery, however, depended upon the ability of the Allies to get their ships across the Atlantic safely.

INDIRECT SALES. After the collapse of France the United States, through a system of indirect sales, released to the Allies considerable stores of munitions remaining from the First World War. To facilitate his program of aid to the Allies President Roosevelt named Henry L. Stimson of New York to be Secretary of War and Frank Knox of Illinois to be Secretary of the Navy. Both men were Republicans and both were strongly pro-Ally.

TRANSFER OF DESTROYERS. Because of the success of German attacks upon British commerce in the Atlantic, the British Navy was in need of additional destroyers. In September, 1940, the administration announced the transfer of fifty overage destroyers to Great Britain in exchange for 99-year leases on eight naval and air bases on British possessions in the Western Hemisphere.

LEND-LEASE BILL. Early in 1941 Congress, over the protests of the isolationist leaders, authorized the President to lend or lease to Great Britain materials needed in the prosecution of the war. The amount of aid which could be given was limited, but the President was given considerable discretion in placing a valuation upon such goods and in arranging the terms of the transfer.

INTERVENTIONISTS. A well-organized minority in the nation had become convinced by the summer of 1941 that the best defense for the United States lay in the victory of Great Britain over Germany. They were prepared to intervene in the war at that time in order to make certain of German defeat.

**National Defense Program.** With the German invasion of the Low Countries in May, 1940, Americans were shocked into a realization of the implications for them of total war. Their earnest endeavor to prepare for full national defense began at that time.

HEMISPHERE STRATEGY. German conquests raised questions in the United States concerning the fate of Dutch, French, and possibly British possessions in the Western Hemisphere.

a. *Rephrasing the Monroe Doctrine.* In a joint resolution, Congress declared (June, 1940) that the United States would not countenance the transfer of any American territory from one non-American nation to another.

b. *Havana Conference.* A meeting of representatives from Latin American countries at Havana (July, 1940) unanimously resolved that any territory whose status was threatened should be placed temporarily under an inter-American administration, and that there should be a general interchange of information concerning Axis propaganda and plots. It also recommended the formulation of plans for closer commercial relations within the American continents. Loans for the expansion of defense industries in Latin American countries were authorized by Congress.

c. *Canadian Co-operation.* Implementing his statement in 1938 that the United States would not permit the domination of Canada by any foreign empire, President Roosevelt joined the Canadian Prime Minister in creating a Permanent Joint Board to study the defense needs of the northern part of the North American Continent.

REARMAMENT APPROPRIATIONS. During 1940 Congress appropriated approximately eighteen billion dollars for armaments. The bulk of this huge sum was earmarked for two purposes: the construction of a two-ocean navy superior to any possible combination of naval power, and the creation of an army of 1,200,000. These two branches were to be supported by an air fleet of 35,000 planes.

COMPULSORY MILITARY SERVICE. The first peacetime conscription was authorized by Congress in September, 1940. All men between the ages of twenty-one and thirty-five inclusive were compelled to register, and from the registrants 800,000 were selected by lot for a year's military training. The National Guard also was called out for intensive instruction in modern warfare. On July 1, 1941, a second registration took place, to include all men who had attained the age of twenty-one years since October 16, 1940.

INDUSTRIAL MOBILIZATION. In May, 1940, the President, acting under the authority conferred by a statute of 1916, appointed an Advisory Commission to the Council of National Defense. The seven members of the Commission were severally responsible for the following divisions: industrial materials, production, transportation, labor, agriculture, price stabilization, and consumer protection. Their task was to carry the defense program from the appropriation stage into action, but they could not enforce their recommendations.

**Foreign Policy and the Election of 1940.** President Roosevelt's close advisers stated that his reluctance to run for a third term had been overcome by his conviction that it would be detrimental to the country to change administrations in the midst of world-wide war.

THE NOMINATING CONVENTIONS. The Republican Convention at Philadelphia on June 24 passed over candidates, like Senator Robert Taft of Ohio and District-Attorney Thomas E. Dewey of New York, who had won political recognition and nominated Wendell L. Willkie, a newcomer to the politicians, who had just transferred his membership from the Democratic to the Republican party. Willkie, as president of the Commonwealth and Southern Corporation, had been a cogent critic of New Deal policies, particularly the electrification projects. His big business connections were balanced by the nomination of Charles L. McNary, senator from Oregon and friend of the farmers, for Vice-President. The Democrats in rather sullen mood permitted the administration leaders at Washington to indicate that the ticket should be Roosevelt and his Secretary of Agriculture, Henry A. Wallace.

THE PLATFORMS. There had been many preliminary forecasts that the campaign would turn on foreign policy, but the platforms offered the voter little choice. Both parties favored a strong national defense, all aid to Great Britain "short of war," protection of the Western Hemisphere against totalitarian aggression; and each promised to keep the United States out of the European conflict. The Republican pronouncements attacked the New Deal domestic policies as dictatorial regimentation and accused the Roosevelt supporters of stirring class antagonism for political advantage. The Democrats stood on the New Deal record and virtually repudiated conservative support.

THE CAMPAIGN. Willkie made the most vigorous campaign which the nation had witnessed since Bryan's first bid for the presidency in 1896. His tour took him into thirty-four states, where he delivered approximately 550 speeches. Accepting the basic theories underlying many New Deal reforms, he attacked President Roosevelt for violating the "third term precedent" and for incompetence in handling the administrative business of his office. He was particularly caustic in his criticism of the President's negligence in defense matters and his failure to keep the country informed of intentions concerning the European war. So effective was the Willkie attack, especially in arousing conservative Democrats and voters who had no regular party affiliation, that the President was induced to make a brief campaign in his own behalf. Much of his appeal was to independent voters and to laboring men, who had been urged by John L. Lewis, president of CIO, to support Willkie.

THE ELECTION. The balloting on November 5 resulted in a third victory for Roosevelt, not so widespread, however, as the result in 1936. Though Willkie secured almost 45 per cent of the popular vote, he received only eighty-two votes in the electoral college, representing ten states chiefly in the farm belt of the Middle West. The Democrats carried both houses of Congress and to the surprise of most politicians increased their majority in the House of Representatives. While the campaign had stirred the country deeply, Willkie promptly called for national unity despite differences of opinion on domestic policies. He was especially insistent that partisanship play no part in modifying the nation's decision to aid Great Britain and to resist to the utmost totalitarian aggression.

**All Aid "Short of War."** The year after Roosevelt's re-election was marked by a bitter battle between the isolationists and the interventionists which in the end was won by the latter.

LEND-LEASE. By late March, 1941, the President was using seven billion dollars, appropriated in conformity with the Lend-Lease Act (page 210), to forward supplies to Great Britain. After the Nazis attacked Soviet Russia late in June, American aid was also sent to the U.S.S.R.

GREENLAND AND ICELAND. By presidential proclamation the United States established a protectorate over Greenland (April, 1941) and American marines were ordered to occupy

Iceland (July, 1941). In each instance it was asserted that the island lay in waters necessary to the defense of the United States.

"FROZEN ASSETS." On June 14, 1941, German and Italian assets in the United States were "frozen" by order of the United States Treasury. About a month later the same treatment was accorded to Japanese assets in this country.

"SHOOT AT SIGHT." The German government tried to prevent us from sending aid to Great Britain and Russia by sinking merchant vessels, which were being convoyed by British warships and such other warships as had escaped from the ports of countries already occupied by the Nazis. When the submarine attack sank the American destroyer *Reuben Jones,* with the loss of seventy-six of her crew (October 30, 1941), President Roosevelt ordered our naval commanders to "shoot at sight" on any Axis submarine coming into American defense waters.

ATLANTIC CHARTER. Meanwhile the United States and Great Britain had defined the objectives of the war in a joint statement, which caused the Axis propagandists to insist that the two countries were already in alliance. Known as "The Atlantic Charter," this statement was the result of conversations between President Roosevelt and Prime Minister Churchill at meetings aboard their respective battleships in the North Atlantic (August 14, 1941). It consisted of the following chief points: (1) neither nation would seek territorial or other aggrandizement after the war; (2) both nations would undertake to disarm any nation which threatened aggression beyond its own frontiers, to respect the right of all peoples to choose their own form of government, to assist in arranging for all nations equal access to the trade and raw materials of the world, to encourage co-operation among the nations for the improvement of labor standards and for social security, and to work for a peace which would make the seas highways of peaceful commerce open to all.

## REVIEW QUESTIONS

1. How did the Roosevelt administration modify the policy of the United States toward Latin America?
2. Why has the American government maintained an attitude of hostility toward the Japanese attempt to create a "new order" in Asia?
3. If you had been a member of Congress, would you have voted for the repeal of the arms embargo? Give your reasons.
4. In what ways have the commercial policies of the United States affected its international relations?
5. Why did President Roosevelt proclaim an unlimited national emergency in May, 1941?
6. Discuss the arguments for and against universal military service.
7. Do you think that the "third term" tradition was an important factor in the election of 1940? Why?

## SELECTED REFERENCES

Bisson, T. A., *American Policy in the Far East*
Buell, R. L,, *Isolated America*
Earle, E. M., *Against This Torrent*
Fenwick, C. G., *American Neutrality*
Griswold, A. W., *The Far Eastern Policy of the United States*
Herring, Pendleton, *The Impact of War*
Johnstone, W. C., *The United States and Japan's New Order*
Wertenbaker, Charles, *A New Doctrine for the Americas*

CHAPTER XVIII

# THE SECOND WORLD WAR

### THE COLLAPSE OF NEUTRALITY

While most Americans were watching the first successful campaigns of the Germans in Soviet Russia, the United States was plunged into the war by the treacherous attack of Japan in the Pacific.

**Japanese Aggression.** Late in 1940 the Japanese government signed a ten-year pact with Germany and Italy, which gave the Asiatic Power a free hand to establish its new order in Greater East Asia.

THREATS IN THE SOUTH PACIFIC. During 1941 the Japanese militarists, now in complete control regardless of the ministry of the moment, grew more truculent. They interfered in the political and economic affairs of Thailand and Indo-China, ruthlessly pressed the war against the unarmed civilian population of China, staged a naval demonstration in the gulf of Siam, and seized the Spratly Islands, only seventy miles from the Philippines.

APPEASEMENT OR COERCION? Unprepared and unwilling to fight Japan in the Pacific, while the fate of Europe hung in the balance, the United States government continued a policy of appeasement until midsummer of 1941. On July 25, having secured the co-operation of the British government and the Dutch government in exile, our State Department finally forbade the export to Japan of scrap iron, aviation gasoline, and other war materials. Many Americans insisted that this step toward economic coercion should have been taken at least a year earlier.

DIPLOMATIC HOCUS-POCUS. The Japanese government kept up a pretense that it desired to reach a peaceful settlement of all outstanding differences between the United States and Japan.

a. *Nomura's Mission.* Admiral Nomura, who was supposed to have many personal friends in the United States, tried in vain to convert Secretary Hull to the idea of an *entente cordiale* between the two nations in the Pacific. He demanded that the United States recognize Japanese control of China.

b. *Saburo Kurusu.* After the extreme jingoist, General Tojo, became premier in October, 1941, Saburo Kurusu came to the United States as a special envoy on a mission of peace; but the peace which he offered meant that the United States would be expected to abandon China to its fate, to recognize the dominance of Japan in its "Co-prosperity Sphere for Greater East Asia," and to reopen trade in all commodities which the Japanese desired.

"A DATE WHICH WILL LIVE IN INFAMY." While Nomura and Kurusu were still discussing with Secretary Hull the possibilities for a peaceful settlement in the Pacific, Japanese airmen carried out a "sneak attack" on American warships and defense installations at Pearl Harbor in the Hawaiian Islands. Next day, December 8, 1941, President Roosevelt asked Congress to declare a state of war between the United States and the Japanese Empire. Three days later Germany and Italy declared war upon the United States, and Hitler gloated that he would now take "a historic revenge."

**Preparing for a Two-Ocean War.** The dastardly attack on Pearl Harbor quickly quieted the arguments over American foreign policy and united the nation in a solemn determination to meet successfully the greatest crisis in its history.

THE INDUSTRIAL FRONT. By the spring of 1943 the American people had converted their peacetime industrial establishment into the "mightiest wartime arsenal" that the world had ever seen. The task was supervised by a War Production Board of nine men, with an able administrator, Donald Nelson, as chairman. Within a year after Pearl Harbor the nation produced forty-seven billion dollars' worth of war material, including 32,000 tanks, 49,000 airplanes, and 8,200,000 tons of merchant shipping. The manufacture of many peacetime commodities was either curtailed or prohibited in order to facilitate war production.

THE FARMERS' PROBLEMS. Despite the bumper crops of 1942, it was difficult to meet the extraordinary demand for foodstuffs. The military and naval establishments were taking 25 or 30 per cent of our total meat supply. In fifteen months we sent to China, Great Britain, and Russia more than seven billion pounds of food in various forms. To continue this program of helping our Allies and supplying our armed forces required careful planning, especially since the farmers were handicapped by a dwindling labor supply and the lack of new machines and machine parts. Domestic consumption was partly controlled through the ration schedules imposed by the Office of Price Administration (OPA), but the entire food problem was directly under the supervision of a Food Administrator appointed by the President.

MOBILIZING MANPOWER. During the first year of the war organized labor generally refrained from strikes and endeavored to settle jurisdictional disputes between the A.F. of L. and CIO. When labor strife flared anew in 1943, Congress finally passed the Smith-Connally Bill, prohibiting strikes in plants which were working on war contracts. American labor, however, scarcely needed such legislation to spur it on to great efforts. Its production record from 1942 to 1944 surpassed any previous record in the nation's history. The results would probably have been less gratifying had it not been for the work of the War Manpower Commission under the chairmanship of Paul V. McNutt of Indiana, which handled the task of apportioning the work of some 70,000,000 men and women (almost 20,000,000 of whom were women) in the labor force.

WARTIME TRANSPORT. If the United States had any secret weapon in the war, it was the marvelous efficiency of its transportation facilities.

a. *The Railroads.* During the First World War it had been necessary for the government to assume control of the American railroads. In 1942, however, they carried 30 per cent more freight and 40 per cent more passengers than they had carried the previous year. This was done with 20,000 fewer locomotives and 600,000 fewer freight cars than they had in 1918. Railroad operators and employees, working harmoniously under the general direction of Joseph B. Eastman, head of the Office of Defense Transportation, carried unprecedented numbers of troops and supply units and hauled, in addition, the gasoline and fuel oil which could not be shipped in tankers while the Axis submarines were taking their heavy toll.

b. *The War Shipping Board.* The United Nations had two answers to the menace of Axis submarines: first, improved methods used by the Allied navies in hunting and destroying both "wolf packs" and lone raiders; and second, the tremendous output of American shipyards. With the approval of Admiral Emory S. Land of the War Shipping Board, Henry J. Kaiser demonstrated the possibilities of the prefabricated vessel, which could be constructed in seventy-eight days or less. Speed made possible the "victory fleet" which kept our service of supply more than adequate after the first few months of war.

c. *Airways*. The commercial airlines, though subordinating their plans to the war needs, managed to maintain many of their normal schedules. Most of the airplane construction was for military purposes. By the spring of 1943 the monthly output was over 5500 planes, as compared with an average of 200 in 1939. The glider industry provided much of the transport space for the Allied air-borne invasions of 1943 and 1944.

FINANCING THE WAR MACHINE. Between January, 1940, and January, 1943, the appropriations for national defense and war amounted to approximately $220,000,000,000, or slightly more than the cost of government from George Washington's inauguration to 1940.

a. *Taxes*. By the second year of the war it was estimated that war's daily cost to the American people was $1.15 for every man, woman, and child in our population, while receipts from taxes were scarcely forty cents per person. Successive tax bills were designed to increase the proportion of the cost of the war which would be met through taxation. This was accomplished by lowering the individual exemptions, thus adding millions of new taxpayers to the lists, increasing the rates of the normal tax and surtax on incomes, and virtually confiscating all corporate earnings which represented excess profits from the war. Congress finally accepted in 1943 a modified version of the Ruml plan to place collection of federal income taxes on a pay-as-you-go basis.

b. *War Bonds*. Despite the increased revenues from taxes, the government relied upon war-savings stamps and war bonds to meet the bulk of the war costs. Prior to July, 1945, the Treasury Department conducted seven successful war bond drives, with aid from millions of citizen volunteers. In anticipation of further huge borrowings, Congress raised the national debt limit to 240 billion dollars.

## THE UNITED NATIONS

Less than a month after the entrance of the United States into the Second World War, representatives from twenty-six countries signed the pact of the United Nations at Washington on January 2, 1942, pledging themselves to joint action until the Axis and Japan had been destroyed.

**Retreat in the Pacific Area.** The first half of 1942 was marked by a series of major disasters to the United Nations in the Pacific.

JAPANESE DRIVE AGAINST THE ENGLISH AND DUTCH. The whole Western World was astonished at the speed of the Japanese advance after Pearl Harbor. Within eight weeks they had secured the entire Malay Peninsula. The great British naval base of Singapore fell on February 15, 1942; three weeks later the Japanese had overrun the Netherlands East Indies and by early May British forces had retreated across Burma into India. Japanese bases on New Guinea and in the Bismarck and Solomon Islands were growing in strength.

THE FALL OF THE PHILIPPINES. Under the command of General Douglas MacArthur, American and Filipino troops heroically defended the Bataan peninsula and the fortress of Corregidor until resistance was no longer possible. At the order of President Roosevelt, MacArthur transferred his headquarters to Australia on February 22, but his men under General Jonathan Wainwright held Corregidor until May 6, 1942.

THE ALEUTIANS. Shortly after the Japanese secured the Philippines, their forces far to the north moved into the Aleutian Islands, occupying Attu, Agattu, and Kiska, which they held for more than a year before American forces threw them out in 1943.

**The Road Back.** By the early autumn of 1942 the Japanese had occupied a million square miles of territory in their triumphant advance, but there the road ended. Their retreat was humiliating and costly in life and treasure.

THE CORAL SEA AND MIDWAY. American bombers, commanded by General James Doolittle, dropped several tons of bombs on Kobe, Yokohama, and Tokio on April 18, 1942. A few weeks later American naval and air forces in the Coral Sea stopped an invading force apparently aimed at Australia. The first real defeat for the Japanese war lords, however, was the rout of a strong Japanese naval force proceeding toward Midway Island (June, 1942).

GUADALCANAL AND TULAGI. On August 7, 1942, the United Nations launched their counteroffensive in earnest, when American marines, supported from the air and sea, landed at Tulagi and on Guadalcanal Island in the Solomons. For the next two years the story in the western Pacific told of the Japanese avoiding battle and suffering costly defeats as island after island fell to the United Nations forces. Americans, under General MacArthur and Admiral Halsey, played a major role in these victories, but they were ably supported by their Allies. From the Solomons they moved into the Marshalls, Gilberts, Carolines, and Marianas; they took Guam and Saipan and prepared for the reconquest of the Philippine Islands.

THE SUPERFORTRESSES. In the spring of 1944 American airplane factories began to produce special heavy bombers, designed for long flights with heavy bomb loads. Based on airfields in China, which Chinese labor had built almost without tools, these "superfortresses" undertook to destroy Japan's industrial centers, a foretaste of the fate in store for the island kingdom as soon as the German phase of the war should be finished.

CHINA. While the United Nations moved northward and westward across the Pacific islands, the Chinese kept up their heroic resistance. They were heartened by increasing air support from General Claire Chennault's forces and by the campaign of Chinese and American troops to reopen the Burma Road. At the same time British Empire forces were gradually clearing the Japanese out of Burma.

**The Invasion of Fortress Europe.** The destruction of Japan's empire was subordinated in the strategy of the United Nations to the defeat of Nazi Germany.

THE BATTLE FOR TUNIS. On November 8, 1942, a British-American armada landed on the coasts of French Morocco. Within three days General Dwight Eisenhower had so disposed his forces that he controlled all Morocco and Algeria to the Tunisian frontier. The Germans fought stubbornly for six months before they yielded to superior forces in May, 1943.

THE ITALIAN CAMPAIGN. During the summer of 1943 the Fifth American Army, commanded by General Mark Clark, and the Eighth British Army, under General Bernard Montgomery, occupied Sicily and several smaller Mediterranean islands. The invasion of the Italian mainland began in September, 1943, more than a month after the Italians had ousted Mussolini and his Fascist regime. The campaign in Italy, despite this revolt, was long and costly. Not until the first week in June, 1944, did the United Nations liberate Rome from the Nazi's control.

DESTROYING NAZI POWER. From the moment the United States entered the war its energies were primarily directed toward the liberation of Europe from Hitler's tyrannical "new order."

a. *"Softening" Germany.* During 1943 the bombing of Germany reached gigantic proportions. The *Luftwaffe* was knocked out of the sky and its production centers were repeatedly bombed and burned; the Ruhr Valley and the industrial Rhineland were all but paralyzed; Berlin, Hamburg, Munich, and Cologne suffered more than English cities had suffered earlier in the war.

b. *Russian Offensives.* While the R.A.F. and American Air Force were attacking Germany's airplane, ball-bearing and oil-refining industries, the Russian armies had launched huge offensives all along the front from the Baltic to the Black Sea. Their primary objective was the destruction of the German armies, but in the process they regained, by the summer of 1944, all the territory which the Germans had occupied and opened routes into the Danube valley.

c. *The Invasion Forces.* During 1943 the British and American navies conquered the submarine and opened the sea lanes to the transport of troops and supplies. By June 1, 1944, Secretary of War Stimson stated that more than two million American troops were in Great Britain awaiting the moment for invasion of that part of Europe which lay behind Hitler's Atlantic Wall.

THE BATTLE OF FRANCE. In the early hours of June 6, 1944, the troops of the United Nations left their bases in Great Britain and crossed the Channel to storm the French beaches in the vicinity of Cherbourg. Preceded by air-borne paratroopers and protected by an awesome bombardment from the huge battle fleet, they soon established beachheads and, with the aid of the air forces, connected their landings into one battle front. Within twelve weeks of these successful landings, the Allied armies had conquered Normandy, over-run Brittany, chased the Germans north of the Seine, and assisted the French Forces of the Interior in liberating Paris. In August new landings were made with slight loss, on the Mediterranean coast of France near Marseilles. On August 26, General Eisenhower announced that the Seventh German Army had been destroyed and warned the residents of Alsace, Lorraine, and Luxemburg that they would soon be in the path of the retreating Nazis. The Battle of France had been won.

THE BATTLE OF GERMANY. German resistance west of the Rhine proved to be surprisingly determined. Not until the armies of the United Nations had destroyed a German counteroffensive (December, 1944—February, 1945) was that resistance broken. On March 8, 1945, troops from the American First Army crossed the Rhine, south of Cologne. For the next two months the armies of the United Nations in the west advanced steadily, under the command of General Dwight D. Eisenhower, while the Russian armies cut through Austria and closed in on Berlin. Nazi high officials, aware that the end was near, either committed suicide or went into hiding. On May 7, at Reims, France, a representative of the German General Staff accepted the terms of "unconditional surrender." V-E Day was announced to an expectant world.

## PREPARING FOR PEACE

Even before the United States became a belligerent, the nations opposed to the Axis Powers had begun to discuss the nature of the peace which they desired after hostilities were ended.

**Roosevelt-Churchill Conferences.** After the promulgation of the Atlantic Charter in 1941 (see page 215), Prime Minister Churchill and President Roosevelt met in conference six times over a period of two years. At Washington, Quebec, and Casablanca they discussed matters pertaining to the conduct of the war, but many of their decisions, reached in an atmosphere of close friendship, vitally affected the formulation of plans for international co-operation after the war.

**The Declaration of Moscow.** Late in October, 1943, Secretary of State Hull flew to Moscow, where he conferred with Foreign Secretary Molotov of the Soviet Union and Foreign Secretary Eden of Great Britain. The result of their deliberations was the Moscow Agreement, in which the three Powers, subsequently joined by China, pledged their word that they would endeavor to establish at the earliest possible date a general international organization, open to the membership of all peace-loving states, for the maintenance of peace and security. This particular article of the Moscow Agreement was approved by the United States Senate by a vote of eighty-five to five.

**Cairo Conference.** Late in November, 1943, Generalissimo Chiang Kai-shek met Churchill and Roosevelt at Cairo. There the three statesmen announced that the war would be continued until Japan's unconditional surrender and that the territory which the Japanese had seized from China during past generations would be restored to the republic of China.

**Teheran.** Teheran in November, 1943, was the scene of the historic meeting of Stalin, Roosevelt, and Churchill. By implication the results of the Cairo Conference were accepted by Stalin, and he agreed with Churchill and Roosevelt that the wartime collaboration between Russia and the two major Western Powers needed to be continued into the postwar era.

**The United Nations.** Several conferences in 1943 indicated the determination of the United Nations to work in harmony during the postwar period. In May representatives of the United Nations Relief and Rehabilitation Administration met at Atlantic City to discuss relief measures for the people of occupied Europe and Asia. In July, 1944, delegates from the United Nations assembled at Bretton Woods, New Hampshire, where they formulated plans to handle international banking and currency problems after the war.

**Dumbarton Oaks Conference.** Representatives of the United States, Great Britain, Russia, and China gathered at Dumbarton Oaks near Washington on the invitation of Secretary Hull, who suggested that there be exploratory discussions of the probable framework for an international association after the war. The Conference prepared tentative proposals for such a postwar organization and the American State Department invited widespread discussion of the proposals.

## PRELUDE TO POSTWAR ERA

**At Yalta.** While the Germans were withdrawing east of the Rhine, Roosevelt, Churchill, and Stalin met at Yalta in the Crimea late in February, 1945, to discuss the concluding phases of the war in Europe, to arrange for the postwar occupation of Germany, and to make sure that the conversations at Dumbarton Oaks would lead to an international organization to safeguard peace. One of their most important decisions was to call a conference to meet at San Francisco on April 25, for the purpose of drafting a charter for postwar security.

**The San Francisco Charter.** Despite the tragic death of President Roosevelt on April 12, 1945, the United Nations went forward with the plans for the Conference at San Francisco of delegates from forty-six nations. As was expected, the representatives of the United States, Great Britain, and the U.S.S.R. dominated the deliberations. The Charter of a World Security Organization was in final form, ready for signatures, on June 26. Whatever the specific provisions of the Charter, almost every correspondent who attended the Conference reported that the peace of the world in the next generation would depend upon the co-operation of the five great powers — the United States, the U.S.S.R., Great Britain, France, and China.

Mindful of the bitter partisan quarrel which developed over the League of Nations a quarter-century earlier, both Republican and Democratic leaders tried to keep the discussions of postwar foreign policy free from the partisanship of the political campaign of 1944.

**Republican Nominations.** During the preconvention primaries Wendell Willkie, who had lost to Roosevelt in 1940, came to the conclusion that he could not again secure the Republican nomination. His position in the party, however, was still strong and he used his influence to counteract the "isolationist" views of such Republicans as Colonel Robert McCormick of the *Chicago Tribune*. Those who were reluctant to make any positive commitments concerning the role of the United States in the postwar world probably would have preferred Governor John Bricker of Ohio, as the party nominee. They yielded, however, to the apparent popularity of Governor Dewey of New York and nominated him with but one dissenting vote in the convention, which was held at Chicago in June. Governor Bricker was unanimously chosen for the second place on the ticket.

**Democratic Convention.** When the Democrats assembled in Chicago in July, they knew that President Roosevelt was willing to be nominated for a fourth term. This they proceeded to do on the first ballot, though the opponents of a fourth term cast some ninety votes for Governor Harry F. Byrd of Virginia. Most of them came from Southern delegations. The drama of the convention came in the fight of Vice-President Wallace for renomination. Though he led on the first ballot, his defeat was finally brought about by an understanding between certain Southern delegates and the leaders of several powerful political machines in Northern cities. Senator Harry Truman of Missouri was named in a stampede on the second ballot.

**The Campaign.** Neither party platform was definite enough to suit the independent voter. Consequently the electorate waited for the candidates to develop their views during the campaign. The position of the President, as Commander-in-Chief of the Army and Navy at the crisis of the war in Europe and Asia, gave him an advantage which he was quick to exploit. Governor Dewey stressed shortcomings in the domestic policy of the administration and indicated through his adviser, John Foster Dulles, that he was determined to promote international co-operation for a lasting peace after the war.

**The Election.** More than 45,531,000 Americans voted on November 7, 1944, giving President Roosevelt a plurality of slightly over three million votes. In the electoral college, however, the President had 432 votes to 99 for Governor Dewey. The greatest Republican strength was in the rural, rather than the urban, counties of the nation.

**The Truman Administration.** President Roosevelt's sudden death on April 12, 1945, elevated Vice-President Truman to the presidency. As soon as he had taken the oath of office, the new President announced that he would be guided by the policies of his predecessor.

CABINET PERSONNEL. Early cabinet changes indicated that the Truman administration was looking to the West for political support. Robert Hannegan of Missouri became Postmaster-General; Tom C. Clark of Texas, Attorney-General; Clinton P. Anderson of New Mexico, Secretary of Agriculture; Lewis Schwellenbach of Washington, Secretary of Labor. All were relatively young men, ranging from forty-one to fifty years of age. After the San Francisco Conference, James F. Byrnes of South Carolina was appointed Secretary of State; Frederick M. Vinson of Kentucky, Secretary of the Treasury; and Robert P. Patterson, Secretary of War.

FOREIGN POLICY. President Truman strongly supported his predecessor's desire to create an international organization for the maintenance of peace and threw the force of his administration behind Secretary Stettinius and the American delegation at San Francisco.

**Victory in the Pacific.** With the collapse of the Nazi regime and the military defeat of Germany, the American government strove to speed up the war against Japan.

THE ASSAULT ON JAPAN. During the spring of 1945 General MacArthur's troops continued to clean up sporadic Japanese resistance in the Philippines and co-operated with the Australians in the attack on Borneo. To the north the combined operations of navy, marines, army, and air forces won Iwo Jima and broke the resistance on Okinawa. The bases for the final assaults on Japan's home islands had been prepared in the early summer of 1945.

THE ATOMIC BOMB. The most devastating weapon of this or any other war was perfected by the co-operative efforts of scientists of the United Nations. On August 5th, American airmen dropped the first atomic bomb on Hiroshima. Three days later a second bomb was dropped on Nagasaki. Both cities were virtually obliterated.

UNCONDITIONAL SURRENDER. During the Berlin Conference, which assembled on July 17, 1945, the United States and Great Britain sent an ultimatum to Japan demanding unconditional surrender. At the same time Premier Stalin informed President Truman that the U.S.S.R. would soon enter the war against Japan. The day after the atomic bomb was used Russia moved its forces against the Japanese in Manchuria. Almost immediately the Tokyo radio broadcast an appeal for peace. After an exchange of notes between the two nations, President Truman announced on August 14th that hostilities had ceased. It was agreed that the Supreme Allied Military Commander would indefinitely rule Japan through the emperor, Hirohito. General Douglas MacArthur was named Supreme Allied Military Commander.

OCCUPATION OF JAPAN. In the early morning of August 29th the peaceful invasion of the Japanese home islands began. Three days later, aboard the battleship *Missouri,* the Japanese signed the surrender documents before the representatives of nine of the United Nations. As the occupation forces moved into control of strategic positions in Japan, it became clear that bombing from the air and naval bombardment had brought that nation to the point of collapse even before the atomic bomb was used.

LONDON CONFERENCE. As Germany and Japan were placed under military control, the Council of Foreign Ministers, representing the United States, Great Britain, the U.S.S.R., France and China, assembled in London for the purpose of formulating the first drafts of the documents which might later become the basis for definitive peace treaties with Italy, Rumania, and Bulgaria.

## REVIEW QUESTIONS

1. Should the United States have imposed economic restrictions on Japanese trade earlier than 1941? Why?

2. For what purpose was the Office of Price Administration created?

3. Why was there considerable criticism of the Administration's policy of extending large-scale aid to Russia through the agency of Lend-Lease?

4. What changes in its tax program were made by the federal government in order to meet the heavy expenses of the war?

5. Was the Administration wise in deciding that the war in the Pacific should be regarded as secondary to the war against Axis Europe?

6. Why were the initial landings in North Africa accomplished with relatively little loss to the Allies?

7. Should the international organization at the end of the war be modelled on the former League of Nations? If not, in what respects should it be modified?

8. Do you believe that the co-operation of China, Russia, Great Britain, and the United States is essential for the maintenance of peace after the war?

## SELECTED REFERENCES

Baldwin, Hanson, *United We Stand*
Boutwell, W. D., *America Prepares for Tomorrow*
McInnis, Edgar, *The War: Third Year*
Peffer, Nathaniel, *Basis for Peace in the Far East*
Romulo, C. P., *I Saw the Fall of the Philippines*
Sprout, Harold and Margaret, *Toward A New Order of Sea Power*
Tregaskis, Richard, *Guadalcanal Diary*
Tolischus, O. D., *Tokyo Record*

# APPENDIX
## Presidents and Secretaries of State

| | | | | |
|---|---|---|---|---|
| 1. | GEORGE WASHINGTON | 1789-1797 | Thomas Jefferson | 1789 |
| | | | Edmund Randolph | 1794 |
| | | | Timothy Pickering | 1795 |
| 2. | JOHN ADAMS | 1797-1801 | Timothy Pickering | |
| | | | John Marshall | 1800 |
| 3. | THOMAS JEFFERSON | 1801-1809 | James Madison | 1801 |
| 4. | JAMES MADISON | 1809-1817 | Robert Smith | 1809 |
| | | | James Monroe | 1811 |
| 5. | JAMES MONROE | 1817-1825 | John Q. Adams | 1817 |
| 6. | JOHN QUINCY ADAMS | 1825-1829 | Henry Clay | 1825 |
| 7. | ANDREW JACKSON | 1829-1837 | Martin Van Buren | 1829 |
| | | | Edward Livingston | 1831 |
| | | | Louis McLane | 1833 |
| | | | John Forsyth | 1834 |
| 8. | MARTIN VAN BUREN | 1837-1841 | John Forsyth | |
| 9. | WILLIAM HENRY HARRISON | 1841 | Daniel Webster | 1841 |
| 10. | JOHN TYLER | 1841-1845 | Daniel Webster | |
| | | | Hugh S. Legaré | 1843 |
| | | | Abel P. Upshur | 1843 |
| | | | John C. Calhoun | 1844 |
| 11. | JAMES KNOX POLK | 1845-1849 | James Buchanan | 1845 |
| 12. | ZACHARY TAYLOR | 1849-1850 | John M. Clayton | 1849 |
| 13. | MILLARD FILLMORE | 1850-1853 | Daniel Webster | 1850 |
| | | | Edward Everett | 1852 |
| 14. | FRANKLIN PIERCE | 1853-1857 | William L. Marcy | 1853 |
| 15. | JAMES BUCHANAN | 1857-1861 | Lewis Cass | 1857 |
| | | | Jeremiah S. Black | 1860 |
| 16. | ABRAHAM LINCOLN | 1861-1865 | William H. Seward | 1861 |
| 17. | ANDREW JOHNSON | 1865-1869 | William H. Seward | |
| 18. | ULYSSES S. GRANT | 1869-1877 | Elihu B. Washburne | 1869 |
| | | | Hamilton Fish | 1869 |

233

| 19. | Rutherford B. Hayes | 1877-1881 | William M. Evarts | 1877 |
|-----|---------------------|-----------|-------------------|------|
| 20. | James A. Garfield | 1881 - | James G. Blaine | 1881 |
| 21. | Chester A. Arthur | 1881-1885 | James G. Blaine | |
| | | | F. T. Frelinghuysen | 1881 |
| 22. | Grover Cleveland | 1885-1889 | Thomas F. Bayard | 1885 |
| 23. | Benjamin Harrison | 1889-1893 | James G. Blaine | 1889 |
| | | | John W. Foster | 1892 |
| 24. | Grover Cleveland | 1893-1897 | Walter Q. Gresham | 1893 |
| | | | Richard Olney | 1895 |
| 25. | William McKinley | 1897-1901 | John Sherman | 1897 |
| | | | William R. Day | 1898 |
| | | | John Hay | 1898 |
| 26. | Theodore Roosevelt | 1901-1909 | John Hay | |
| | | | Elihu Root | 1905 |
| | | | Robert Bacon | 1909 |
| 27. | William H. Taft | 1909-1913 | Philander C. Knox | 1909 |
| 28. | Woodrow Wilson | 1913-1921 | William J. Bryan | 1913 |
| | | | Robert Lansing | 1915 |
| | | | Bainbridge Colby | 1920 |
| 29. | Warren G. Harding | 1921-1923 | Charles E. Hughes | 1921 |
| 30. | Calvin Coolidge | 1923-1929 | Charles E. Hughes | |
| | | | Frank B. Kellogg | 1925 |
| 31. | Herbert C. Hoover | 1929-1933 | Henry L. Stimson | 1929 |
| 32. | Franklin D. Roosevelt | 1933-1945 | Cordell Hull | 1933 |
| | | | E. R. Stettinius | 1945 |
| 33. | Harry S. Truman | 1945 - | E. R. Stettinius | |
| | | | James F. Byrnes | 1945 |

# States, Territories, and Dependencies

*Original thirteen states indicated in capital letters*

| State | Settled | Area Sq. Mi. | Entered Union |
|---|---|---|---|
| Alabama | 1702 | 51,998 | 1819 |
| Arizona | 1580 | 113,956 | 1912 |
| Arkansas | 1685 | 53,335 | 1836 |
| California | 1769 | 158,297 | 1850 |
| Colorado | 1858 | 103,948 | 1876 |
| CONNECTICUT | 1635 | 4,965 | 1788 |
| DELAWARE | 1726 | 2,370 | 1787 |
| Florida | 1559 | 58,666 | 1845 |
| GEORGIA | 1733 | 59,265 | 1788 |
| Idaho | 1842 | 83,354 | 1890 |
| Illinois | 1720 | 56,043 | 1818 |
| Indiana | 1733 | 36,045 | 1816 |
| Iowa | 1788 | 55,586 | 1846 |
| Kansas | 1727 | 81,774 | 1861 |
| Kentucky | 1765 | 40,181 | 1792 |
| Louisiana | 1699 | 45,409 | 1812 |
| Maine | 1624 | 29,895 | 1820 |
| MARYLAND | 1634 | 9,941 | 1788 |
| MASSACHUSETTS | 1620 | 8,039 | 1788 |
| Michigan | 1650 | 57,480 | 1837 |
| Minnesota | 1805 | 80,858 | 1858 |
| Mississippi | 1716 | 46,362 | 1817 |
| Missouri | 1764 | 68,727 | 1821 |
| Montana | 1809 | 146,131 | 1889 |
| Nebraska | 1847 | 76,808 | 1867 |
| Nevada | 1850 | 110,690 | 1864 |
| NEW HAMPSHIRE | 1623 | 9,031 | 1788 |
| NEW JERSEY | 1664 | 7,514 | 1787 |
| New Mexico | 1537 | 122,503 | 1912 |
| NEW YORK | 1614 | 47,654 | 1788 |
| NORTH CAROLINA | 1650 | 48,740 | 1789 |
| North Dakota | 1780 | 70,183 | 1889 |
| Ohio | 1788 | 40,740 | 1803 |
| Oklahoma | 1889 | 69,414 | 1907 |
| Oregon | 1838 | 95,607 | 1859 |
| PENNSYLVANIA | 1682 | 45,126 | 1787 |
| RHODE ISLAND | 1636 | 1,067 | 1790 |
| SOUTH CAROLINA | 1670 | 30,495 | 1788 |
| South Dakota | 1794 | 76,868 | 1889 |
| Tennessee | 1757 | 41,687 | 1796 |
| Texas | 1686 | 262,398 | 1845 |
| Utah | 1847 | 82,184 | 1896 |
| Vermont | 1724 | 9,124 | 1791 |
| VIRGINIA | 1607 | 40,262 | 1788 |
| Washington | 1811 | 66,836 | 1889 |
| West Virginia | 1727 | 24,022 | 1863 |
| Wisconsin | 1670 | 55,256 | 1848 |
| Wyoming | 1834 | 97,548 | 1890 |

## Territories and Dependencies

| | Acquired | Area Sq. Mi. |
|---|---|---|
| Alaska | 1867 — purchased from Russia | 590,884 |
| Hawaiian Islands | 1900 — annexed | 6,449 |
| Philippine Islands | 1899 — ceded to U. S. by Spain | 127,853 |
| Puerto Rico | 1898 — ceded to U. S. by Spain | 3,435 |
| Virgin Islands | 1917 — purchased from Denmark | 133 |

# BIBLIOGRAPHY

## GENERAL

Dewey, Davis R., *National Problems* (1907).

Dunning, William A., *Reconstruction — Political and Economic* (1907).

Oberholtzer, E. P., *History of the United States* (4 vols.) (1917-1931).

Ogg, F. A., *National Progress* (1918).

Peck, H. T., *Twenty Years of the Republic* (1905).

Rhodes, James F., *The McKinley and Roosevelt Administrations* (1922).

Sparks, E. E., *National Development* (1907).

## THE POLITICAL SCENE

Bowers, Claude, *Beveridge and the Progressive Era* (1932), and *The Tragic Era* (1929).

Burgess, J. W., *The Administration of President Hayes* (1916).

Chamberlain, John, *Farewell to Reform* (1932).

Cleveland, Grover, *Presidential Problems* (1904).

Corwin, Edward S., *The Twilight of the Supreme Court* (1934).

Dewitt, B. P., *The Progressive Movement* (1915).

Earle, E. M., *Against This Torrent* (1941).

Fish, C. R., *The Path of Empire* (1919).

Fleming, D. F., *The United States and the League of Nations* (1932).

Fleming, W. L., *The Sequel to Appomattox* (1919).

Ford, H. J., *The Cleveland Era* (1919).

Herring, Pendleton, *The Impact of War* (1940).

Hill, H. C., *Roosevelt and the Caribbean* (1927).

Howland, H., *Theodore Roosevelt and His Time* (1919).

Johnstone, W. C., *The United States and Japan's New Order* (1940).

Latané, J. H., *America as a World Power* (1907).

MacCormac, John, *Canada: America's Problem* (1941).

McMaster, J. B., *The United States in the World War* (2 vols.) (1918-1920).

Malin, J. C., *The United States after the World War* (1930).

Millis, Walter, *The Martial Spirit* (1931).

Peffer, Nathaniel, *Basis for Peace in the Far East* (1943).

Seymour, Charles, *Woodrow Wilson and the World War* (1919).

Shotwell, J. T., *At the Paris Peace Conference* (1937).

Tolischus, Otto D., *Tokyo Record* (1942).

Welles, Sumner, *The Time for Decision* (1944).

White, William A., *Masks in a Pageant* (1928).


## SOCIAL AND ECONOMIC TRENDS

Allen, Frederick T., *Only Yesterday* (1931).

Armstrong, L. V., *We Too Are the People* (1938).

Beard, C. A., *The Open Door at Home* (1934).

Beard, C. A. and M. R., *The Rise of American Civilization*, Vol. II (1929).

Beard, M. R., *Short History of the American Labor Movement* (1928).

Black, J. D., *Agricultural Reform in the United States* (1929); *Parity, Parity, Parity* (1943).

Brooks, Robert R. R., *Unions of Their Own Choosing* (1940).

Buck, S. J., *The Agrarian Crusade* (1919).

Burns, Eveline M., *Toward Social Security* (1936).

Chase, Stuart, *Men and Machines* (1929).

Corey, Lewis, *The Crisis of the Middle Class* (1935).

Croly, Herbert, *The Promise of American Life* (1909).

Douglas, Paul H., *Social Security in the United States* (1941).

Emeny, Brooks, *The Strategy of Raw Materials* (1934).

Faulkner, H. U., *The Quest for Social Justice* (1931).

Hendrick, B. J., *The Age of Big Business* (1919).

Hicks, J. D., *The Populist Revolt* (1931).

Kendrick, B. B., and Arnett, A. M., *The South Looks at Its Past* (1935).

Laidler, Harry, *Concentration in American Industry* (1931).

Lloyd, H. D., *Wealth versus Commonwealth* (1894).

MacDonald, William, *The Menace of Recovery* (1934).

Mitchell, W. C., ed., *Recent Social Trends* (1932).

Moody, John, *Masters of Capital* (1919), and *The Truth about the Trusts* (1904).

Nevins, Allan, *The Emergence of Modern America* (1928).

Orth, S. P., *Our Foreigners* (1919), and *The Armies of Labor* (1920).

Post, L. W., *The Challenge of Housing* (1938).

Schlesinger, A. M., *The Rise of the City* (1932).

Slosson, P. W., *The Great Crusade and After* (1930).

Sullivan, Mark, *Our Times* (4 vols.) (1926-1932).

Thompson, Holland, *The New South* (1920).

Tugwell, R. G., *Industry's Coming of Age* (1927).

Wallace, Henry A., *America Must Choose* (1934).

Ware, Norman J., *The Labor Movement in the United States, 1860-1895* (1929).

Webb, W. P., *The Great Plains* (1931).

## BIOGRAPHIES

Baker, R. S., *Woodrow Wilson, Life and Letters* (4 vols.) (1927-1931).

Barnard, Harry, *Forgotten Eagle, John Peter Altgeld* (1937).

Barnes, J. A., *John G. Carlisle* (1931).

Bowen, Catherine D., *Yankee from Olympus* (*O. W. Holmes*) (1944).

Browne, W. R., *Altgeld of Illinois* (1924).

Bryan, W. J., *Memoirs* (1921).

Caldwell, R. G., *James A. Garfield* (1931).

Cortissoz, Royal, *Life of Whitelaw Reid* (2 vols.) (1928).

Croly, Herbert, *Marcus Alonzo Hanna* (1912).

Dennett, Tyler, *John Hay* (1933).

Flynn, J. T., *God's Gold* (*John D. Rockefeller*) (1932).

Fuese, Claude, *Carl Schurz, Reformer* (1932).

Hagedorn, Hermann, *Leonard Wood* (2 vols.) (1931).

Haynes, F. E., *James Baird Weaver* (1919).

Hendrick, B. J., *The Life of Andrew Carnegie* (2 vols.) (1932), and *The Life and Letters of Walter Hines Page* (2 vols.) (1922).

Holt, Rackham, *George Washington Carver* (1943).

Howe, George F., *Chester A. Arthur* (1934).

Johnson, Gerald, *Roosevelt, Dictator or Democrat* (1942).

Kerney, James, *The Political Education of Woodrow Wilson* (1926).

La Follette, Robert M., *Autobiography* (1913).

Lynch, D. T., *"Boss" Tweed* (1928).

McAdoo, W. G., *Crowded Years* (1931).

Milton, G. F., *The Age of Hate* (*Andrew Johnson*) (1930).

Nevins, Allan, *Henry White* (1930); *Grover Cleveland, A Study in Courage* (1932); *Hamilton Fish* (1936); *John D. Rockefeller* (1940).

Palmer, Frederick, *Newton D. Baker* (2 vols.) (1931).

Pringle, H. F., *Theodore Roosevelt* (1931); *William Howard Taft* (1939).

Robinson, W. A., *Thomas B. Reed, Parliamentarian* (1930).

Roosevelt, Theodore, *Autobiography* (1913).

Steffens, Lincoln, *Autobiography* (2 vols.) (1931).

Stephenson, N. W., *Nelson W. Aldrich* (1930).

Thayer, W. R., *Life and Letters of John Hay* (1915).

White, William Allen, *Calvin Coolidge* (1931).

# Index

48; 1892, 65-66; 1896, 72; 1900, 90-91; 1904, 1908, 118; 1912, 130; 1916, 148-149; 1920, 166; 1924, 167-168; 1928, 169-170; 1932, 171-172; 1936, 172; 1940, 212-214; 1944, 229-230
Election laws, 31
Electoral Commission, 26-27
Electoral Count Act, 38
Electricity, 99
Eliot, Charles W., 101
Elkins Act, 110
Enforcement Acts, 7
Esch-Cummins Bill, 163-164
Espionage Act (1917), 152
Evarts, William M., 30
Expedition Act, 109
Export-Import Banks, 205

Fair Labor Standards Act, 198
Fall, Albert B., 166, 167
Far East, 209-210
Farm Bankruptcy Act, 192
Farm bloc, 167, 175
Farm Bureau Federation, 175
Farm Credit Administration (FCA), 192
Farm Mortgage Corporation, 192
Farm Mortgage Moratorium Act, 192
Farm Mortgage Refinancing Act, 192, 202
Farm Security Administration, 192
Farmers' Union, 64
Federal Alcohol Control Administration, 183
Federal Deposit Insurance Corporation, 199
Federal Emergency Relief Administration (FERA), 189-190
Federal Farm Board, 176
Federal Farm Loan Act (1916), 137
Federal Food Administration (World War I), 151
Federal Fuel Administration (World War I, 151
Federal Housing Administration (FHA), 197
Federal Power Commission, 196-197
Federal Reserve Act, 134-136
Federal Reserve System, 199
Federal Securities Act, 199
Federal Trade Commission (1920), 136, 164
Federal Water-Power Commission, 177
Federation of Organized Trades and Labor Unions, 57
Fenian movement, 76
Field, Cyrus W., 18
Field, James G., 65
Fifteenth Amendment, 7
Filled Milk Act, 175
Finance, government, 30, 67, 151, 166-167
Financial reforms, 198-200
Fish, Hamilton, 22, 74, 83
Fisheries, 76, 78-79
Fisk, Jim, 22, 40
Foch, (Marshal) Ferdinand, 153
Folger, Charles J., 32
Foote, Arthur, 105
Foraker Act, 91
Forbes, Charles R., 167
Fordney-McCumber Tariff, 173-174
Foreign Debt Commission, 185
Forests, national, 112-113
"Fourteen Points," 155

Fourteenth Amendment, 4, 7
France, 75, 117, 152 ff., 225
Free silver, 63-64, 70-72
Free-silver movement, 63-64
Freedman's Bureau, 3
Frelinghuysen, Frederick T., 32
French, Daniel C., 104
Frohman, Charles, 105
"Frozen assets," 215
Frye, William P., 87
Futures Trading Act, 175

Galveston commission plan, 122
Garfield, James A., 29, 31-33
Garfield, James R., 111
Garland, Hamlin, 104
Garrison, Lindley M., 148
General Munitions Board, 151
Geneva Award, 76
Geneva Conference (1927), 186
General Disarmament Conference (1932), 187
George, Henry, 52, 104
Germany, 114, 117, 145 ff., 208 ff., 217 ff.
Gibbs, Josiah W., 104
Gibbs, Wolcott, 104
Gilman, Daniel C., 101
Glass-Steagall Act, 184, 199
Glavis, L. R., 126
Goethals, George W., 116
Gold, 11-12, 96
Gold Clause Act (1935), 200
Gold Conspiracy, 22
Gold reserve, 66-69
Gold Standard Act (1900), 98
Gompers, Samuel, 57
Gorgas, William C., 116
Gould, Jay, 18, 22, 40, 97
Grain Stabilization Corporation, 176
Grange, 20-21
Granger cases, 42, 43
Granger laws, 21-22
Grangers, 20, 175
Grant, Ulysses S.: administration of, 22-26; election of 5-6, 23
Gray, Asa, 104
Gray, George, 87
Great Britain, 78-80, 114, 139, 146, 225
"Great upheaval," 59
Greeley, Horace, 23-24
Greenback movement, 63
Greenback party, 26
Greenbackers, 43, 63
Greenback-Labor party, 43, 62, 63
Greenbacks, 6, 20, 25, 68, 98
Greenland, 214-215
Guadalcanal, 223
Guam, acquisition of, 87
Guatemala, 77
Guiteau, Charles J., 32, 33

Hague conferences: 1899, 89; 1907, 114
Haiti, 142-143, 205
Halfbreeds, 29
Halsey, (Admiral) William F., 223
Hancock, (General) Winfield S., 32
Hanna, Marcus A., 69-70, 118
Hannegan, Robert, 230
Harding, Warren G., 165-167
Harmon, Judson, 129
Harriman, Edward H., 97
Harrison, Benjamin, 48-50, 66
Harrison, Francis B., 93
Harte, Bret, 104